UNDERSTAND

DARE

THRIVE

How to have your best career *from today*

Diana Parkes

Understand: Dare: Thrive
by Diana Parkes

ISBN: 978-1-912092-24-6

First published in 2021
by Arkbound Foundation (Publishers)

Arkbound is a social enterprise that aims to promote social inclusion, community development and artistic talent. It sponsors publications by disadvantaged authors and covers issues that engage wider social concerns. Arkbound fully embraces sustainability and environmental protection. It endeavours to use material that is renewable, recyclable or sourced from sustainable forest.

Arkbound
Rogart Street Campus
4 Rogart Street
Glasgow G40 2AA

www.arkbound.com

UNDERSTAND

DARE

THRIVE

How to have your best career *from today*

Diana Parkes

To Gracie
For making me the best person I can be

Contents

Figures

Tables

Acknowledgements

When I sat in the City Business Library in London reading a Harvard Business Review article on Eagly and Carli's *Through the Labyrinth. The truth about how women become leaders*, I had no idea where the sparks it set off in my mind would take me, nor how many people would be involved in making this outcome possible.

That was 2007 and my daughter Gracie was 6. She is now 20, and without her absolute belief in me, and her incredible support and patience – way beyond her years – you would not be reading this. Gracie, thank you darling, *yous incredibles* (as we say) for putting up with my crazy hours researching, studying for my psychology degree and running my business. When I was on the verge of giving up because I was struggling to make it all work, you told me about Edison's discovery of 10,000 ways that didn't work to make a light bulb, but which inevitably led to the one way that did. You said, "don't give up Mummy". Thank you so much for your wisdom, strength, immense sense of humour and Microsoft Office skills!

The power of this book comes from the 45 leaders who didn't know me from Adam (or Eve) and yet gave me their time and open reflections on the lessons of their careers. What an immense privilege and extraordinary experience. Thank you for your candour, and for keeping your door open. Nancy Kline, thank you for taking that support further with the mentoring conversations, encouraging me to find my voice. Your words and your work have been guiding lights.

While it has taken many years to come to fruition, I'd probably still be in the coffee shop transcribing the 260 hours of interview recordings if not for Linda Fenwick who saw the importance of this project and funded the transcriptions, as well as hosting the thank you event for the interviewees and launch of The Women's Sat Nav to Success back in 2011.

Professor Alice Eagly, thank you for being accepting of my naïveté and allowing me to grow, providing me with insights and research papers along the way, and even the extraordinary opportunity to spend time with you and your husband when you were in London. I

1

am also grateful to the many academics, professional institutes and authors in this field who have shared their perspectives and research.

I'm indebted to those who have worked on my words with tact, skill and care: Mindy Gibbins-Klein, Sara Fox, Karin Karian, Carolyn Waterworth, all the first reviewers, and Jamie Nixon, Mónica Martin and Steve McNaught at Arkbound Publishing, and Tasmin Briers and Sarah Spargo for their design work. And to the special friends, clients, business partners, and men and women in my professional network whose interest and encouragement over the years have kept my momentum going and self-belief intact.

And finally, thanks to my sister Georgina for her practical advice, tangible support and no-nonsense outlook; and to Dr Elizabeth Bridger, for showing me what women can achieve, even in the toughest circumstances – thank you Mum.

In memory of Emma Fox and Olivia Burt.

Crowdfunding supporters

I'd like to say a special thank you to everyone that pledged their support for Understand: Dare: Thrive.

Gaby Allen	Mike Banks	Atty Bax
Rebecca Booth	Rebekah Bostan	Richard Boyles
Peter Breakell	Elizabeth Bridger	Sarah Brooke
Wendy Browne	Hannah Butland	Richard Clissold-Vasey
Alison Cole	Babz Cope	Joanna Cudlipp
Alison Dewey	Sam Duffy	Kim Eeles
Gary Ford	Carrie Foster	Rachel Gardiner
Rachel Gibson	Natalie Gorman	Georgia Halston
Debby Hammond	Paul Harris	Euan Holwill
Kate Hunter	Katie Ireland	Karin Karian
Lesley Keets	Nancy Kline	Katie Marlow
George McKerracher	Karen Mee	Amy Miles
Sarah Mitchell	Victoria Mountain	Deborah Mudway
Paul Newberry	Ann O' Shaughnessy	Shaheena Pall
Georgina Parkes	Gracie Parkes	Haydn Parkes
Christina Patterson	Kerry Priday	Sean Raw
Heidi Roper	Lynn Roseberry	Faye Sanders
Heather Shearer	Lisa Simmons	Bente Stubbington

Nikki Thornley	Sophie Townsend	Mike Walczak
Caroline Weaver	Lucy Weedon	JJ Weeks
Kelly Williams	Florence Wood	

The interviewees

Name	Position(s) at time of interview	Organisation
Anna C. Catalano	Board Director	Kraton Corporation, Willis Towers Watson
Anon	Managing Director	A US bank
Barbara Follett	Member of Parliament	British Civil Service
Barbara Harris	Head of HR Operations	CPS
Belinda Gooding	CEO	Duchy Originals
Beverley Bell	Traffic Commissioner	Department for Transport
Celia Adams	Financial Director	Range of interim directorships
Charmaine Stewart	Joint Managing Director	eConsilium LLC
	Programme Transition Manager / Change Lead	BP
Claire Walters	MD	Unipart Logistics
Clare Kavanagh	Director	Transport for London (TfL)
Clare Maurice	Senior Partner	Maurice, Turnor, Gardner
Collette Dunkley	Founder	XandY Communications
Fiona Kendrick [now Dame]	Chairman and CEO	Nestlé UK and Ireland
Dana Skelley [now OBE]	Director of Road Network (Engineer of the Year 2006)	Transport for London (TfL)

Fiona Hagdrup	Director & Senior Fund Manager	M&G Investments
Gill Adams	Head of Supply Chain	Carphone Warehouse
Jane Walton	Innovation Futures Group Director	Colgate-Palmolive
Jill Caseberry	General Manager	Premier Foods
Karen Guerra	Président & Directeur Générale	Colgate-Palmolive, France
Laurence Vallaeys	Partner	Odgers
Lavinia Carey, OBE	Director General	British Video Association
Lin Phillips	Global Head of Operations	Shell Gas
Maggie Stilwell	Partner	Ernst & Young
Mandy Pooler	CEO	Mindshare Worldwide
Marion Cowden	Director Corporate Services	Commonwealth Secretariat
Mhairi McEwan	Managing Director	Brand Learning
Miriam Jordan-Keane	Global Brand Officer	Weight-Watchers International
Morag Blazey	CEO	PHD Media Ltd: UK Group
Morwenna Angove	Sales and Marketing Director	Merlin Entertainments Group (Alton Towers)
Nancy Kline	President	Time To Think
Peggy Montana	Executive Vice President	Shell
Prof. Dorothy Griffiths	Deputy Faculty Principal	Imperial College Business School
Prof. Karen Kirby	Director of Science, Director of Graduate Studies	Dept Electronic Engineering, University of Surrey

Rebecca Salt	Group Director of Communications & Marketing	CEVA Logistics Ltd
Ruth Waring	Founder	Women In Logistics
Sally Wells	Managing Director	Origin HR
Sara Fox	New Building Director	Swiss Re
Sarah Brooke	Legal Consultant	National Health Service
Sarah Lewis	Commercial Director	Diageo
Sharon Kerr [now QPC]	Head of the Flying Squad	Metropolitan Police
	Senior VP Security	American Express
Sharon Thomas	MD	Unipart Consumer
Simon Hughes	CEO	Mothercare
Suzie Allwork	Executive Chairman	Aerial Systems Ltd
Victoria Mountain	Director	Bis Henderson

(Bios are available at https://womenssatnav.co.uk/the-book.php)

PART 1

INTRODUCTION

Chapter 1

Understand: Dare: Thrive

I live just ten houses away from a beautiful sandy beach with a promenade that stretches for more than eight miles. The view is stunning. There can't be a more perfect setting in which to go running. I even have the added impetus of two demanding dogs that need exercising twice a day.

Typically, I would wake up anticipating my morning run and my mind would swing into action, presenting me with a swathe of get-out options, even before I'd put my running gear on. It would start with: *'Don't do this now – another day maybe. Look, the weather app says it might rain. Probably best to leave it till tomorrow.'* If the voice that argued in favour of the run won the debate, it then faced its next set of potential push-backs when I began jogging. It would be just moments before that other voice chipped in to say: *'This hasn't started well. First few metres are a struggle. Best to stop now. I'm clearly having an off-day.'* But I would probably keep going because I'd feel stupid walking the dogs in running kit. So, on I'd go, and then that voice would make more unhelpful observations: *'You're tired; your knee feels a bit dodgy; you can't go much further; I think you really better stop now. Your body isn't up for this today.'* There would be some more exchanges about the potential of running a bit further before finally giving up and walking.

But now it's a different experience and outcome. Now I apply – if somewhat grudgingly – the philosophy for success that I've distilled through my years of research developing this book. When that defeatist voice tells me to give up, I try to make myself check it out – to understand the truth of the situation with my body. What am I actually feeling in my legs and my lungs? Almost every time what I find is that my legs are not really hurting that much, they're just warming up; my lungs are doing OK and I'm not overheating. So, I discover a rather different truth: the little voice in my head is deceiving me and I shouldn't listen to it, and that I'm fine to keep going and maybe I could actually go further (or, perhaps, faster) than I had thought, hoped or planned.

However, that voice can be quite relentless. So, I have to remind myself of how good it will feel to complete my run and how bad it will feel if I give up. Thrive or dive? That's my choice. So, I *dare* myself to keep going. It feels like taking a risk and stepping into the unknown. Will I really be able to make it? But I do. I run all the way and I get home feeling energised, proud, and strong.

However, each time I succeed, I collect more evidence of what I really can do and how amazingly good it feels. I know that when I understand and when I dare, I thrive. Now I'm able to see the reality of the situation, and to challenge the doubts that could stop me achieving my goal. I can dare to keep going when I'm not sure whether I can succeed and relish the satisfaction of what I've achieved.

'*Understand: Dare: Thrive*' is a powerful formula. It will help you to navigate barriers by enabling you to understand clearly what their nature really is. It will help you make the daring leap, or the little steps that add up to a leap, allowing you to secure the intrinsic and extrinsic rewards that will really enable you to thrive.

Dare a little. Thrive a lot!

Henry Ford insightfully said, "*if you always do what you've always done, you will always get what you have always got.*" So, to make different things happen, you will have to try new approaches. Often you will need a bit of courage to try something that is just outside your comfort zone: asking for something you've never asked for before; going into a new environment that makes you feel a bit scared; speaking up when you don't know how your contribution will be received. However, once you have dared to try – even if it's just a tiny new step – you will find that the experience and outcome weren't actually anything like you had anticipated or feared. The experience is similar to the prospect of taking something back to a shop. You imagine the push-backs and the resistance of having to confront someone quite publicly when you don't feel sure of your position. You work yourself up, going through the possible scenarios in your head and developing a range of scripts to try to secure the outcome you want. Then as you start your script with the employee, they smile broadly, say that they are so sorry for the inconvenience, and of course you can have your money back immediately.

What's so important about applying that tiny bit of courage is that it gives you access to something that's really worth having. When you experience the benefit of taking a different step you will feel bolder in future, and the scale of the 'dare' will diminish, but the size of your step will comfortably increase, as will your reward. You will be able to gain more of what you want, leaving behind a less productive approach. It becomes a virtuous cycle taking you onward and upward. You will have greater self-belief and therefore greater confidence because you will have evidence of what you *can* do and what it *will* bring. This will raise your sense of self-worth and increase your resilience to fuel momentum towards what you really want and deserve.

Making it happen:

This is your space to explore what this chapter means to you, and what difference those insights can make for you.

Can you think of occasions when you haven't done something that it would have been beneficial to do, when in reality it was only that little voice of self-doubt that stopped you from doing it? Things like picking up the phone to ask for something; or making a presentation; or putting a point forward at a meeting; or putting yourself forward to lead a team; or applying for a bigger job?

Do you recognise that you could have done it?

What difference would it have made if you had challenged that voice to understand that reality differently? Could you then have dared to do it? And, if so, what benefit would it have brought you – what would your 'thrive' experience have been, and what could it have led to?

What have you got coming up that might fall into this category?

What will you take from this first chapter, to put yourself in a better position to create a thrive outcome and how are you going to apply it to your situation?

What options do you have to address them, prevent them, or circumvent them?

Chapter 2

What to expect and why this will make differences that really matter to you

The purpose of this book is to enable you to have your best career, **starting today**. It aims to equip you with the insights and strategies you need to have your best working life. It's about a great, fulfilling journey – not just the final destination. It is for women at any stage of their career. It can be a companion across your work-life adventure, whatever your current situation or starting point.

It could be that you are in a full-on, turbo-charged momentum phase with few other commitments. Perhaps you are at a relatively early point in your career with real clarity about where you want to get to and a determination to achieve everything you aspire to, so you are laser-focused delivering that plan. You want to learn all you can to be equipped to get there smoothly and speedily with the best rewards and maximum job satisfaction. Or it could be that you've had your head down doing your very best – having assumed, as many do, that your career will find its own way – but now you want to take control and make more informed choices.

However, it could be that you're encountering barriers, detours, swampy terrain, setbacks, or even dead ends that your male colleagues and friends don't seem to be experiencing. While this may happen further down the track for those in well formalised and structured organisations, it can be shocking when you transition from university to paid employment.

Along the way, there may be opportunities to get involved with great projects or high profile assignments. For a whole host of reasons that I address later, you may not recognise that you are perfect for the role. And when you do, landing opportunities like these can be a challenge when candidate selection defaults to the expected profile, namely male and pale!

Or maybe you are at home, going stir-crazy looking after your kids and wondering how the hell to get back to doing stuff you really loved doing at work. Like many others, you may be deeply concerned about whether you've got what it takes to do it anymore – whether the world has moved on.

Or, like another vast group of working women, you could be feeling quietly but deeply frustrated that you don't seem to be recognised, respected and valued for what you do. You have got a number of years under your belt, so you have great experience; you work hard and do well and yet opportunities seem to knock on other people's door. You could be one of the many women who want to do more exciting, stretching and rewarding stuff, with more stimulating people, but wondering how you can pitch to make that leap successfully.

Or conversely, you could be one of the silent and significant population of women doubting what you can really achieve and dismissing opportunities that you don't believe are relevant to you. Whatever your stage or your mindset, this is about getting the most out of your working life. To give you the best time at work – fulfilling, stimulating, rewarding – based on your definition of success.

This book shares the insights that matter to real women who want to have their best possible working life with success based on the real world – not some paint-brushed, digitally enhanced celebrity exception. It's the book that I wish I could have read in my twenties or thirties. It would have helped me to translate the signs around me more accurately so that I could navigate a faster, smoother, less stressful course through working relationships, meetings, projects and job negotiations to make the very best of every stage of my career. I might have fought different battles, accepted some red lights with less angst, and seen more clearly the terrain I was navigating. Many of the setbacks and times I was not heard or supported were actually a response to my gender, with all that it subconsciously implies about what people expect to be my strengths and limitations in different types of work, career stages and roles, and even in specific situations.

I don't want you to spend a lifetime working out how this career thing really works – I want you to know what you need to know NOW and then just get on with it – have fun and great success – whatever 'success' means to you.

So, this book is firmly rooted in the reality of the workplace – not some varnished version represented on TV, in films and advertising. It is rooted in the reality of women's lives – tough choices, huge pressure to be everything to everyone, the expectation that you must make it to the top and, if it works out that way, that you are a perfect 'mother' – not to mention that you must have the perfect figure, be ageless, and so forth.

I did not want the book to represent one woman's success. Instead, it's developed from my structured interviews with over 45 women who have made it in a cross-section of different types of roles, sectors, professions and workplaces. The 260 hours of their words were painstakingly analysed to identify the most important strategies for successfully navigating the workplace for a fulfilling career. It's not flowery, pink or idealistic. It's grounded firmly in reality, which is sometimes grim, but it's what we have to deal with.

Understand: Dare: Thrive hasn't been written to give you a short-term boost – to fill you with energy for an hour, a day or a week and then to be forgotten as real life overwhelms what you experienced through a few pages of motivational hype. The aim is to give you deep insights and pragmatic strategies that will guide, support and sustain your progress across your work-life journey. To do this, I had to understand the true underlying psychological causes of the detours, diversions and dead-ends women experience trying to navigate the career labyrinth. So, after the research interviews and analysis, I took a degree in psychology – studying it through the lens of gender and the workplace, to get to the *root* causes of the challenges that persist, as it's only through understanding the causes that we can develop sustainable solutions. This means I know for sure, based on the most contemporary scientific research and stress-tested psychological principles, why these issues persist.

The truth is that it's *still* harder to succeed as a woman in the world of work. According to the consistently reported numbers, progress is slower, support, recognition and opportunities are scarcer, and rewards are lower. If it was truly a level playing field for women today – as you might expect given the time that has elapsed since sex discrimination legislation was passed in many countries (in the UK the first Sex Discrimination Act was passed in 1975) – the make-up of boardrooms, technology companies, law firms, parliaments, etc, would be very different. Nor, half a century after equal pay legislation (the UK's Equal Pay Act was in 1970) would we still be seeing headlines about gender pay gaps and governments having to legislate to expose organisation-specific gaps, in some sort of attempt to shame them into addressing gender inequalities. One interviewee brought this impact to life: she said that, had she been paid the same as her male peers as she rose through the ranks, she would have had enough money to either buy a second home in London, or to use as the capital to inject into her start-up business without the need for external funding. And she was spot on, as the average gender pay gap across a woman's working lifetime is the value of an average house at current prices. If you include the much more significant gap in discretionary pay, such as bonuses, this could pay off your mortgage, *and* buy you a holiday home.

Let me be clear, this book is not about taking up arms against men, who are vital allies in driving workplace change. The issues that persist are primarily down to the embedded, subconscious understanding of the world that we all share and unconsciously conform to through our expectations, attitudes and actions. My ambition is for you to be able to take control of your own destiny to make the right things happen at the right time and with the best rewards for you. Hence, reading through the chapters, you will discover:

- Insights into the reality and reasons behind the surprising lack of women across a wide range of fields and functions as well as in leadership positions.
- Clarity and confidence that women are not only as capable

of leadership as men but also arguably better placed to be great leaders in this multi-cultural, multi-stakeholder world – bringing not only prosperity to the organisations they run and represent but also creating fulfilling and engaging workplace cultures.

- The myths that persist about why women aren't the best fit for certain roles.
- Confirmation that it's not 'just me', as many women feel is the case. The challenges individual women experience are common. They are driven by well documented and researched psychological phenomena that cause biased decision-making in favour of men.
- Practical, comprehensive answers to the question 'so what can I do about it?' Parts 3, 4 and 5 take you through the most potent and pragmatic approaches to enable your success.
- Inspiration, reassurance, strategic and practical options through the stories and approaches of women who have made it in male-oriented organisations, sectors and roles.
- A range of coaching-based questions to enable you to assess where you are against these enabling strategies, and to help you develop clarity on what you could or should do to move closer to your definition of success as you travel through your working life.

Chapter 3
What is success?

My original definition of career success came from 15 years in the consumer goods industry. Success was all about driving the top line (sales) as cost-efficiently as possible to deliver the best possible bottom line (net profit) and getting your brands higher up the rankings. It was also measured by numbers and defined by hierarchical status – my income, bonus, title and the material evidence of my status – cars, home, holidays, clothes and the places I frequented. So, career success was about progress towards the top and about how much I earned, which embodies the contemporary, consumerist model.

At the beginning of my research, I found that many women looked at what it meant to be at the top and didn't like what they saw: unacceptable behaviour towards other people and irrational hours that no amount of pay or perks could justify.

> *"I'd rather poke pins in my eyes than behave like they do towards the people in this company"*
>
> **Anon Interviewee's rationale for turning down the offer of a main board position.**

We need to widen the definition of 'success' to something that feels more like 'fulfilling'. We should focus on the rewards of our journey, not how we feel at specific destination points. We should ask: *was it a fulfilling day, week or month? And, if not, what needs to change?*

What I found through all these conversations was that there are many types of work that women, like men, really love: logistics, engineering, IT, advertising, law, politics, medicine. So, workplace **fulfilment** is actually also about finding and doing the work you really love. Work that is stimulating, stretching, exciting, novel, challenging or maybe deeply analytic, complex and intense. Whatever it is that feeds you. We need the buzz of doing the work we love, and we will thrive in an environment which is healthy but wither in a toxic culture. And as humans, we need recognition and seek it from the earliest days of our lives. Recognition communicates our competence and boosts our self-esteem, so it is important to our mental health and well-being. However, a despairing comment I've consistently heard from women over my 16 years of focus on this subject is *'if only I could just get some recognition for what I do'*.

My research has shown that this lack of recognition of the value of women's work and potential sets off a negative cascade of long-term career and fulfilment consequences. It undermines belief in capability, which then delays women considering and applying for roles, and can diminish their impact when they 'pitch' for those roles. It leaves women behind, in roles they can deliver with their eyes shut, which is dull and draining of energy and which can then promote the perception that *'she doesn't want to get stuck in'*. If you're in that situation when babies come along, why hurry back? Then you can slip into being the lower wage earner and your career no longer becomes the one to back or defend. Thus, the descent becomes entrenched.

My definition of success has three dimensions which provide a framework that reflects the things that matter to have your best working life:

Success is:

- **Doing the work you find the most fulfilling,**
- **In a healthy culture,**
- **With appropriate recognition, support, progression choices and rewards.**

Having a successful career means getting the most out of your whole working life. This is likely to mean different things at different life stages. So, it's healthier to be open to alternative characteristics that deliver meaningful success. This flexibility and openness to change means that you can see new ways forward and embrace them, rather than holding on to the picture you had of what a successful career looked like when you entered the world of work.

The pace of change has never been faster – not just technologically speaking but also in how things get done and by whom. And the pandemic threw every workplace and working day norm out of the window. So, to assume that what we envisaged five years ago will be there in the same form is asking for a painful crunching of gears; it's asking for frustration and being ill-prepared for the inevitable changes coming down the track.

We all hope that we will never experience the seismic impact of being hit by an asteroid the size of Covid-19. Most of us had to rapidly re-calibrate everything, to adapt in order to navigate a new framework of possibilities and impossibilities.

> *"It all comes down to defining success in life. Why am I working? What am I being employed to do? How does it match what I want to do? Do I work to achieve a certain title and position, in which case the only reason I am working is to get to that position and role, so therefore these are my stakeholders, and this is the environment in which I work and these are the things that will help me get there.*
>
> *I don't work within those parameters. I work for myself and I am employed to come in and deliver. I want to do interesting work and I want to deliver certain things. How am I going to do that? It is not about getting to a certain position. You talk about success and you talk about leadership. If you put the focus on yourself too much it is not good. I don't often see those people getting ahead or they make the wrong choices because they get waylaid by what they are trying to do. Or they are easy to attack. If you are in that traditional framework of working, people are looking to attack, so you are an*

> *easy target for attack. They just can't work out why*
> *they are not achieving what they need to achieve. If*
> *they took out the self-interest it might actually help*
> *them make a right decision with the right people." –*
> **Charmaine Stewart**

So, **what constitutes a fulfilling career is unique for everyone and it can differ at each life stage**. Some want to make it to the top; others want to be able to focus on work they really love and enjoy; sometimes we just want to take time out for other stuff that really matters. It's down to you to understand what success means and to try and make that happen.

> *"The day I don't jump out of bed in the morning*
> *passionate about going to work, is the day I give up."*
> **– Fiona Kendrick**

Chapter 4

YOU have to actively manage your career

"My boss who has just retired, he thought I was the best person he has ever had working for him. He persuaded me to come and work here. He was looking for a director a few years ago, the role that I am now doing. He was sitting with me at the table saying, 'who do you think would be a good person for this job?' He was naming all of these men in the industry. I was sitting there thinking: 'am I going to say it?' But I didn't. I was so cross with myself for not saying: 'what about me?'

I am always doing it. My partner is always saying: 'of course you could do that. I am absolutely convinced you could do that.' I will be saying: 'no, I haven't got this or that or I would need to do that first.' Always.

I have been overlooked for promotion and other people have been recruited for the wrong reasons. I have had a lot of this and have been completely crushed by it and considered leaving the industry, considered slamming the door and swanning off."
- Dana Skelley

In some types of organisations and professions, and often at more junior levels, there are very structured processes and unambiguous frameworks that ensure employees work their way up, around or across the organisation based on competency levels and performance. However, it is frequently the case that when careers start entering more senior levels these rigorous structures and processes start to crumble, and then develop gaping holes, and even disappear. This means that 'getting on' requires your active management over and above delivering the role objectives that were previously measured to ascertain your readiness for the next pay level or promotion. In other types of organisations and professions you have to adopt this approach from day one. The risk of not doing so is that other people put themselves in a better position to be considered for roles that you might want to be considered for, and then they get those roles. That could leave you – like it left Dana Skelley – feeling like walking out of the door.

But whose responsibility is it? If the people that make the decisions didn't know what you wanted, then that's mainly down to you. It is your responsibility to decide what you want and then make the best moves.

> *"I look after my people and I promote them by making sure everybody knows what they are doing and what they are achieving, I also look out for new opportunities for them. I'm expecting my senior management to be doing that for me, but it doesn't happen often. I feel it's better to be self-sufficient; that way you are never disappointed.*
>
> *I think that is the difference between men and women: women often forget to look after number one; they assume that someone is looking out for them."* – Lin Phillips
>
> *"You do get to a point where you realise that it's not enough to expect that people will notice the good things you've done and reward you. That is a fact of life."* – Lavinia Carey

We live in a culture that is still uncomfortable about women pushing themselves forward, which means that we have to be even more thoughtful than our male colleagues about how we do it. And it's equally true that decision-makers are less likely to see you as an option if you are a woman in a profession or role that is typically considered male or even gender-neutral. Hence, it's essential to take control of your own destiny and be firmly on the front foot to drive forward. If you don't, you are in danger of being left behind with all the associated financial, fulfilment and self-esteem collateral damage.

It's important to be circumspect about the views, opinions and direction of well meaning 'others' such as friends, family, network members, peers, recruitment consultants. They simply don't know enough about your work, skills, potential, values and what you really enjoy, to advise you on how good you are, how far you can go or what you could or should do next.

You must do the research and the analysis, and you must make the decisions. They can be there to support those decisions and remind you how brilliant you are at the times when you start doubting yourself or when your plans hit setbacks, but if you are really going to be fulfilled in what you do then your choices must be down to you.

A woman who became a dear friend as we recently studied for a psychology degree together graduated in style, with a first-class honours degree. At 40 she discovered that she's even more clever than she had an inkling of when she was at school. But her parents didn't see it. They didn't expect a woman to have a career – she should be the wife, the mother, the carer and the support, and that's what she's been. Her life is the way that others wanted it to be, and the structure of her family life is deeply embedded. Now she has to look at her life and ask how she lives it now, given that she has opened the doors to the proof of her potential. The signs are that she is creating a distinct path that is compatible with her values and family, and enables her to use that incredible brain and to feel great about it – proud, liberated and fulfilled.

So, the bottom line is: you are the best person to manage your career. You've been there the whole time, you've experienced everything you've been through first-hand and you are the one who has to live with the decisions you make. I'm not a great fan of Neuro

Linguistic Programming, but there are a few great tools within its portfolio, and one of my favourites is this:

Imagine you've come to the end of your life and you're standing outside the Pearly Gates (or the equivalent) and Saint Peter (or the equivalent) asks you to answer a question before he/she lets you enter paradise. It is:

> *'Have you lived your best working life?*
> *No? Then what's the difference between your best working*
> *life and your current reality?'*

Two huge and sobering questions. And I use 'working life', rather than 'career', because the latter seems to imply that you have to have your foot hard down on the gas to drive as fast as you can throughout. That approach may not be right for you at some (if any) stages of your working life, so it's not going to be helpful in supporting you to define what is really your best.

Given you are still alive – and not at the Pearly Gates - reflect on your current situation and path ahead. You *can* make positive choices to ensure the answer to that first question is always going to be 'yes'. You need to understand yourself well, and the following sections will help you do that.

> *"I could have gone [for promotion] a lot sooner and been a bit more ambitious. I did twenty odd years before I even considered higher command. I should have been thinking about that after five years' service. I just wasn't interested. I had a couple of tentative approaches and thought it wasn't for me.*
>
> *Me: What was the feeling?*
>
> *I just wanted to get on and learn the job. I think that is another thing that women tend to say: 'I want to learn about the job I am in before I go for the next one.' And then everybody overtakes you." –*
> **Sharon Kerr**

The reality is that most people's career paths are a series of accidents. You bump into a job opportunity for which you might be qualified and go for it. You do that job and along comes a promotion or a different opportunity and off you go along that track until something else bumps into you, or you bump into it.

Can we possibly have our best and most fulfilling career by accident? Is it likely we'll fall over cultures that match our values; roles and recognition that give us the greatest buzz; opportunities, support and development that enable us to reach our potential?

When we set out on working lives, we have very limited information and exposure to inform our choices. The truth is that we probably spend more time planning our annual holiday than planning our career!

However, as you go along, it's important to reflect on what you are experiencing and to note what aspects of your working life tick your boxes. As you understand the ingredients of your recipe for a great working life, you can test opportunities that come up against this unique formula. Does the potential new role / boss / department / organisation give you the range of things that work best for you? And where is the evidence that it can deliver, beyond what they say or promise? What's the evidence; where have they done it before; how does it work; who has benefitted? You decide. Don't fall into something, or be sold a story of a reality that doesn't exist.

Bear in mind that your formula for 'best' is likely to change across your lifetime and as the things that are of importance to you change. You have to work out what is best at each stage, and that means investing time reviewing, reflecting and rethinking. Doing that work and refreshing your formula will give you the clarity to follow what is uniquely right for you. Knowing that you have prioritised your values, thought about what you want from work, and what it needs to give you in the broadest sense, and weighed up options means that you can be more certain about what is in and what is out. You can focus on what you need to look for, or you can mould what's available, or even create what is right for you, if it doesn't already exist.

PART 2

UNDERSTAND THE CAUSES TO NAVIGATE THE EFFECTS

There's an old adage in business which is fundamentally important in the context of having your most fulfilling career:

'You can't manage what you don't know'

In other words, you can only take action on things that you are aware of. For example, if there is a meeting where the agenda covers items that affect you and your work, but you are not invited, then you are underprepared at best and disadvantaged in any scenario. You can't influence the discussion and what decisions are made. Actually, you probably won't just be disadvantaged, you'll also experience a range of thoughts and even negative emotions when you find out about the situation, which may then have a direct effect on your behaviour. That may be limited to feeling irritated or – depending if this was a one off or part of a pattern – it may extend to you disengaging with the people involved in the meeting, the project or even the organisation. Was it just an oversight because those topics don't usually crop up and the people involved aren't familiar enough to know that you are key, or did people know of your involvement but think you were unnecessary? If you had known about the meeting and the agenda but not been invited, then you could have tried to find ways to ensure that your position and content were represented. Knowing about the meeting provides the opportunity to find a way in, and therefore a way to influence outcomes. So, you stay in control, engaged and on-track.

This is the principle for securing the best outcomes on your career journey, and for maintaining a positive perspective to support your momentum. You want to be in the best position to know, recognise and ideally anticipate potential obstacles. You want to have options in place ready to navigate or remove those obstacles or to make the choice of another route altogether. With this knowledge, obstacles are minimised, smoothing your progress and reducing angst.

This section of the book will help you understand why and when obstructions to your progress may occur so that you have the best possible chance of anticipating them and managing or minimising them, to keep your career journey positive, progressive and pain-free. These obstructions can range from everyday situations such as finding that your contributions in certain meetings consistently go unheard, to milestone situations such as assessing the reality of a potential new role where the culture could enable you to flourish, or cause you to fail. The situations may be external, like the two I just mentioned, or they may be internal, or both. When I say internal, I mean such things as your level of self-belief, resilience, perception of your capabilities and your potential. These internal factors are critical as they affect your ability to even consider opportunities, and the levels of confidence, credibility and commitment that you can communicate to ensure you succeed. When you have a good understanding of what may cause a delay, diversion or dead end to your plans, you'll be able to identify the most appropriate strategies to navigate this reality to your best advantage.

Chapter 5

Gain a psychological advantage

The psychological advantage I'm referring to is not some sort of ability to surreptitiously manipulate people or situations to your advantage. It is the development of relevant insights into human psychology that will enable you to anticipate the way both you and others may think and behave in given workplace situations. With this knowledge you can interpret behaviour in the right light and plan how to manage those situations for the best outcomes in the short, medium and longer term.

There are certain situations that women find themselves in at work – often some form of having been overlooked or valued less – which they may quite naturally interpret as due to a personal shortfall, thinking, 'it's just me' or 'maybe I'm just not good enough'. These situations may seem very small and yet be intensely frustrating – such as getting the point you made in a meeting glossed over in favour of a different point, or in favour of your point, but only when it's made by a different person. Or they could be big and materially significant, such as not being considered for an opportunity that you should be a contender for. When these things happen in an environment or with a focus which is predominantly male or generally associated with men, you can be reassured that it is not a reaction to you as an individual. What has happened is that unconscious gendered 'thinking' has taken place. The decision or behaviour has been driven by ingrained cultural expectations of women as a whole. It was a response to your gender, not one based on you as an individual.

People behave in a way that's driven by the generalised 'model' they have in their head (the stereotype) of who should be doing what, *not* by the reality of the person in front of them. If the stereotype that we have of someone delivering your role doesn't look like you, then your contribution can have less credibility.

Unfortunately, gender really does throw up obstacles in the form of gendered beliefs and expectations, which exist both in your subconscious and in that of others. And because these expectations and beliefs (or biases) are rarely recognised by individuals, and therefore not explicitly articulated, you need to be able to understand and predict when these implicit unconscious biases may affect thinking and behaviour. Extensive psychological research shows that unconscious biases affect the extent to which:

- People are listened to.
- People's work is valued.
- People's contributions are considered.
- People's work and contributions are remembered and correctly attributed.
- People are trusted.

Given we all absorb the same models of the world, we share the same biases and unconsciously apply them to ourselves. So, we may:

- Speak up less, or more tentatively.
- Believe that certain opportunities are not relevant.
- Under-rate our capabilities.
- Fail to see our full potential.

So, let's take this opportunity to be really clear what these obstacles are and look at the most powerful proven strategies to overcome them, avoid them, diminish them and / or prevent them affecting you.

Humans subconsciously and automatically categorise everything.

Try to imagine what life would be like if you walked along a high street passing buildings with glass fronts, open doors and items on display inside, but had no concept of the term 'shop'. Can you imagine the impact of having to assess each store front individually to work out if it's a place that you're free to go into, to look around and to exchange money for items on display? What if you had to work out that the person standing behind a counter was the one with whom you could carry out a purchasing transaction?

How slow, repetitive and mind-numbingly painful would life be if we had to work out each element of every scenario we encountered!

Our amazing brains develop this astonishing ability to group things together into categories from soon after birth. We then constantly refine and expand our portfolio as new information enables us to do so. My sister gave me a very endearing example of how her son, Hallam, as a two-year-old, was confronted with this opportunity. From picture books he had learnt that things with four legs, a head and a tail were called rabbits – or 'babbits' in his terminology – and this led to some confusion the first time she took him to visit a children's farm. He proudly walked up to the guinea pig pen, pointed and said "babbits". He then excitedly repeated this with the lambs, calves, ponies and even piglets – becoming more and more disconcerted as he was told each time they were not 'babbits', but rather a differently named animal. This meant he had to find ways of distinguishing them from *babbit*s, forming new categories of animals using such things as height, head shape, fur, ears, tails, and noses. It became obvious quite quickly that once he had learnt these new categories, he also needed to learn what to expect from them.

Some animals he could pick up and hold. Some he could sit on and ride. Some he could feed with a bottle; others he had to be careful of as they might bite or kick.

Associating each category with these characteristics meant that he could understand how he should and should not behave towards them. And so it is with the people we encounter. Young Hallam would have learnt that there are *adults* and *children*, and to expect different things from these two groups. He would have sub-divided adults into teachers, parents and others. He'd have learnt indirectly and directly that you behave slightly differently with these sub-groups and that they have different and sometimes overlapping roles in his life. He knew pretty quickly that it's best not to run up to your teacher and fling yourself into her arms for a great big cuddle, and that you'd stay out all day in the garden at home if you waited for a bell to ring to tell you it was time to come indoors.

So, humans automatically organise the inundation of multi-sensory information about objects and people into categories with common characteristics to help make decisions about how to interact with them safely and successfully in everyday life. Some examples:

- This is a chair. I sit on it rather than try to eat it, talk to it, or use it to send emails.
- This is a piece of IT equipment with a screen and no keyboard, so I probably have to touch the screen to make it work.
- This is a doctor. If I have a bad cough and the doctor has asked me to take my top off to listen to my chest, then that's OK.

When it comes to people, we create many categories to help us work out how to feel about them, what to think about them and how to interact with them. We may think doctors are clever and authoritative. They may make us feel a little timid and that we need to heed what they say, perhaps with little challenge or questioning. But meet that doctor out of context and without knowing their profession and there may be another category that we will employ subconsciously to work out how to think, feel and behave around them. Maybe you are queuing for tickets at the cinema with the show about to start and this person (that you don't know is a doctor) is standing there at the front of the queue holding everyone up sorting out tickets for a rather large family – how are you categorising that person now? What information are you using? How are you feeling and what sort of behaviour are you considering? Does the specific environment also have an effect?

And tell me something else. What gender is this doctor of yours that you have in your mind's eye?

If you said 'male', you would share that conclusion with the majority of people. It's simply what you've grown to expect given the many sources of 'information' you are exposed to, although the least influential of these sources is our direct experience! In the UK, female GPs have outnumbered male GPs since March 2014 (Bostock, 2018).

Every day we interact with far more people than we probably realise, and we use these categorisations and their associated characteristics – which form our stereotypes – to help guide our thinking and behaviour towards them.

Think of a typical journey to work (if you have one) maybe in a car, on foot, on the train, the bus, the tube. As you look around (though not if you're on the London Tube!) you will inadvertently, instantly and unconsciously pop people into categories. Now, the word 'judge' seems quite strong, but we are constantly making judgements about those people and we use the characteristics we associate with those categories to make our judgements. If I see a young man driving a car with sports trimmings of some sort, I'll assume that he is going to drive fast. I'll think he will be impatient and probably not be paying full attention because his music will be on full blast. I may put my senses on higher alert as I may need to take evasive action. Very occasionally I'm right, and – like the human I am – I'll use those 5% of occasions when a young man in a sports car cuts me up to reassert that my stereotype is right, and all young men will behave like that.

Fresh from an experience like that, or after reading a headline about a crash involving young people, it's quite normal to make a comment and perhaps add an opinion, such as 'it would be safer if men weren't allowed to drive till 25'. You can imagine the social media posts. Those reading it may have come across similar comments or news stories in the past, and all these comments subliminally connect.

This is the creation of an unconscious association between a notional category of people (young adult males) with a specific set of characteristics. Henceforth, the unconscious brain is primed to accept and connect further information confirming the stereotypical behaviour of this group. It will also disregard first-hand evidence about the thousands of young male drivers who drive safely. But there are consequences. Perhaps, in this example, sons reaching 18 are subtly deterred from learning to drive. What are the effects if young men can't access that form of independent travel when young women can? Perhaps that cancels out options for certain universities; perhaps it's unfeasible to get to interviews for certain jobs. Alternatively, they may become a really nervous driver and then crash as a result of indecision.

We categorise people whenever and wherever we encounter them. Significantly, the first level of categorisation we make is gender. This person is male and therefore will have certain characteristics, whilst a female person will have others. I therefore expect these things of them, and I will act according to these expectations.

Many years ago I was a sales rep. My patch was the East Midlands in the UK and part of my job was cold calling businesses to try and make appointments. On one occasion, a slickly dressed young male rep was just ahead of me entering a business unit in some out-of-the-way industrial estate. He went up to reception and said to the woman that he needed to speak to the Managing Director (MD). She asked what it was about, and he said that it was a matter for the MD alone. The woman pressed him a few more times about what he wanted to see the MD in connection with, but he was insistent that it was only for the MD's ears. The exchange came to an abrupt halt when the woman said: "I *am* the MD, and *you* can leave." While I wouldn't have used the same 'pitch', I knew that the truth was that I would have patronised this woman to some degree, had I not found out that she ran the business and was not the receptionist. A sobering lesson!

Professor Karen Kirkby was one of the women I interviewed. She is an electronic engineer and at the time was the Director of Science for the Surrey Ion Beam Centre, as well as Associate Dean for Research and Enterprise for the Faculty of Engineering and Physical Sciences at the University of Surrey. As a world leading authority, her work involves travelling the globe to present at conferences as the Keynote Speaker. She also happens to be an attractive woman with long blonde hair. This is what she shared about how the stereotypes she 'fit' create a barrier that she has to overcome before even speaking a word.

"You meet so many people who come in with all those assumptions. I find I have to spend the first half of the meeting actually almost proving to the presenters that I can actually do the job. The number of times I have been taken as the secretary. People then get incredibly embarrassed when you say, 'Actually I'm Professor Kirkby.' It happens all the time.

It is quite useful having a name badge on because you can occasionally point to it. You do find all the time that nobody can believe that you are in the role you are in."

- Professor Karen Kirkby

What Prof. Kirkby is describing is an example of overt things that can happen when the stereotype we have of a person doing a specific job role doesn't match the stereotype of the gender in front of us.

As you read the following sentences, take a moment to picture the person you'd associate with the jobs mentioned – which gender automatically springs to mind?

- We have stereotypes of job roles but also for job functions – think of examples like HR, Sales, Finance, Operations, Admin, or functions more familiar to your own workplace or sector.
- We have stereotypes for job levels – support staff, management, leadership, board directors.
- We have stereotypes for technical specialisms – think of IT / tech, distribution, research.
- And we have stereotypes of people working in whole industries and professions. Think of science, engineering, law, banking, medicine, nursing and social work.

In your minds-eye you see a man or a woman for each type of work. In some cases, this gendered aspect is even built into the role name: salesman, fisherman, fireman, tradesman, policeman, chairman. And even though the titles for all of those jobs have moved on to embrace either gender, associations for many are stuck fast and, all too often, irrationally defended.

The implications of the assumptions and expectations that go with these gendered stereotypes are far reaching, both for those that fit those stereotypes and for those that don't – because stereotypes are not just descriptive; they are also prescriptive. Your name or picture tell me you fit this gender stereotype, which tells me you have these characteristic behaviours and strengths, and therefore you will be good at these things, but less good at those things.

Now you have gained a grounding in the causes and consequences of stereotypes, you can start to identify situations when they might come into play and consider ways to counter barriers that they could create. As Prof. Kirkby demonstrated, something as simple as a name badge displaying her title was immensely powerful in preventing a barrier going up.

Making it happen:

Which stereotyping scenarios have occurred to you while reading this section?

What options do you have to address them, prevent them, or circumvent them?

Categorising is 'used' as a source of well-being which makes the walls built around categories harder to breach.

Given this book is in your hands, it means that I finally finished it, and it will have become a source of positive self-esteem for me. I'll have moved myself into the category of people called 'published authors' which is a tiny segment of the population who can attach themselves to very specific positive characteristics. They have to be disciplined and articulate, for example. There is an underlying implication that people outside the 'published authors' category do not have enough of these special qualities to join this 'elite' group. So, if I now identify as a member of the published authors group, I can use this comparison to feel special, which feels good and boosts my self-esteem.

Before you slam the book down because you are starting to loathe me, I should make it really clear that it would actually be very rare for these thoughts to be consciously articulated. But you know I'll have a glow inside when I step onto a platform and am introduced as the author of *Understand: Dare: Thrive*.

Using this '*I'm in a special group, compared to them*' comparison is something all human beings are subconsciously driven to construct in whatever way they can, as it's a reliable strategy to maintain or bolster self- esteem.

Humans are driven by a few basic physical and emotional needs. Food, water, shelter and warmth are obvious physical ones. And psychologists believe that we also have a strong and continual drive to develop and maintain a sense of positive self-esteem – a feeling that we are a worthy, valuable human being. Research is clear that when self esteem is low, particularly over a prolonged period, it affects our thinking about a wide range of aspects about ourselves, and our lives, which in turn affects our behaviour and contributes to depression. This can become a negative spiral, as we interact less with people, and those limited interactions happen when feeling down about ourselves, which can reflect back in people's involvement and behaviour towards us. We become more withdrawn and see life through a negative lens, making everything seem worse than perhaps it is, and so it goes on in the downward spiral of declining mental health.

The perception of our self-worth triggers a chain reaction that can result in mental and physical illness. Hence, through evolution, humans have developed an innate drive to secure positive self-esteem, leveraging clever strategies for building and maintaining it which are unconscious, powerful and relentless. This mental health and well-being strategy is incredibly efficient because it dovetails with the categorisation mechanism that is also working on our behalf in the background. They combine as a super-fast, energy and attention-free decision-making machine to help humans survive and thrive. And we benefit from it every day, be it through sourcing top-ups of self-esteem, or enabling us to successfully navigate workplace and social interactions. However, there will be times when this fundamental mechanism will also work against women (and members of other stereotyped social categories). This comes back to the critical fact that the first categorisation we make when we meet someone is gender. You would find it very hard to identify any culture or country in this world where women are considered the superior, rather than inferior, of the two categories. What happens is that difference in status is unconsciously processed and 'used' by men as a steady and reliable source of feeding their self-esteem. However, it's a source that also needs defending, as to lose it would be a threat to their healthy levels of self-esteem. Maintaining and defending this reliable and ubiquitous source of self-esteem requires a range of ongoing strategies to be activated, and these cause many of the barriers, dead-ends, delays, pitfalls and detours that women face.

But where do these insights fit in with having your best career? Well, these types of comparative categorisations artificially construct superior groups and their comparator, inferior group. So 'published authors' is an example of a superior social group that psychologists term an 'in-group', which distinguishes characteristics that members of that group have in common and which they consider to be different to, and better than, those of people outside that group (the 'out-group'). In-groups amplify the positive qualities they have in common and exaggerate the differences these represent compared to the characteristics that they identify as negative and less worthy, and typical, of out-group members. This leads to the thought, that '*I'm better than them*'. It is this relative sense of value that is the core ingredient of self-esteem.

There have been horrific examples throughout human history where these constructions are politicised to infer and entrench benefits to the privileged in-group, with dire penalties for the out-group. Consider, for example, the Nazi and Apartheid movements. It was in trying to understand how humans could act to one another as these people did that psychologists developed the insights about the drivers of human behaviour that I'm sharing with you here.

Humans use categorisations of people in even the most fleeting moments. Many tiny parts of our daily lives are used to make subconscious comparisons and to try and ensure that those comparisons are favourable to ourselves. We try to align ourselves with positive, 'superior' in-groups in any given situation and will seek to align ourselves with the groups that give us the best outcome. A situation as 'straightforward' as having a drink in a coffee shop or a meal in a restaurant leads us to making split-second, unconscious categorisations of the people around us, based on what little information we scan to decide where we can fit them on our pecking order. Their hair, clothes, level of personal grooming, accent, posture and facial expressions all provide this information.

On Friday April 5th, 1968, the day after Martin Luther King was assassinated, Jane Elliott, a teacher at an all-white school in a small town in Iowa, ran the first of her exercises to help white children (8 and 9-year-olds) understand what discrimination feels like. It's recognised as a landmark of social science.

She separated children with blue eyes from children with brown eyes and explained to them with clear examples and scientific 'evidence' how children with blue eyes weren't as clever or quick as those with brown eyes. She used examples from history and culture of brown-eyed people who had achieved great things and of whom Americans could be very proud. She also constructed special privileges such as five minutes of extra play time. The effect was dramatic. There was an instant behavioural response in both groups. The superior group became arrogant and bossy towards the blue-eyed children, who in turn became noticeably more timid, withdrawn and subservient after some initial resistance. Even performance changed, with the brown-eyed children doing better than they normally had in maths and reading tests, while the brown-eyed children scored more poorly. On spotting that Jane Elliott has blue eyes, one brown-eyed child said: "Hey, Mrs. Elliott, how come you're the teacher if you've got blue eyes?" Before she could answer, another child replied: "If she didn't have blue eyes, she'd be the principal or the superintendent."

On the following Monday (and, yes, that all happened in just one day) Jane Elliott reversed the test, saying that, of course she had got it the wrong way round and it was obviously people with blue eyes that were better. The impact was the same. The self-esteem and confidence rose in the blue-eyed children, while the drooping shoulders and lowered heads of the brown-eyed children were obvious physical demonstrations of their loss of self-esteem. However, the blue-eyed children were noticeably less nasty to the new out-group. The exercise ended with the teacher asking these children to reflect on what it meant to be a member of a supposedly superior or inferior group. The impact on them has lasted a lifetime, as they still go on record to testify to this day.

Despite a hostile response from white Americans, Jane Elliott continued these exercises at school and went on to become a famous speaker, trainer and author about racism and sexism. And this experiment set in train a whole new paradigm in social and cognitive psychology, with a focus on understanding the causes and consequences of these arbitrary social constructions.

When does our thinking about gender start to see differences and to discriminate between men and women? I'd suggest it's before a child is even born. A common question of expectant parents is whether they know if it's a boy or a girl. Why? Because then we can start to think about what to expect of that child and what that means for the parents.

Making it happen:

Just take a moment to think about this one. Perhaps make a note of your answers to these questions, being as honest with yourself as possible.

What do we expect of the life ahead of a baby boy compared to a baby girl? What are our expectations about their behaviour as a baby, a toddler, a child, a teenager?

What's OK and what's not OK? What do we assume about what games they should play and what they shouldn't play? How do we expect them to interact with friends? What would be normal? If a boy wrestles in the playground with another boy, is that OK? What if he wants to sit quietly and read or play or do ballet? What if a girl wrestles with another girl in the playground – is that OK? What happens if she cries? What happens if he cries? When is that OK? What about the sort of relationships they will have? With friends, and, as they grow older, with lovers? What sort of jobs do we imagine them having? What will their roles be if they have children? What should their work-life or career aspirations be?

We start to build very different pictures of what's 'normal', and what we are comfortable and uncomfortable with. Saying to a boy or a man that he's behaving like a girl or woman is often considered an insult, and used as such. A UK research study (Banerjee, 2009, p. 153) brings the power of this perception home. This research showed that while it's OK for a girl to be a 'tomboy', it's really not OK for a boy to act out of his gender-role stereotype, and behave in ways we stereotypically associate with girls. It showed that this is considered such a dreadful thing that the males closest to them specifically their fathers and their friends – will 'ridicule' and actively punish such behaviour, with the goal of forcing compliance to gender-norms. The bottom line is that in our society men are the superior 'in-group' and women are relegated to the inferior 'out-group'.

The implications of superior and inferior category membership are colossal. Women are born into a position of lower value, so they face an uphill struggle to build self-esteem to a healthy level and maintain it. Throughout their lives, women are exposed to micro-messages confirming their position in society. Our gendered roles, responsibilities, potential and values are communicated through literature, the media, advertising, film; through what we see and hear of the world in the news; through the construction, nuances and use of language which maintains the social power balance. All these things assign positive adjectives to describe male qualities, and negative ones to women: men talk, women gossip; men are assertive, women are bossy; men are passionate, women are emotional and erratic; men are analytical, women are indecisive. Our society uses men as the benchmark for normal and this includes everything from how leadership is best delivered to what an IT expert looks like; to the dummy to practise CPR on to the size of smart phone and the vocal pitch virtual assistant AI technology (such as Alexa) was trained to recognise.

You may have heard of an alternative film classification methodology called the Bechdel Test, which assesses movies for a very basic level of female representation in a film. It asks three questions of a movie and it must meet all three positively to pass the test:

- Does it have at least two named female characters in it?

- Do they talk to each other?
- About something other than a man?

These are relatively undemanding questions. Characters don't even need to be lead roles and they just need to have a conversation that isn't about a man. If we turned the test around to see if films could pass for male characters, it would be laughable. In 2020, the analysis of 8,574 films across all genres – including children's and adult's films – revealed that over 4 in 10 failed to pass the test (The Bechdel Test Movie List, 2020). Over 50% of Oscar winning films have failed the test.

What message does that give out about the significance of women and their role in life? And what is the impact of films continuing to fail the Bechdel Test? This is stuff our children, employers, partners, colleagues, politicians and families are absorbing, and it is just one simplistic measure for a single medium.

A few years ago, when my daughter was nine, she was selected to attend a special event put on by my city's libraries to motivate children to read. If they read six books across the summer holidays, they were in the draw to attend. I went with my daughter and listened behind around 50 children seated on the carpet in front of a young author who developed a story using suggestions the children called out. This author from London was probably in his early 30s and clearly successful, clever and articulate. The children lapped up his story. It was a story about a farm. But what stood out most was that, of all the characters, only two were female. And, of all the many characters, only two were not given a name. You've guessed it: while all the male animals were given names, the one female animal (a cow) was just called 'the cow'. The other character that didn't warrant a name was 'the farmer's wife'.

This wasn't Dickens or Shakespeare, but a young, cosmopolitan author. These were the next generation that were lapping up a presentation of the world as one in which males are ubiquitous and females a minority in the background, who are not even worthy of a name. According to the Drawing the Future Report (N. Chambers, 2017), by the age of seven, children's aspirations appear to be shaped by gender-related stereotypes about who does certain jobs:

boys aspire to traditionally male-dominated professions and girls show a greater interest in nurturing and caring related roles.

From that point I started observing and listening very carefully to how the world is presented to my daughter – the news, stories, school hierarchy, books she read, advertising, colour and nature of clothes and shoes, how people talk to her, and what they comment on. It quickly became alarming. One of my greatest concerns is that the evidence showed we are far from the brink of breaking out of gendered roles and the lifetime limitations – for boys and girls – that they represent.

While it can initially feel depressing to learn that these psychological drivers are deeply embedded, understanding what influences the thinking and beliefs of the people around you, including your own thinking, is actually a source of real power. When you understand that we have these mental models of the world and that these drive expectations of where people fit (and where they 'need' to fit to make us feel good about ourselves), you can anticipate worst case scenarios and develop approaches to address these biases to reduce their impact on your daily life as well as your longer-term goals.

It's not just about other people's expectations of genders – it's about yours too. 'What gets fired together, gets wired together' is a simple phrase from the world of neuropsychology used to describe what happens when we make associations between things. For example, when we see a blue sky on a warm day, neurons in our brain fire simultaneously when taking in these two bits of information. These small electrical pulses connect to create a neural pathway between the two elements – 'blue sky' and 'warm'. When information arrives that reinforces that association, the same neural pathway gets used again and becomes more established each time. Just like a well-trodden path across a field, it's easier and quicker to use than walk through long grass over rough ground. And this is how it works with information we receive together, in whatever form, however subtly and unconsciously. If we are consistently given information that men are farmers, or scientists, or heroes, we will then develop that default association deep in our brains so that if we think of a farmer, or a scientist or hero, we will automatically and instantly think of a man.

The lesson from neuropsychology is that we will have formed deep unconscious associations about aspects of working life, which will include the characteristics that we associate with certain job roles, levels of management and leadership, and certain key tasks such as presenting, negotiating, chairing, decision-making and dealing with complexity. So, when there is an opportunity to go for a role unconsciously associated with being delivered by a man, you may not even see it as an opportunity! If you do register it and go for it, then you are likely to have some level of doubt in your subconscious about how well you can do it because of this 'evidence' that you are not the natural fit. Fortunately, it may not manifest itself unless something brings your attention to evidence of female role expectations, such as being asked to take the meeting notes, or organise the coffees. This unconscious representation of a different profile for suitable candidates can prevent you from recognising yourself as an individual with relevant experience and potential.

Making it happen:

Try this challenge to explore your unconscious associations:

The police are searching for an armed robber and have got a tip-off that the villain, nick-named Johnny-Trigger, has taken refuge at a specific address, which they then plan to raid. When they get there, they find five people around a table playing poker. One is a decorator; one is a software engineer; one is a dentist; one owns a shop; and one is a company director. Without a word being said the police swoop, and instantly grab Johnny-Trigger.

- Your question: How did they know who to arrest?
- Answer: They knew who to arrest, because Johnny-Trigger was the only man seated round the table, all the rest were women.

Assuming you struggled with this, like most people, it demonstrates that 'what gets fired together gets wired together' and that we all learn the same view of how our world works. Our expectations, our beliefs and our behaviours, – like those around us, are subconsciously formed by these associations.

Having these insights is your psychological advantage. Now you can step back and look at what is really behind any reluctance you feel to put yourself forward. You can step up with more strength and conviction, focusing on your strengths and what they say about your potential as an individual, and subtly counter potential gendered stereotypes that might influence decision-makers.

Reflect back on opportunities you've hesitated about or dismissed, however big or small. What were these opportunities?

To what extent could this have been about your gender expectation for the role?

What could you do differently next time to consider the opportunity based on the reality of you as an individual rather than you as a member of the 'female' category?

Gendered 'schema' also affect your thinking and actions.

A schema is a dynamic stereotype. So, it's a commonly held view of something typically done or how something typically works. We have schemas for many facets of our lives. Consider the schema for something as simple as going to a coffee shop. We know how to recognise one from the outside – we see people around tables, on comfy seats or at bars, who have cups and saucers, or mugs in front of them. They are often with other people and are chatting. When we go inside, we expect to go to a counter to order drinks and we may need to queue till it is our turn to be served. We ask for what we want and wait for it, either at the end of the counter or at a seat if they bring orders to your table. We drink our drinks in a relaxed atmosphere and potter off afterwards, or power back to work. We'll have schemas for going to the cinema, and the dentist. We'll have them for catching a train; for attending a meeting. We'll have them for how the working day starts; and for many of the regular aspects of our working day and the interactions with other people in our working life. We use this clever mechanism that beavers away in the background, to help us navigate the world successfully without having to give it too much thought, so we can save our limited mental energy for higher priorities.

Schemas include what, where, when, how and who you most commonly associate with the situation in question. They are constructed through words and images (TV, films, books, what others say) that you've absorbed over time. Like stereotypes, direct experiences that counter the assumptions are often insufficient to change the mental construction that already exists.

So, you may know female company directors, politicians, lawyers, plumbers, doctors, and so forth, but your schema won't budge. And our mental motion picture carries a lot of detail. It will show how people in these roles behave with other people: subordinates, peers, superiors, clients. We have a view about the sort of language; their mannerisms; their work ethic; their integrity; their attitudes; what they might do in their spare time; the sort of people they associate with and maybe even something about the nature of those relationships.

We use schemas to compare what we know about ourselves with what we 'know' about potential roles to help guide our choices. Can I chair a meeting? Can I be a manager? Can I be a director? To be considered, should I be like that? Do I need to talk like that, behave like that? Does that mean I should or shouldn't pursue that direction?

Given that men have a vast history of doing the whole gamut of paid jobs, most career schemas are based on men, and therefore the embedded view will include a dimension that suggests something innately masculine is required to successfully deliver those roles. For women, their subconscious thinking can therefore go along these lines: 'men must be better at that job because it is men, not women, that you see doing it. So, there must be things about being a man that make them better able to do that job. As a woman, I'm less likely to be able to succeed. There's no point in going for it now. I'll work hard to build the evidence that shows me and them that I could do that job'.

For men, their subconscious thinking goes along these lines: 'I can see lots of people who look like me doing this job. So, I should have a good chance of succeeding. I'll apply now.'

One of the women I interviewed had been a marketing director for a large and successful company which was part of a wider group, and had been offered a job on the main board when we met. She would have been the first woman there. But she turned the job down and was intent on leaving the company and her highly paid role without another job to go to. When I asked her why, she said "I'd rather poke pins in my eyes than behave like they do towards the people in this company". She believed that their behaviour towards people was what was required to fit in as a main board director and to be considered successful. The idea of trying to challenge and change that behaviour as a lone female in a group of powerful men would have been immensely daunting and perhaps unrealistic – even given the enormous strength, confidence and capability of this particular individual.

To change the gendered element of role schemas, women have to carry out those roles in sufficient numbers and for long enough to create a new view. A view which automatically associates how the job is delivered with the needs of the role, and not mythical gendered characteristics. For example, that '*engineers are analytical, structured and highly qualified*' not that '*engineers are men, hence they are analytical, structured and highly qualified*'. Having female role models is an important step on this journey, showing women what is possible and creating a pipeline of women who will be part of re-defining the schema.

Chapter 6

Distinguish the facts from the fiction, the myths and the mantras

Psychological research shows that members of an 'in-group' adopt strategies to maintain their privileged position, with its range of benefits including, as we've just seen, higher self-esteem.

When we think about the in-group in this context – men in the workplace – the membership benefits include easier access to progression and senior jobs, higher status, higher salaries, wider opportunities, freedom from domestic constraints and so on. These are the sort of membership 'perks' which provide more tangible motivation for defence than perhaps the more profound benefits of self-esteem and confidence. Research shows that the drive to defend this higher ground is intensified by men's greater need for 'social dominance' (the desire for one's own group to dominate other groups). Men also have higher scores on what is known as the 'homosocial reproductive tendency' which is the desire to be with individuals with a similar social profile.

Over time a range of myths and mantras have developed as a series of protective walls around the 'in-group'. Much like some medieval castle, these defences prevent invasion and the loss of precious resources. The walls must be solid to maintain clear boundaries. Something less definite could mean a blurring of who were insiders and who were outsiders, leaving the property vulnerable to gradual infiltration and the dilution of resources, or even a complete takeover.

These myths and mantras have been repeated for so long, by so many people, that they are embedded in our culture as fundamental truths which are so 'obvious' that you would be stupid to challenge them. But I'm playing the child in the Emperor's New Clothes and shouting out that the Emperor is completely naked. I'm going to expose these myths and mantras for the nonsense they are, by providing you with the evidence of the contrasting truth.

I want to address these head-on so that you know the truth to start the un-shackling process to free you from fake societal frameworks that limit access to opportunities and fulfilment. These clear, fact-based insights will help liberate potential that may have unknowingly been held back. They will increase your positive self-belief, confidence and resilience.

My experience is that when you start to share the real facts, most people – women and men alike – will gradually open up, listen and engage. Many even become champions of the new model.

> *"I feel that we are probably much more forerunners than we actually think we are; we are pathfinders, striding out."* – Lin Phillips

Myth 1. Men are natural leaders, hard-wired through evolution.

'Men are hard-wired to be leaders' is an evolutionary theory. Like many other theories about the impact of evolution on behaviour, it is fundamentally flawed because there is no evidence to support it. Cave paintings may show men running around with spears, but any conclusion about what this means about modern behavioural differences in men and women is purely speculation. To move from speculative theory to fact requires significant, substantiated evidential data. There is none in this case. Therefore, we can speculate to our heart's content about the impact on the behavioural evolution of women from pre-historic societies in which women were cave-centric in comparison to men who were hunters, but it can only ever be speculation.

What we can and must work with is evidence. Where this has been done, it has resulted in the development of the Biosocial Origin Theory of Psychological Gender Differences (A. H. Eagly L. C., 2007, pp. 34, 35) which shows that the behaviour humans exhibit depends on the roles society assigns and which biology may determine. Historically, roles were very physically driven, with men using their greater upper body strength for manual work, while women conceived repeatedly in the absence of contraception. To survive in their respective roles, men had to use the traits, attitudes and behaviours best suited to the demands of their environment whilst women had to use rather different elements of the same human portfolio of traits, attitudes and behaviours to survive in theirs.

The crucial point here is that humans have a repertoire of traits, attitudes and behaviours which they are able to apply selectively dependent on the needs of the situation. On a daily basis we all adapt and modify our behaviour according to the situation we are in. We will talk and behave differently with different categories of people – children, adult partners, parents, work colleagues, bosses, customers, shop workers, people on social media platforms and so on. To successfully negotiate different environments and situations we may have to curb or avoid certain attitudes and behaviours – but critically, it doesn't mean that they do not exist in a person's repertoire.

Darwin's core principle for certain species surviving while others became extinct is most accurately termed 'survival of the adapted' – rather than the populist version 'survival of the fittest' – as it was the ability to adapt to new, different and changing environments that determined species' success or demise.

So, we need to think about this in the context of the changes over the last century which have been bringing down the barriers that have stood in the way of women's access to education, healthcare and to the wider world of workplaces. At the beginning of the 20th century, most types of work were simply closed to women; they could not own property and they had no political voice. The Suffragette movement and two World Wars – where women had to do the work men had previously done – made seismic changes. Through persistent struggle and not without a great deal of retaliatory oppression, women gained political power, and access to new roles which they could do well. In the 1960s came the contraceptive pill and many women then had control over their reproductive biology and could decide if, when and how many children they would have. These social changes and biological freedoms resulted in huge numbers of women entering the workplace and delivering roles they had never held before.

However, one facet of the response to this has been criticism for behaving in 'unbecoming ways' because they are 'acting like men'. Women in leadership are commonly scrutinised and criticised for behaviour perceived as masculine. But what if they are simply behaving like leaders? What if this set of behaviours that we've been wired to associate with masculinity is actually a set of behaviours we should wire to the demands of the role and the environment? Leaders have to be decisive. They have to be clear and unambiguous and often direct. They have to keep ahead of multiple sources of rapidly moving information, projects and communications. They have to make hard decisions which may be unpopular and assert their influence to make necessary changes. They have to successfully compete. So, when women (or men) display these characteristics, they are not being masculine, they are simply using the situationally appropriate traits, attitudes and behaviours in their repertoire – up-weighting some and down-weighting others – to navigate that environment successfully.

"I've worked with relatively enlightened people. They were certain I was right to be Managing Director, they were certain I was right to be CEO. But it didn't come without unnecessary criticism being levelled at me.

Telling me to stop doing my job in such a masculine way.

Telling me just to be me, that I didn't have to keep up with them.

It was patronising. I was doing the job the way I felt was the best way and with unparalleled success. We achieved things that no other agency had done before – we were recognised by all the trade press titles as agency of the year. That had never happened before. My boss, who was in New York, would fly over on the odd occasion and tell me off, then fly back. He would say 'stop trying to be so male about this. You'd be better at your job if you were more female'. His way of dealing with me making difficult decisions was to tell me I was odd!" **- Morag Blazey**

These leadership behaviours would be utterly unhelpful, self-defeating and unsuccessful if applied to the job of looking after small children. To survive and thrive with babies, toddlers and young children, carers have to be patient. They have to learn to live life in the slow lane. They must tolerate demanding and difficult behaviour. They must learn to cope with the relentless repetition of tasks requiring no brain power and delivering no mental stimulation. They must be on call 24 hours a day, 7 days a week, without holiday or pay, and remain positive to support the learning of our little people.

Today many women find the adjustment from fast-paced exhilarating careers to baby-carer incredibly hard. They have to learn and adapt if they are to survive in that foreign role which requires the instant 'parking' of the characteristics that previously made their days stimulating and rewarding. They have to dig deep to successfully care for these demanding individuals. Letting go of one's established identity, lifestyle, independence and income – however briefly – requires an enormous re-calibration and comes as a hell of a shock.

So, there is no evidence that women are born nurturers and men are born leaders. We simply adapt our behaviour to fit the occasion, accentuating some characteristics and minimising others to bring about the best outcome. Childcare and organisational leaderships require different characteristics sourced from the same foundation repertoire, as many fathers have now experienced while working at home during the pandemic.

> *"Roles have powerful effects on behavior and personalities."*
>
> **Eagly and Carli (Through The Labyrinth) (A. H. Eagly L. C., 2007)**

When you compare the personality traits that have been identified as key to effective leadership, men and women are the same. However, there are some subtle differences in what are currently recognised as the sub-traits (A. H. Eagly L. C., 2007, pp. 40-44). Within the main trait of 'extraversion' (important in building relationships), women over-index on the sub-traits of warmth, positive emotions, gregariousness and activity; while men over-index on the extraversion sub-traits of assertiveness and excitement-seeking. What this shows is simply that women and men have slightly different routes to achieving the same goal. So, if building relationships is key, then it would be splitting hairs to try and infer that one route was better than the other, since the objective will be achieved.

Unfortunately, decisions about recruitment and promotion are often made on _how_ people lead, rather than the degree to which they are successful in achieving the desired outcomes. And, as fallible humans, we assume that the way that leaders have delivered success in the past is the way it needs to be done in future.

> *"An observation that a colleague on that board made to me was, 'Marion, the rest of us open our*

mouths on the basis that we'll be right one third of the time. You open yours one third as often on the basis that you'll be right every time.' I would spend time on that board and watch and listen to the men questioning the chief executive or one of the business heads and I'd be thinking, 'Come on guys, they told us that and went through it in painstaking detail two meetings ago. Weren't you listening?'" **- Marion Cowden**

"Successful leaders most often have an androgynous balance of traits that includes gregariousness, positive initiative and assertion, social skills, intelligence, conscientiousness, integrity, trustworthiness, and the ability to persuade, inspire and motivate others."
(A. H. Eagly L. Carli, 2007)

Of the very few gender differences, there is one set of real significance: that women rate higher on emotional intelligence, empathy and a concept called 'theory of mind', which is the ability to understand what is in someone else's mind and therefore explain and predict their behaviour. Research indicates that these are the key reasons why teams with a significant proportion of women have measurably higher collective intelligence than teams with a small proportion, or an absence of women altogether (Woolley, 2010). Women use these abilities to evaluate what other team members are feeling – engaged, concerned, eager, irritated, disengaged, etc – to manage their contributions better and to create a level playing field on which everyone can add value.

Teams that are made up of many clever people will not necessarily make a clever team. When conversation is dominated by a few people, teams are less collectively intelligent than those with a more equal distribution of contributors. Interestingly, research has also shown that having a significant proportion of women in virtual teams using conferencing technology, where only voices are heard, also raises the level of team intelligence significantly (Engel D & doi:, 2014). These qualities may also be significant in accounting for research findings which show that where teams need to be innovative, they are the most successful when there is gender balance.

> *"I have a very strong belief that business relationships are relationships in business. If you treat your clients and your colleagues with the same measure of respect and affection and sometimes the same humour and irreverence that you would treat a friend or a partner, you have a much better chance of succeeding. I spent nearly 20 years in agencies and one of the things I was proudest of was that I was never asked off of an account. Because it is a perennial thing in agencies for clients to say, 'I don't want that person on our account anymore.' I think I always believed that it is very easy to fire an agency and very difficult to fire a friend.*
>
> *I think that was a real driver for me. When I ran departments and when I ran my agency people genuinely liked working with me. People years later have said, 'My friend used to work with you. You were a fantastic boss.' Everything to me has been about relationship building. I would say that I probably did that better a lot of the time because I was a Miriam, not a Malcolm. I believed all my life that great things happen by having strong powerful relationships, and by working with people and not working against people. I would say that even though I have spoken about the intellect being so important, I would say that on balance the EQ has been as important to me as the IQ."* - **Miriam Jordan-Keane**

Studies of empathy, EQ and Theory of Mind also reveal a slightly different emphasis on how power is perceived and used. While men are more likely to look for personal power and the competitive situations and hierarchical structures that enable levels of power to be visible and exerted, women tend to seek a version of power which is through teams and through cooperation.

"Be true to yourself, enjoyment and fulfilment is important. As we all know, women have a broader deck of skills, we are more multi-faceted – conversely men tend to be more single-minded. This allows women to be more agile and along with strong emotional intelligence, we have an incredibly powerful skill set." - **Fiona Kendrick**

These characteristics come together to bring the right resources together and ensure all contributors have a voice. These may be the driving forces behind the worldwide evidence that businesses with a critical mass of women at the top consistently deliver significantly better financial performance (McKinsey, 2007).

"One that I would always put on my leadership model would be creativity. In fact, that is a subject I have discussed with female colleagues before. We do feel that we are different because we are more creative. We draw in all of those around us who can help us turn that creative thought and idea into something tangible. We don't fly solo, we think differently; we think far more broadly about an issue and engage with those who can help us deliver." - **Sharon Kerr**

The following example from Prof. Karen Kirkby shows that the impact of these subtle differences in approach can mean a difference of millions of pounds in academia, where funding is fundamental to an institution's existence.

"It is more about being inclusive rather than exclusive.

There was a crucial turning point, and the first time for a completely new approach to the university.

The university, believe it or not, had never actually built up teams of people to put together large bids. You would be tasked with one area and then they would just leave it to someone to do it on their own.

63

My view was that this was far too important.

A bid that we put in involved people from across the whole of the university. We used the marketing department, we used the research and enterprise department, I used academics from three of the faculties. It was a big bid and it pulled in a lot of the different departments.

Me: So the convention before that bid was to let people do their own thing.'

To leave people on their own with no support. Whereas, what is very important is actually putting the team in place; different people doing different jobs. So you create the thing together. There were some bits that could only be written by one person, but no one person feels that it is all down to them and they have been left on their own to do it.

We won that bid with my new approach, because we had a much better chance now of getting it. The university has a science and innovation group, who are of the great and the good. We sent it out to them a number of times and got some very good comments back. They had never been involved before in one of these bids. A lot of them are industrialists. We knew that one of the bids was going to be read by industrialists. We were too close to it to be objective. We asked them to have a look at it and give us some feedback on what they thought was good, what was bad and what needed improving. Again, a lot of it is stating the obvious. But it's about actually making it happen.

Money is very important in universities.

At that time, my name was on the grants worth

£20 million, with about six million already secured. That makes more of a statement. I was one of the university's highest earners.

It is about the type of research that I do and also because in some ways putting together a team is a harder job.

In some ways it is easier to go off and do something yourself and you might get it and you might not. But you don't have to form a team and have the satisfaction of getting that team working. It is tremendous, especially if you feel you are giving the people who are doing a lot of the work the support they need to do it properly. They will do more that way than they could otherwise. There is a lot of satisfaction to be had out of that.

You are always aware that you are writing something you should be, but that there may be holes in it. The problem is that if you are too close you can't see them. It will happen when it goes into the research councils and other people read it. I would much prefer to have it evaluated beforehand, get some feedback and improve it. You will get other comments, but you will know that you have used the best resources available to you to get as good a result as you can. When these bids went off, what was said by all the people involved was, 'If we don't get it, we know we couldn't have done any better.' If we don't get the funding, we know there are bids above it that are better and they were put together by people who can do better than us. But we know we couldn't have done any better with the resources that we have got. You can't do any more than that."

- Prof. Karen Kirkby

Not only are men not hard-wired to be leaders, but evidence shows that women over-index on the leadership style, widely agreed and shown to be the most effective style in this era.

In 2007 Eagly and Carli published their seminal work, *Through the Labyrinth*, which is arguably the most comprehensive analysis of the research into the questions around women and leadership. Part of what makes their work so powerful is that they carried out meta-analysis of research into every important aspect of women and men vis-a-vis leadership. Meta-analysis is the equalising of a representative range of research studies addressing the same main question to identify what the overall insights really are. It's hugely powerful because it doesn't rely on or over-weight the evidence of individual studies. Through this enormous undertaking they were able to identify that women over-index on Transformational Leadership, while men over-index on Transactional Leadership, as evidenced in Figure 1.

Figure 1: Overview of Transactional and Transformational Leadership (Eagly, 2003; A. H. Eagly L. C., 2007)

Measurement Dimension	Description of Leadership Style	Effect Size + score higher = men; - score = women higher
Transformational Leadership		
Individualised consideration	Attends to individual followers' needs, focuses on development: mentors followers	-0.19
Inspirational motivation	Exhibits optimism and excitement about goals and future states that inspire, include and motivate others to perform beyond expectations	-0.02
Idealised influence	Demonstrates qualities that motivate respect and pride from association with her/him. Communicates values, purpose and importance of the organisation's mission	-0.09 to -0.12

Intellectual stimulation	Examines new perspectives for solving problems and completing tasks. Challenges assumptions, solicits followers' ideas	-0.05
Transactional Leadership		
Contingent reward	Provides rewards for satisfactory performance by followers. Relies on standard forms of inducement, reward, punishment and sanction to control followers	-0.13
Active management by exception	Attends to followers' mistakes and failures to meet standards	0.12
Passive management by exception	Waits until problems become severe before attending to them and intervening	0.16

"Transformational leaders…are those who stimulate and inspire followers to both achieve extraordinary outcomes and, in the process, develop their own leadership capacity. Transformational leaders help followers grow and develop into leaders by responding to individual followers' needs by empowering them and by aligning the objectives and goals of the individual followers, the leader, the group, and the larger organisation." (Bass, 2006)

It's easy to see that Transformational Leadership is the more powerful leadership style, enabling teams and organisations to anticipate and meet the demands of our rapidly changing global economy fuelled by diverse cultures. We have to listen, engage, influence and seek win-win situations, rather than dictate terms.

Looking at the evidence I've shared here, it also becomes easy to see why organisations with a critical mass of women at the top are so significantly outperforming other organisations. Not only are women as suitable for leadership as men, but they also provide a nuanced approach that looks further into the future and gets the best out of their people to meet that future successfully. It's an edge that makes a very significant difference. So, acting on the premise that men are hard-wired to be leaders is also damaging to the health of an organisation, its employees and stakeholders if it's acted upon. This is why the governments of so many nations are flexing legislative muscles to accelerate the realisation of gender balance in leadership.

Myth 2. Women have babies, so they're a costly risk.

"We shouldn't employ women of child-bearing age," the Financial Director of the management consultancy I worked for said to me. I was a rare creature in that business as a female management consultant and I was eight months' pregnant. The company's strategy for excellence was to recruit from 'the best'. Companies like the Mars Group, Procter and Gamble, and Unilever. To do this, it offered a superior package than those purple chip companies – higher salary, better pension, better insurance, better healthcare, better car. However, it had no maternity or paternity policy. And it bumped along the bottom providing the legal minimum. The board made it crystal clear to me that if I wanted anything beyond the statutory minimum then it was up to me to create a policy for their approval, or put up with this remuneration anomaly, as none of the all-male board would consider accepting or owning the task. It was my presentation of the policy that generated that statement from the Financial Director. They finally signed it off two weeks before my maternity leave needed to start.

Through my analysis of the policies of peer organisations, it became clear that they recognised that if you reward employee loyalty by looking after people at important life stages, then employees show even greater loyalty in return. Why would you go anywhere else when you get so well looked after, supported and rewarded? These leading companies saw the economic sense of investing in keeping the people they'd carefully selected to work for them, rather than incurring the greater cost of recruitment (which can be as high as 50%-60% of an employee's annual salary), training and waiting for newbies to get up to full speed, which is six months on average for management roles.

From an employer's point of view, there can be significant benefits from having employees who take career breaks. Unlike new starters, returners hit the ground running and have a fresh perspective on the organisation they know well, which is a unique opportunity that can benefit all stakeholders, as Sarah Lewis explained to me.

> *"I am a great believer in that whilst there are a lot*
> *of barriers for women in business, we sometimes do*

have some amazing life opportunities that men don't which put us in a much better place to continue to develop and grow. I would put maternity and maternity leave really high up in that box. I think there are significant benefits from maternity leave that men just never get.

Me: What do you mean by that?

I think the big one is that it's a life change and you also have this marvellous opportunity to have been away from the business for anything from five months to a year with the legal obligation from the business to give you your job back. You come back with this amazing ability to look at the business again as if you were an outsider looking in. Everybody knows who you are and what your skills are, everyone can still value you in the same way, but it is like you are starting fresh. If you can harness that in the right way...I didn't quite get it right the first time. The second time I came back I did absolutely. I had a three month window of enormous opportunity where I was seeing things in a different way, because I hadn't been there for six months. It is not a long enough period for things to have changed massively, but it is a long enough period to take a fresh look and think about how you want to do things differently. Certainly from my peers and people who work for me and probably from senior people, you have a real permission to actually come back and do things differently. If you do behave differently people say, 'That's because she's been on maternity leave.' They are absolutely right it is. Enjoy and get the benefit from me being different. So my style shifted probably as a result of maternity; but not just maternity because there is an emotional change from having children but because there is a window of time where you get the opportunity to stand back at a distance and look at the business. Things take on a different perspective and importance. Harnessing things like that is really valuable. It was probably not conscious, but when I look back it made a big difference to my leadership style, and I did start doing a lot less management and direction and a lot more supportive coaching and stretching kind of leadership style. The other thing that it made me do, was be really clear that I had limited time and therefore I had to make choices about where I spent my time." - **Sarah Lewis**

When people talk about women, work and babies they seem to assume that they must write off all women as a potential risk. We have to push back on this gross misrepresentation of the size of this 'risk' and to challenge the assumptions about women (and men) relating to parenting which can otherwise lead to very poor decisions about managing and developing talent.

To put this in perspective, 0.01% of the working population of the UK is pregnant on average each year (Equal Opportunities Commission, 2015) (ONS, 2018) and in the UK, USA and Australia families have an average of only 1.7 children over a lifetime. The global average was 2.45 in 2019, which has halved since 1950 (World Bank, 2019) and it's on a downward trend that will continue.

The truth is that not all women can have babies, many do not want babies, and an increasing number of women reach a situation in life where a baby is not viable (they don't meet the right partner, or not at the right time, or their income can't support a child at a time when they could have one) and not all women who have children are the primary carers. Figure 2 shows the reported levels of sharing of domestic responsibilities for men and women with children under 17; for about half of parents this a team effort. These equal sharers also reported the highest levels of engagement with their employer compared with other profiles of sharing.

Figure 2: Sharing of domestic responsibilities (Parkes, *The Credibility Crunch, Sat Nav to Success Research Report, 2020)*

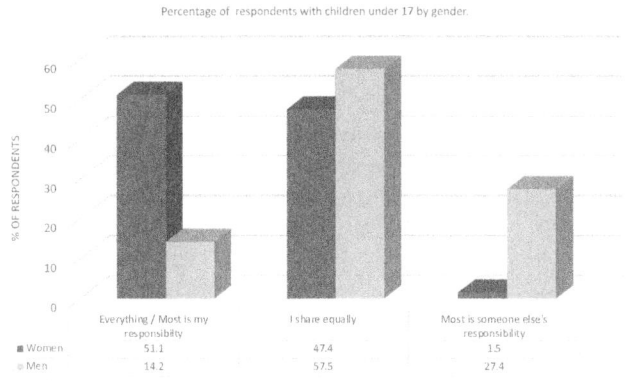

Morag Blazey describes the employer's perceived problem:

> "*Women are seen as too high risk. Women will be interviewed, and they will be thinking, 'Are you of childbearing age? Do you want to have kids?'*
>
> *I ran a company where 50% of the employees were women, all of whom were within childbearing age, bar one. When you divide 235 people up into skill sets and capabilities, you end up with quite small teams. You think 'Shit, if somebody goes missing from that team, we're going to have difficulty managing. And they'll be gone for a year.' You can see yourself getting into that way of thinking. This is a client servicing business. A client will come back and say, 'I want Laura.' And you have to say, 'Laura's having a baby.' Then we say, 'There's a chance of her doing three days a week.' And they say, 'No. We'll have somebody else.' And we say, 'But you want Laura.' And they say, 'Not if she's doing three days a week I*

*don't. I want somebody who does five days a week.'
So what do we do with Laura now? In the service
industry you are at the behest of the clients' call. And
women are frequently the best people for the job. The
chances of enticing the women back, making sure
their hours weren't so onerous that they couldn't
possibly stomach it and would just leave (as many
did) is very small. My colleague [female] and I
were always looking for ways of making this jigsaw
puzzle work. But we struggled through. We needed
the culture of women in the organisation and often
they were better at their jobs and worked hard. But
you can imagine if there were a man at the top, and
put a recession on top of that. They would probably
be thinking, 'I'd prefer to have a less talented person
who can do five days a week.' That is awful, but that
is what they would be thinking."* - **Morag Blazey**

Parenthood, which is usually synonymous with motherhood, is frequently seen as a problem, which many managers and leaders would rather not have. There are the implications in terms of covering that person's role, and in some cases, a cost to bear of paying for that leave and paying for the role to be covered in the woman's absence. And there are implications in terms of keeping pace with the rules and regulations and nuanced approaches to managing maternity leave conversations which can feel like very risky territory because of the perceived consequences of getting it wrong.

This challenge will become more common as more fathers take up their share of parental leave, as recorded across richer nations (Yekaterina Chzhen, 2019). Indeed, the Covid-19 experience has driven changes in paternal attitudes and expectations with their sudden immersion into family life – creating a new appreciation of both how hard it is to work and look after children, and how rewarding it can be for parents and children.

The loyalty to be gained from treating potential parents positively, openly and with integrity would more than repay the cost of paid leave. And the continuity of new parents returning to work far out-weighs the short term management task of covering a role short-term. There are organisations seeing this not only as a direct benefit with existing employees, but also as a source of competitive advantage to attract talent.

Organisations should work to create reasons and incentives to come back, making it a positive choice for parents. They should be talking to men and women about the realities and options when it comes to entering parenthood. Too many women (and men) are frightened by how their employer might respond if they have an honest conversation about their family aspirations. Too few organisations see the benefit of engaging with the reality that adults reproduce, so too few open their minds and apply their creativity to construct an environment which can make it a win-win-win for all parties.

Making it happen:

What do you take out of these new insights about women and parenting?

Even if they don't directly relate to your personal circumstances, is there anything you want to do differently or are there any changes you want to make as a result of what you've learned?

If there are actions you want to take, why do they matter and to whom?

So, when will you act?

Myth 3.   Women aren't as ambitious.

Comprehensive research shows that women are as ambitious as men as they enter the world of work, and the higher their educational achievement, the longer their expectations remain set at the highest level. However, as their careers progress, reality bites, with clear evidence showing that, as women, they are less likely to fulfil their ambitions. It's an objective evaluation of the most likely outcome based on the current reality of gender ratio imbalance increasing further up hierarchies and deeper into many specialisms. **This means women's expectations change, not their ambitions.**

The overall picture is that women work hard to achieve the best possible academic results and they expect to have the fulfilling career that their dedication should secure. They take the task of securing the first step on their career ladder after university more seriously than their male peers. They research hard, complete applications thoroughly, paying attention to detail and prep conscientiously for their interviews. The result is that newly graduated women are securing more of the available jobs and they secure the best entry roles, and the higher pay that goes with them.

Catalyst's report *Women and Men in U.S. Corporate Leadership* (Catalyst, 2004) published insights from a survey of 705 senior women and 253 senior men with similar backgrounds (such as education) and similar characteristics (such as age). They found that 55% of women and 57% of men wanted to get to the top job (CEO or the equivalent). They also found that having children at home made very little difference to the level of women's ambitions. A similar European study (Catalyst, 2014) of 124 women out of 526 full-time employees with MBAs with an average age of 36 found that 95% of women and 97% of men 'aspire to the top'. Again, no significant difference.

Catalyst's longitudinal research of thousands of MBA graduates from Asia, Europe, Canada and the USA shows that men and women's ambition is matched through their twenties – but then women start experiencing such issues as differential support (less access to mentors and sponsors) and less constructive feedback – factors which enable men to advance more rapidly. After this stage, the pay and progression lines on the graph representing women and men diverge.

These studies provide robust evidence that what we are seeing is the impact of biased management behaviour, not a lack of ambition. People who don't experience these barriers don't see that they exist and assume that if women wanted to get on then they would, so the lack of women at the top 'simply' means – as far as they are concerned – that they don't want to be there.

Many women reach the decision to get out of corporate life altogether, setting up their own business, where they can determine the culture, values, behaviours and rewards. As Eagly and Carli's research identified: "The main reason women leave corporate life is to advance their career." (A. H. Eagly L. Carli., 2007).

> *"This thing about women starting their own businesses (including probably my choice to do that) was a lot to do with furthering their career. And a lot of the reasons for women deciding to start their own businesses were because their heads were bleeding too much from banging them against the wall over and over again. This has blown up in a lot of corporation's faces, because after work there is no life left when you struggle like this all of the time. We all know the argument – acquisition versus retention – particularly in organisations; to have senior staff in whom you have invested walking away because you are not able to capitalise on their greatest strengths. That to me is a tragic waste."*
> **- Miriam Jordan-Keane**

Allied to this situation, there is evidence that when women approach the very highest levels, they take a critical view of the wider impact of the culture at those levels – the crazy working hours, the travel, the stress – and weigh up the costs and benefits to decide if both the intrinsic and extrinsic rewards are sufficient. Will it feel good enough? Will the material rewards be sufficient to compensate for the loss of a life outside work? What do I need? What do I want? What choice should I therefore make?

The rationale for leaving is completely understandable – women face more 'hazards' than men (Lee, 2012). And while it makes complete sense, these talented women become less visible, adding to the perception that if women were ambitious then there would be more of them at the top of the biggest and highest-profile corporations.

Research carried out by my business over the last four years has made it clear that women are remarkably tenacious in the face of these additional 'hazards'. Sector-specific research, such as in STEM (Sibley, 2016) (The Smith Institute, 2011), shows that there is only so long that women can persist where progression is thwarted, access to work they have taken years to qualify for is blocked, and the culture is unpleasant or even toxic.

So, while women are still lacking at the top, and in functions and specialisms typically thought of as male, this situation cannot be attributed to a lack of ambition. Different dynamics are at play, which are primarily rooted in the gender-biased beliefs and expectations of the gatekeepers of opportunity. Many of whom genuinely believe that they have no such bias, but of course these biases operate unconsciously, so people cannot see them or measure the extent to which they affect their decisions (without taking special unconscious bias assessment tests). Despite the cause of these obstacles, there are many strategies that organisations can employ to successfully reduce and overcome their impact.

Making it happen:

Notes on the insights and implications of this section:

Myth 4.   Women are hormonal and less capable of being objective.

In 2008 the global economy suffered the biggest financial meltdown since the Wall Street Crash and subsequent Great Depression. According to analysts it was primarily caused by financiers' flawed risk evaluation and out-of-control risk taking. The notoriously male environment of the financial markets led to 'Group Think' that got carried away unchecked. To prevent a recurrence of such a disaster there was a dramatic escalation of financial regulation in some parts of the world. One specific measure sought by the European Commission was to impose gender diversity quotas to break up and prevent Group Think:

EU Commissioner Barnier stated: "I believe it's essential that there is more diversity on boards of banks and other financial institutions, in particular more women. The issue is not just one of better gender equality, but also one of better corporate governance. We need to break the Group Think approach, which has been far too prevalent in the past, with the disastrous consequences we have all witnessed." (Treanor, 2011)

Evidence from the field of neuroscience is very clear that testosterone has a detrimental effect on the cognitive ability to assess risk, which becomes exacerbated under situations of stress.

"*In a competitive environment, testosterone level increases significantly, leading to greater risk taking than in a non-competitive environment. Overall, this study underscores the importance of the endocrine* [hormone] *system on financial decision-making. The results of this study are relevant to a broad audience, including investors looking to optimise financial performance, industry human resources, market regulators, and researchers.*" (Nofsinger JR, 2018)

The impact on decision-making is an even greater issue among men between 16 and 30 when testosterone levels are at their peak, although levels only decline gently by an average 1% a year from then on. This everyday hormone impairs the judgement of risk, making judgement worse under pressure, and in the absence of specific balances, checks and measures, causes undue risks to be taken.

Gender balance in leadership delivers consistently better business performance.

Michael O'Sullivan, UK Research and Global Portfolio Analysis Managing Director at the Credit Suisse Research Institute, gave a very powerful message to investors on publication of their 2012 report, which presented evidence from analysis of 2,360 companies across the world that those with more than one woman on the board had consistently outperformed those with no women on the board by 26% over the previous seven years covered by their data (Credit Suisse Research Institute, 2012).

"Most of that performance comes from the post-credit crisis period: introducing women to the board gives better decision-making and better vigilance in terms of what's going on in the company. A mixed-gender board allows for a better mix of leadership skills and access to a wider pool of talent. It improves corporate governance, and tends to be more risk-adverse than companies with male-only boards, the report showed. According to the research, people, including investors, also believe companies with women are better businesses and people work harder when there is gender diversity in the workplace."

The report concluded: *"In testing the performance of 2,360 companies globally over the last six years, our analysis shows that it would on average have been better to have invested with corporates with women on their management boards than those without".*

The 2019 Credit Suisse Gender 3000 report, tracking the extended base of 3,000 companies back across their 12 years of data, showed consistently that as gender diversity increased, so performance against key financial measures such as operating margin, credit ratings and cash flow return on investment increased. (Credit Suisse Research Institute, 2019)

For centuries women were (and sometimes still are) considered to have physically different and inferior brains, consequently making them incapable of logic and objectivity. Let's boot that gendered myth out of the stadium.

Psychology is all about human behaviour and therefore it has a major scientific focus on human decision-making. One of the big questions in this field is whether humans are capable of logical evaluation. The short answer is that only a minute subset of men and women are capable of being truly logical. Vast bodies of research have shown repeatedly that people fail to be able to apply the rules of logic, and only those with an immensely high IQ are capable of truly logical thinking. This seems to be partly because they are able to suspend, or partition, the prior experiences or expectations which can sway reasoning, while the rest of us factor in stuff that we assume we already 'know' and therefore don't have to consider. While women perform better academically at the key stages and at degree level, there is no evidence that women's IQ is higher. So, let us leave the question of logic as one that exists in the domain of the super-intelligent, be they male or female, but which will always be beyond the vast majority of us.

This takes us to the next question about objectivity and subjectivity – a vast topic which has also been closely researched. For all of us, objectivity in the evaluation of information, people and situations to help us make the best possible decisions is an elusive utopia. The overwhelming problem is that our phenomenal brains are structured to make shortcuts to speed up our decisions and minimise demands on the limited capacity of our conscious brains, so they can attend to more important stuff. This automated corner-cutting system is a huge asset, but it has flaws. It makes systematic errors due to the tendency to rapidly pull in and over-weigh the familiar, the recent and the easily accessible. The result? We all consistently and systematically make errors of judgement. Psychologists have defined and measured over 150 distinct types of systematic errors of judgement (cognitive biases). The consequence on the quality of decision-making in organisations is so significant that a whole sphere of study has emerged called Behavioural Economics. As McKinsey stated in their research *The Case for Behavioural Strategy* (Sibony, 2010): "*cognitive biases affect the most important strategic decisions made by the smartest managers in the best companies.*" Therefore, organisations must create strategies to minimise exposure to the vast and sometimes devastating costs incurred where decision-making lacks the necessary rigour.

Many people, even apparent experts, over-estimate the accuracy of their judgement. This is so common that it has a name – the

Overconfidence Effect. An effect for which there is no research evidence of greater prevalence in one gender. Psychological research (Ayton, 2010) has found that experts who fail to follow up on the outcome of their decisions make poor decisions more often than they believe they do, hence they also fail to learn from their mistakes or sub-optimal decisions. It's worrying given this group included doctors. Weather forecasters are rather different: they learn immediately whether their forecasts were accurate, and can therefore analyse and learn from their errors to become increasingly accurate and better at calibrating the likelihood of getting components of their forecasts right.

How often do managers and leaders really evaluate the impact of their decisions? How often do they articulate the measures and dimensions of their intended outcome and then go back and measure how well they have done? Very rarely, in my experience – and I'm sure in yours too.

As with stereotypes, cognitive biases are caused by the lightning-speed application of unconsciously constructed mental models of how the world works, based on what we are exposed to. We hang onto our model and the components that make it up, because if we change them, we risk chaos and confusion because they are all interdependent. So, when we are confronted with evidence that challenges our mental models we tend to ignore, disregard or find a way to dismiss the 'anomaly'. And conversely, when we stumble across a real anomaly which supports our model, we immediately pay attention to it, and re-confirm our belief. So, we are drawn to information that confirms our bias while doggedly ignoring the other 95% which proves it wrong!

However, I was fascinated by the comments of some male CEOs (Chief Executive Officers) of FTSE 100 companies about women on boards, gathered by the authors of *A Woman's Place is in the Boardroom* (Graham, 2005). They observed that the presence of a woman, ideally more than one, increased objectivity and reduced the issues and impact of testosterone-fuelled behaviour in board meetings.

> *'There's less ego around – less positioning. We're all bloody kids. Boys are boys. Women bring calmness and objectivity; not all the time, but generally they're calmer and there's less jostling for position."*

> *"Any team with a mix [of genders] is better, because it stops the 'testosterone high'."*

- Two male CEOs (Graham, 2005)

What we have to conclude is that **women aren't more hormonal, nor less capable of being objective than men**. The male hormone testosterone can have a detrimental impact on risk assessment (Apicella, 2015). Women's ability to be objective has been shown to be no better or worse than men's across many types of rigorous scientific studies. Perhaps the most revealing insight is that all humans struggle to make objective decisions because they cannot escape their unconscious cognitive biases.

Making it happen:

Your notes on the insights and implications of this section:

Myth 5. Women aren't good at IT, maths or science.

According to meta-analysis of one hundred US research studies, representing results of over 3 million people's mathematics performance, there is no significant difference between men and women's ability: "females outperformed males by only a negligible amount" (Hyde, 1990).

Research entitled *Investigating Gender Differences in Mathematics and Science: Results from the 2011 Trends in Mathematics and Science Survey* (Reilly, 2019) reported results from an international assessment of 13- and 14-year-old students' achievements, attitudes, and beliefs across 45 participating countries. It found small to medium-sized gender differences for most individual countries in both mathematics and science achievement. However, the direction of difference varied i.e., in some countries boys were better, in others girls were better, and **'there were no global gender differences overall'**. The variation of the direction of differences by countries was concluded to be **'incompatible with the notion of immutable gender differences'**. Interestingly, they identified differences between OECD and non-OECD countries, with girls scoring higher than boys in mathematics and science achievement across non-OECD countries. So, these differences in achievement outcomes must be driven by differences in cultures and their impact on attitudes, influences, choices and practices – not innate capability differences.

Despite the scale, weight and consistency of evidence to the contrary, there is an enduring and very widespread perception that females are poorer at maths, IT and science than boys. This cultural perception is communicated and reinforced by parents by such actions as steering children to gender-stereotypical play and subjects (Tenenbaum, 2008) and by their non-verbal language. For example, buying games and play materials attuned to maths and science for boys more than girls (Bleeker, 2004) and offering unsolicited help with maths homework to daughters and not sons (Javanoic, 2005). Likewise, teachers and teaching materials are vulnerable to reinforcing academic gender stereotypes, in the absence of rigorous and conscious checks and challenges. These messages are absorbed from a young age, resulting in girls believing that they are innately inferior at these subjects, which will therefore be harder for them. And when people anticipate a poorer outcome, they will attend (i.e., focus) less, and therefore remember less, and they will give up more quickly with challenges.

Research on another key influence is a phenomenon called 'stereotype threat'. This is widespread in its impact on individuals, with a large body of research behind it (Steele, 2010). The 'threat' arises in a situation where you could be associated with a stereotyped group considered to be less competent in relation to the focus of the situation. The threat is the anticipation of the response of those who see themselves as more competent, based on direct previous experiences and indirect knowledge. Awareness of a threatening situation raises levels of anxiety about confirming the negative stereotype. This raised anxiety then needs to be controlled in order to carry out the task successfully and disprove the stereotype. However, this requires a level of cognitive effort which diverts cognitive resources, and the result is poorer than it would have been in the absence of this perceived threat. So, the threat has a material and detrimental impact on the outcome.

The threat of the specific stereotype of males being better at maths and females being better at languages has been shown to undermine girls' performance in maths from the age of six. At that age kids are still in the mode of seeing their 'group' as being the best at whatever is the topic – my Dad is bigger than your Dad; we built the best den; our team can run faster than your team, etc. However, their unconscious has absorbed and processed messages that boys are better at maths, and this correlation is strong enough to undermine performance at maths tasks when there is a 'cue' in their environment that triggers the connection (S. Galdi, 2013). In this research the cue was colouring in a picture at the start of the test: one group had a picture of a boy resolving a maths question on the board, with a girl in the scene failing to respond; a second group coloured in a picture reversing the genders' i.e., the girl resolves the maths question, the boy doesn't respond; and the third – the control condition – was a picture of a landscape.

Boys' maths performance was unaffected by any of these

precursor cues. Girls' performance was unaffected by the landscape cue. However, girls' performance was lower with the 'boy succeeding' cue. What is also very interesting, and positive, is that girls' performance was higher than the neutral, control condition with the 'girl succeeding' cue. This boosted performance even higher.

This pattern of results is consistent for girls and women with maths and has been measured across other negatively stereotyped groups in triggering situations. Unfortunately, the circumstances that are most likely to trigger the stereotype threat response are at 'the next frontier of their skills', which means the times when people need to prove their capability. For example, a white male athlete who has made it through to his highest level of 100 metre race; a person of colour sitting their Oxbridge entrance exam; a woman interviewing for an IT role (Steele, 2010, p. 41).

The good news is that strategies are emerging which can counter stereotype threat (which I share in detail in Chapter 11). As illustrated just now, a positive cue countering the stereotype (the picture of the girl solving the maths problem) has an immediate and opposite effect. In my own research with adults, having a picture of a well-known, successful female mathematician within the immediate working space had the same impact on maths performance. Another study (Nicola J. Pitchford, 2019) showed that introducing control of the content and delivery of maths teaching to prevent unconscious bias in delivery by using interactive apps on handheld, individual students' devices, eradicated any difference in gendered outcomes for both maths and reading.

Figure 3 graphically illustrates the maths capability myth: it's the A-Level (pre-university exams taken at 18 years old) uptake and achievement picture in England in 2019. Bubbles to the right of the vertical axis indicate that more boys than girls took these subjects (and more girls to the left) and bubbles above the horizontal axis show where boys' results are better than girls. While girls do better at more subjects, more boys do maths and maths-based subjects, and boys did better at maths and chemistry. The size of the bubbles depicts the relative number of students taking the exam.

Figure 3. A-Level entries and attainment (Education Policy Institute, 2019)

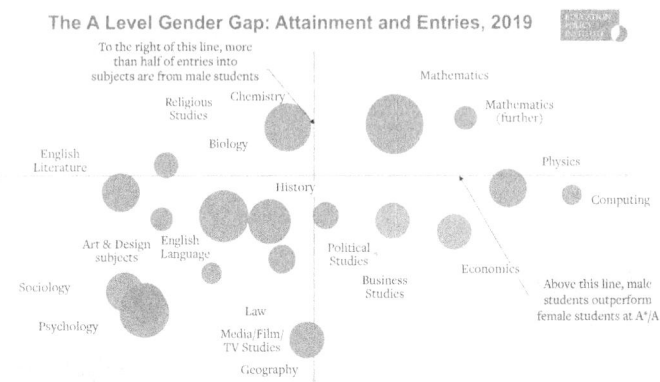

Recent research (D. Storage T. E., 2020) has focused on investigating explicit and implicit (unconscious) stereotyping around high levels of intellectual ability ('brilliance' is the research term used to encompass this concept). This focus has been driven by the determination to understand and help address the underrepresentation of women in fields that are perceived to demand high levels of intellectual ability such as the sciences, technology and maths.

Preceding research identified that 'gender-brilliance' is an umbrella stereotype which covers any domain considered to require this high level of intellect. It also shows that while women are increasingly considered to be equally intelligent – 85.9% agreed in a nationally representative US poll, undertaken in 2018 (A. H. Eagly C. N., 2019), it is not the case with high level intellect. Research in 2016 (D. Storage Z. H., 2016) showed that the more a field was believed to require this level of intellect, the lower the proportion of women in it.

A methodology for testing implicit associations and the strengths of those associations has been refined by psychologists over several decades, giving us absolute confidence in their results. Known as

Implicit Association Tests (IATs), they are computer-app driven, using the speed of reaction to different stimuli (different words or pictures representing different attributes, such as funny, serious, strong, creative, clever, slow, etc) when paired with the core subjects (such as men and women). They use algorithms to measure the differences in response times and patterns to identify associations and their strengths. People are faster at pairing concepts and attributes that are strongly linked (associated) in their subconscious mind, even if consciously they would not recognise these 'beliefs', because these are automatic associations. Attempts to consciously control responses in these tests are instantly apparent, as conscious thinking takes longer.

Daniel Storage used this approach to research implicit association and also collected data on participants' explicit associations. The results showed that there is a robust implicit association between 'men and brilliance', and not 'women and brilliance' (this included women from a wide range of racial and ethnic profiles). Participants reported recognising that society generally believes men to be more brilliant, but said that they personally didn't. However, their actual unconscious biased association was strong and clear. The difference between the explicit and implicit results indicated that people know this type of belief is a highly socially sensitive issue and therefore distance themselves from it.

The research also showed that children (9 and 10 years of age) shared this 'male=brilliant' association. The research team made clear that it's vital to understand, scope and quantify this association in children as well because of the implications:

- These implicit associations are able to predict and explain differences in their achievement.
- Certain subjects are considered to require more intellectual horsepower than others (specifically maths and physics).
- It may be an obstacle to girls' success in fields where they perceive this trait to be valued (i.e., girls may opt out, or be pushed out of pursuing brilliance-oriented professions).

These embedded beliefs have a stark and very tangible impact, in addition to those we've seen already, which is that when girls are able to make decisions about what they study then they drop these subjects in favour of ones they believe are more likely to be successful, as Figure 3 demonstrates in terms of the gendered take up of A-Level maths, which is a compulsory subject to 16. These researchers also pointed to the continual cycle sustaining this stereotype.

Because of women's exclusion from the professions that have delivered high profile advances in the sciences, medicine, engineering and so forth till the most recent era, the vast majority of the great pioneers that we all know so well are men. The narrative accompanying this profile both fuels and supports rationale that the cause is superior male brain power. Children are led – with the best of intentions – to what is believed to be the best fit for them. But, as we can see, this perception of 'fit' is fundamentally flawed. The impact, however, is very serious for individuals fulfilling their life potential and for societies to thrive.

> *"From 7th to 12th grade*, my secondary education was entirely in an all-girls school, so no competition from men, only from other girls. It is a very different environment to being in a mixed gender school. You get a far better chance, as a woman, if you go to an all-girls school in my opinion, because of the stereotyping. The teachers expect boys to be better at maths for example. Guess what, there aren't any boys, so the best person in the class at maths is going to be a girl.*
>
> *I think it teaches you to be competitive and that it's OK to be competitive. I think the difficulty is that boys are testosterone driven and they never sit still. They are out there rough-housing, they are beating each other up; there is always a game to be played and teams to be created. I think we had the freedom to be competitive in a girlie way rather than having to be competing on boys' terms of what competition means; having to constantly prove yourself in a physical way, or constantly having to be there with*

your hand going, 'I know! I know!'

Six years in a girls' only school I think was very good for self-confidence." - **Sara Fox**

*approx. 12 to 18 years of age.

"The pipeline starts leaking at schools really. Not very many women do Physics A-Level. So, you are always fighting as a minority. But having said that, compared with thirty years ago, it is different. We don't think it is wonderful here [at Imperial College], but it is different from thirty years ago.

I am sure there are still many organisations that are very unpleasant for women to be in. The engineering trade would be one of those. In the 70s it was trendy to be a woman in a manual trade. God knows what happened to all of that. There are still some plumbers, electricians and carpenters around. It is the same with engineering; we get women on engineering courses, but not British women. We get Asian women. They are pushy.

I am sure there are parts of the college where it is not nice to be a woman. Departments where they have very few women and there is outright sexism. I know that is the case in some places because I end up talking to some of these women and trying to do something about it. That is part of the battle. We haven't done it yet." - **Prof. Dot. Griffiths**

According to a report in Harvard Business Review (Sibley, 2016) women account for 20% of US engineering graduates and yet just 13% of the US engineering sector's workforce, with an estimated 40% of graduates leaving or never entering the profession. To understand why this 40% figure exists, a longitudinal study tracked 700 undergraduate male and female engineers. Clear issues started emerging as teamwork – so fundamental to engineering activities – commenced during undergraduate studies. Women reported being treated according to gender stereotype: being side-lined for the 'real' engineering work, to do the admin and similar 'menial' tasks. This treatment was also experienced in interactions with the academic staff and on work placements and internships. These engineers were not being given the chance to do engineering and could clearly see the prospects for the road ahead.

UK data has highlighted the impact of the same set of issues. In 2008 there were 620,000 female science, technology, engineering and maths graduates, but less than a third (185,000) were actively employed in those fields. In 2010, nearly 100,000 women with these degrees were not actively using these qualifications (The Smith Institute, 2011).

In conclusion, maths – the underpinning discipline for the sciences, IT and engineering – is a subject in which there is no difference in capability and performance by men and women, or boys and girls based on meta-analysis of global data. Evidence in the STEM industries (Science, Technology, Engineering and Maths) shows that those young women that pursue their interest and ability in these subjects to professional level are then challenged when they enter the workplace to endure what is all too often a closed-minded culture towards professional women. As a result, many leave not only a specific employer but also the industry.

The pressure is on parents, educators and leaders of these sectors to change the picture they present to girls (and boys). Great initiatives are now coming to the fore to attract young female talent, perhaps because these industries are now struggling to find sufficient talent to meet their growing needs. Competition may be the one factor that ultimately forces the implementation of the cultural, behavioural and structural changes needed for them to attract, retain and progress female talent. However, given that culture changes slowly, the pressure is also on women in these sectors to hold onto the work they love, to tough it out and change the culture from the inside for the sake of the women behind them.

> "*Britain is gripped by an engineering skills crisis. In order to plug the yawning gap, we need to double the number of engineering graduates coming out of*

our universities each year, for the next twenty years. If we don't, our high-technology companies will be out-invented by the international competition. Our exports will virtually disappear and our wealth will plummet. We will have lost forever the ability to engineer and make things. It's a problem that we can't ignore, but we can't begin to solve it if we discount half the population based on myth. It is simply not true that women don't 'do' engineering."
- Sir James Dyson. The Guardian, August 2014

- In 2015 Dyson opened his engineering university in the UK – The Dyson Institute of Engineering and Technology – paying, not charging, students.
- In 2018, over 40% of the undergraduate intake were female (versus 15.1% average across UK engineering undergraduate courses).
- Dyson estimated that Britain will be short of 1.8 million engineers by 2025.

And, while ***the scientific evidence wholly undermines the myth that women aren't good at IT, maths or science*** it is important to be aware that, for all the reasons I've described to this point, there is and will continue to be bias in the media's reporting of findings about gender differences that will seek to interpret findings in favour of men's 'superiority'.

Making it happen:

Note your insights and their implications from this section.

Are there any assumptions you make about your capabilities or those of men and women or boys and girls around you that you need to challenge?

What do you want to do differently as the result of your reflections?

Myth 6.   There is no discrimination –'they can get on if they want to, like anyone else'.

A couple of years ago I hired a camper van and toured the South Island of New Zealand with my daughter for three fabulous weeks. Camper vans were everywhere, and I was a complete convert to the total freedom and flexibility they afforded, and I wondered why they weren't popular in the UK. Then I got back to the UK and found that camper vans seemed to be everywhere I looked. They were popular but they had never been visible to me before because they'd never been relevant.

And that's the way it works with spotting discriminatory behaviour (both words and actions). If it's not something you experience, it's simply not going to be visible on your radar. So, if you are a white male in a predominantly white country, it's not something you are aware of, because it's not something that happens to you. As far as those people can see, there is no impediment to progress because they have experienced no such impediment to their progress.

> *"More than half of all men (55%) think gender equality has been achieved at work, compared to 42% of women."*
>
> **(Eurobarometer 465, 2017) Survey and report for the European Commission report on Gender Equality**

That's 26,479,000 more men than women thinking the job's done.

Today there is a relatively high awareness of the unacceptability, and legal risk, of blatant forms of sexism (as well as other kinds of discrimination). Hence overtly discriminatory behaviour has reduced dramatically. Those with strong biases tend to be aware of them and how they are seen.

More moderate levels of bias (as measured by implicit association testing) may only make themselves patent under certain circumstances (such as being tired or stressed, or under pressure). Individuals with this level of bias may feel that they are balanced, understanding and open without any prejudices. Unfortunately, none of us are free of the associations that our culture subliminally communicates. So we all have a level of bias. What matters is whether that bias then affects what we say, do and decide – to the benefit of some and detriment of others.

Most of the behaviours that express our subconscious beliefs about members of stereotyped groups are very small in scale, hence they are called micro-behaviours. Those micro-behaviours that communicate our 'view' that someone is of less value, i.e., unequal to others, are called micro-inequities. And while they are small, their impact can be very significant, undermining the individual on the receiving end. They are subtle, often unconscious, messages that devalue, discourage and exclude.

> *"We send anywhere from 40 to 150 micro-messages to each other in an average 10-minute one-to-one conversation and 20 to 40 in that time in a mid-sized meeting".*

> **Stephen Young, Insight Education Systems. Author, *Micromessaging: Why Great Leadership is Beyond Words***

Micro-inequities can be conveyed in a myriad of ways. Through facial expressions (rolling of eyes, looking elsewhere in a conversation); gestures (turning away, using hand signals to involve or exclude in meetings); tone of voice (patronising; unnecessarily loud); choice of words (using a nickname or general term like 'love', or 'girl' while referring to other people by name); talking over and interrupting; and through relative nuance, minimising the value of one contributor versus another – being "damn[ed] with faint praise" as Alexander Pope called it. A message can even be conveyed by doing nothing – ignoring or passing over someone, engaging in selectively informal situations such as conversations waiting for a meeting to start, or walking through the office. The impact is compounded when others receive clear, positive verbal and non-verbal messages, called micro-affirmations.

> *"Organizations have done a great job at controlling the big, easily-seen offensive behaviours but have*

been somewhat blind to what is rarely observed. Organizations have done great work at controlling the few elephants, while being overrun by a phalanx of ants." - Joyce Tucker *'The DNA of Culture Change',* (Tucker, 2004)

Being on the receiving end of micro-inequities can wear you down. It may stop you in your tracks and gradually erode your belief in your capability and worth to the point of making you feel like giving up.

However, they are notoriously hard to pinpoint, to describe and to cite as significantly problematic without appearing to yourself and others as over-sensitive or just plain paranoid.

As part of my research strategy, I set out to measure the scale of difference in the degree to which men and women's contributions are valued in the workplace, and to quantify the impact of the micro-inequities. Hence, I've been able to measure the extent of this difference, which I term the *Contribution to Value Gap.*

Figure 4 shows these gaps at entry level, in middle management and at senior management, for men and women. At entry level, there is about the same sized gap between the proportion of men and women consistently contributing and the proportion having their contributions consistently valued.

However, in middle management women report a crushing 26.9 percentage point *Contribution to Value Gap,* given that 83% of women report that they contribute whenever they could or should, but only 56% report that their contributions are consistently valued. There is virtually no gap for men: 80% are consistently contributing and 77% consistently valued.

In senior management and leadership, women report a gap that is virtually the same as women at entry level. For men at this level, the gap is negligible. This is consistent with the research on the gendered stereotyping of 'brilliance' (D. Storage T. E., 2020) that I shared with you on pages 88 and 89.

Figure 4: Contribution to Value Gaps by gender and career level

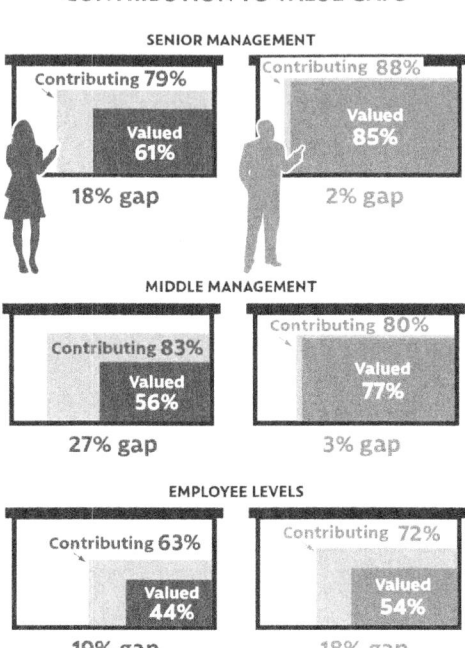

CONTRIBUTION TO VALUE GAPS

SENIOR MANAGEMENT

Contributing 79%
Valued 61%
18% gap

Contributing 88%
Valued 85%
2% gap

MIDDLE MANAGEMENT

Contributing 83%
Valued 56%
27% gap

Contributing 80%
Valued 77%
3% gap

EMPLOYEE LEVELS

Contributing 63%
Valued 44%
19% gap

Contributing 72%
Valued 54%
18% gap

Every employer should be deeply concerned about the impact of unconscious discrimination communicated via micro-inequities, if only because of the differential impact on engagement and therefore on performance.

- At entry level and in middle management, twice as many men as women increase engagement as a result of the extent to which their contributions are valued.
- In senior management and leadership, it's seven times as many men as women.

Organisations which don't address these micro-inequities also leave holes in their talent pipeline, as far more men than women report an increase in their motivation to progress.

- At entry level and in middle management, twice as many men as women increase their motivation to progress as a result of the extent to which their contributions are valued.
- In senior management and leadership, it's eight times as many men as women.

So, 'no', in answer to the title of this myth, they cannot 'get on if they want to, like anyone else'. Firstly, because organisations value significantly fewer women than men, and secondly because the impact of this reality results in significantly more men than women increasing their motivation to progress.

Making it happen:

Notes on the insights and implications of this section.

What actions, if any, do you plan to take as a result of what you have learned?

Myth 7.   Quotas would be wrong – women should just get on based on merit.

Women should get on based on merit. It's just that they don't. The question of quotas has been a hot potato since 2003 when the Norwegian Government lost patience with businesses and imposed legislation which stated that at least 40% of board members in limited companies must be of either sex. In 2010, the UK's newly elected Lib-Dem/Conservative coalition government took action, prompted by the growing body of data on the performance benefits of having a 'critical mass' of women on company boards (McKinsey, 2017). It was so concerned about the impact of not having the best of the best leading the UK's top companies, and the consequences for the performance of the economy, that it set up the Lord Davies 'Women On Boards Review' to analyse why the boards of FTSE 350 were so homogenous (male and white), whether there was a problem to be fixed, and how to fix it. Lord Davies' position about the review was:

> *'This is not about aiming for a specific figure and is not just about promoting equal opportunities, but it is about improving business performance. There is growing evidence to show that diverse boards are better boards, delivering financial out-performance and stock market growth.*
>
> *Board appointments must always be made on merit, with the best qualified person getting the job. But given the long record of women achieving the highest qualifications and leadership positions in many walks of life, the poor representation of women on boards, relative to their male counterparts, has raised questions about whether board recruitment is in practice based on skills, experience and performance.*
>
> *Government must reserve the right to introduce more prescriptive alternatives if the recommended business-led approach does not achieve significant*

change.' - **Lord Davies of Abersoch, CBE. Women On Boards Review 2011 (Davies, 2011)**

The review showed that even the biggest and most successful companies in the UK had failed to make the best decisions in recognising and progressing its talent to senior management and leadership. Lord Davies' recommendations were implemented, including changes in corporate governance and reporting, but stopped short of quotas and instead suggested FTSE 350 companies adopt gender ratio targets for their non-executive director group. The Hampton-Alexander Review of 2019 took over the annual review of FTSE progress on gender balance at the top, and added teeth to the recommendations, targeting the executive pipeline and the executive board to change the balance of leaders working in (not just on) these businesses.

Research by Professor Emilio Castilla at the MIT Sloan School of Management (Castilla E. J., 2016) identified a further issue existing in the best-intentioned organisations, which he calls **The Paradox of Meritocracy.** It showed that robust strategies to ensure the best talent is recruited, rewarded and progressed – including formalised performance appraisals and a rewards processes with company communications about its commitment to valuing all talent – actually creates a culture in which biased decisions can, and do, flourish.

Castilla's controlled experiments had mock companies presented as either valuing and rewarding performance equitably (i.e., a meritocracy) or leaving reward decisions to managers' complete discretion. The meritocracy model in the 'equitable' companies resulted in men getting 12% higher pay awards than women for equal roles and equal performance. Men also end up having better outcomes in recruitment, progression and termination decisions. In the companies without the hint of any such goal, there was no measurable gender bias.

> *"When managers believe their company is a meritocracy because formal evaluative and distributive mechanisms are in place, they are in*

fact more likely to exhibit the very biases that those systems seek to prevent." - **(Castilla E. J., 2016)**

Castilla suggested that individuals making these key decisions were likely to give less scrutiny to their own decisions because the system and culture create a *false sense of confidence* that their decisions in such an environment would be fair, objective and impartial. This leads to little self-examination in identifying any hidden demographic biases. Thankfully, his research also identified additional strategies of transparency and accountability that can mitigate these paradoxical outcomes (Castilla E. J., 2016).

In 1968 a psychologist called Philip Goldberg carried out an experiment, which is repeated to this day in many different fields and formats, all with the same findings. It has become known as **The Goldberg Paradigm.**

Goldberg asked university students to evaluate an undergraduate essay. All participating students were to evaluate the same essay using the same marking criteria. However, there were two versions distributed for evaluation. The single difference between the two versions was the name at the top. One version had a woman's name; the other had a man's name. There was no other difference – the essays were identical. You've guessed the outcome already and you are right. The version apparently written by a woman received lower marks than the version apparently written by a man! So, the impact of disclosing gender affected the assessment of the capability of the individual, for the sole reason that the author was perceived to be a woman. You really have to pause at this point and consider the implication: without any other information, a woman's work was not considered as good. So, if what was true in 1968 still applied today then you should assume that sending your CV in for a job or posting it online would mean that yours would get adversely judged compared to a male with the same credentials. But surely this can't still be the case?

Yes, it can. A meta-analysis study (a highly controlled study of a wide number of studies) of experiments investigating this issue was published in 2020 (A.J. Koch, 2015). It analysed studies about gender bias in workplace decisions and showed that there is still bias in favour of men in male-dominated occupations, with men showing greater bias towards men, but no bias either way for female-dominated occupations. Research has shown that not only are women viewed as less qualified than men where capability is the same but also, where capability is different but equally valid, a justification will be constructed for the male's profile being selected as the best fit. This even happens in research where these profiles are switched (the male switched to the female's profile which had been rejected), resulting in the male profile being selected again. This is evidence that in recruitment and promotion "people may creatively redefine job criteria to fit the qualifications of the candidate whose gender seems to fit the job" (A. H. Eagly L. C., 2007).

Additionally, research by the psychologist Dr Pete Jones, who developed the Implicitly™ unconscious bias tests, shows that people who show low (inactive) gender bias in relation to women managers in support roles and functions may exhibit active levels of bias favouring men in operational management and in leadership roles. This relates to the 'brilliance' stereotype, and a type of bias called 'gender benevolence', which is applied to decisions made to 'protect' women from work that might be too difficult for them!

Therefore, evidence overwhelmingly shows that a presumption of the existence of meritocracy being effective for gender equality is naïve at best. Such a myth is especially pronounced in:

- Sectors such as advertising, academia, construction, engineering, farming, government, haulage, information technology, judiciary, logistics, medicine, science, politics, technology and many more which are considered either male domains or gender-neutral.
- All functions which aren't 'pink' (typically pink = HR, marketing and support staffing).
- Senior management and leadership levels given that they are culturally considered 'masculine'.

According to Deloitte's analysis of the board composition of 8,648 companies across 66 countries (Deloitte, 2020), women hold 16.9% of board seats worldwide: a 1.9% increase from 2017. At that rate, it will take until 2050 before there is gender balance. Their analysis also shows that having women on the board catalyses greater gender diversity at senior leadership level, providing a broader pipeline of talent from which to populate board positions. They also identified that "homogeneity spurs homogeneity". Catalyst's research quantified this insight, showing US companies which have increased numbers of women at the top and have shown a 45% increase in women in the next two layers down compared to companies without women on their boards. If creating and maintaining a meritocracy is extraordinarily hard (due to being undermined by invisible human bias), how do we go about trying to achieve it? Do quotas represent a good idea – such as imposing legislation to make it compulsory to have a certain representation of either gender?

Taking such 'radical' corrective action is too controversial for many people, who will cite issues such as women not wanting to appear as being meritlessly promoted just to 'tick boxes' and make up the numbers. However, the experience of women in the country that took the lead (Norway) is that any question of tokenism evaporated rapidly: the new female leaders excelled in their positions, Their performance provided all the evidence of merit necessary.

> *"Certainly, with all the talk around diversity, there are a lot of women who feel like they have been given a job because they were a woman. That already starts to undermine their confidence. They start to think they got the job because the company needed to meet a target. What I tell women is they need to let go of that thinking. I tell them that I have been on hiring panels forever and I have never been in the situation where we have said 'That lady is really not qualified but we are going to give her the job anyway.' It doesn't happen. I tell them to set that aside. We look at all the qualities and there are pros and cons. Do we take a risk on some people? Yes. Do we take a risk on some men and some women? Yes. Do they all work out? No. There is too much angst*

individually with women about why they got the job.
It is relating to this thing about not going for the job
unless they are 85% sure. 'It didn't meet my hurdle
but it obviously met somebody else's, so maybe I got
it even though I'm not qualified.' That just drives
me absolutely nuts. I may have felt that way earlier
in my career. They said to me 'We want you to be
the first woman process manager.' I remember
when I first got the woman process manager job; the
guy I was replacing told me 'It is going to be OK. I
talked to all the foremen and they said they are OK
working for a woman.' I know he thought he was
doing me a favour. I said 'You know Rick, that is
really interesting, but they don't have a choice. I'm
the boss." - **Peggy Montana**

The situation for most women across the 'developed' world is that they are highly educated; they over-achieve compared to men academically, and yet they are promoted more slowly with access to senior positions proving illusive for the many reasons we've explored.

Women are ready. There is no capability gap. They are stuck in what has been called the 'Marzipan Layer' (Graham, 2005), very near the icing on the cake. Touching the top, but never being on the top.

[In response to being shown data illustrating that,
at the current rate, it will take another 70 years
until there is gender equality at the top of FTSE
companies]

"That's scary. I remember in my 20s being very
convinced that women were going to break through
the glass ceiling." - **Gill Adams**

Another artificial barrier is an obsession by boards and those who recruit for them to seek people with experience of running a 'P & L', which means running a business unit or operation for which they are profit responsible. However, these roles have exactly the characteristics that make women the least likely to be considered for them. This is mind-bogglingly blinkered thinking, as it assumes that only certain roles can develop the necessary competencies for board level success, instead of recognising the obvious reality that there are many other routes to developing and demonstrating those competencies. These can easily and successfully be transferred into other environments and bring the huge added benefit of fresh thinking and new perspectives. In Norway, the 40% quota legislation fostered innovation in finding suitable candidates. They not only succeeded in sourcing talented women but also accessed talented men that would have been off the conventional radar.

> *"Criteria widening – not weakening: Nomination committees and owners were forced to broaden the criteria, and many new and interesting board candidates appeared, including younger female specialists, in technology, finance, law or some other field highly relevant to companies' strategy."* (C. Seierstad, 2015)

The debate about quotas was raging in the immediate years after the 2008 global financial meltdown, which was followed by such governmental responses as the UK's Lord Davies Review and recommendations. Unfortunately, it receded as softer strategies appeared to be making some progress. And the focus on gender balance through non-executive directors (NEDS) (directors who attend board meetings but aren't working in the business otherwise) was an easier 'fix'. This limited benefits to that one group, as they are not part of the day-to-day fabric of organisations, nor are they visible as role models to potential female talent. As one interviewee told me of one of her NED roles: "it took me four years to understand the business, given that I was interacting with it a handful of times a year".

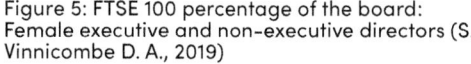

Figure 5: FTSE 100 percentage of the board:
Female executive and non-executive directors (S.
Vinnicombe D. A., 2019)

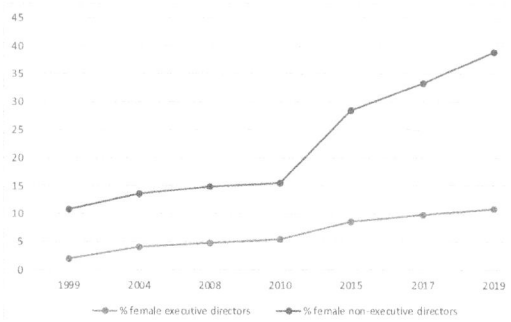

In 2019, only 10.9% of FTSE 100 board executive directors were women (S. Vinnicombe D. A., 2019). These are the people that change companies, not NEDs. Clearly, the top companies aren't leading the way, and others are ticking the gender box by appointing female NEDs and assuming 'one is done', as the 2019 Hampton-Alexander Review concluded (The Hampton-Alexander Review, 2019).

Quotas by gender for executive directors and the immediate leadership tier below would result in the consistent presence of women at the most senior level of leadership across the most visible organisations. The consequence would be the removal of the gendered association with leadership. This is what happened in Norway: "gender balanced boards spread to other companies where it was not enforced [privately owned limited liability companies]" (C. Seierstad, 2015). This change would encourage more women to go for the roles they really aspire to and their chances of success would be much closer to equal as the stereotypes and schemas recede, setting in motion a self-perpetuating virtuous cycle.

> *"I led the executive committee to 50/50 gender balanced.*
> *Within two years of my departure, all the women I hired*
> *had left.*

> *Overall, progress on executive board level gender balance has stalled. We have to take action, action we know works where softer strategies have failed, and that means quotas: at least 40% men, at least 40% women."* – **Dame Inga Beale, DBE former CEO of Lloyd's of London.**

In 2012 the European Commission's proposed quota legislation for a minimum representation of 40% of either gender on boards by 2020 failed to make it into law. It was blocked by a number of countries, including the UK, pointing to initial progress with existing measures and the need to leave balance to the equivalent of market forces. Given that such 'optimism' was misplaced, the progress that would have been guaranteed through quotas failed to happen. In March 2020, the European Executive stated that it would be reviving the proposal as part of a wide-ranging five-year equality strategy, "*otherwise we will wait another 100 years for things to change by themselves*" (Helena Dalli, EU Commissioner for Equality (Dalli, 2020)). Then the pandemic hit.

So, are quotas wrong? Not while meritocracy remains virtually unachievable, and the appetite for investing sufficient money and resource to make inclusive gender balance happen is still absent in most organisations.

Making it happen:

What has struck you as you've read through this section?

What do you want to act on as a result? And what do you want to be the outcome?

What will be your first steps?

Myth 8. Women should use their looks to help get on – if you've got it, flaunt it

"I always used to say to the women who worked with me in [advertising] agencies...about short skirts and high heels – only wear them if you've got a brain like a steel trap (really sharp, probably like a guillotine really). If you haven't, use them with caution. Because if you are really, really smart then it is nice to do feminine as well; I don't mean exploiting that you are a woman, but acknowledging and celebrating it.

Maybe if the male senior director came in in safari shorts and he is running a serious corporation, nobody is going to take him seriously either. Because you are giving the wrong signal. You are not surfing on the beach, you are in the boardroom.

At Saatchi and Saatchi one of the American men who was very senior and of a different generation said to me, 'I like you very much Miriam. Can I just give you a tip?' I remember I was wearing leggings, a velvet shirt and high boots. He said, 'The Procters don't like people who dress like rock star's wives.' My immediate reaction was anger. And then I thought about it for the weekend, and I thought, 'OK it is just another part,' and I went out and bought a black suit. Actually, within two or three months it was obvious that the Proctors were more interested in your brain than whether you are dressed like a rock star's wife or not, but I understand that sometimes you have to wear the costume that fits the part.

Then you realise it is just a costume. I don't think men go through those dilemmas. They don't even have to because they have their uniform set from day one. They don't have to question that. They

> *know the signals they are sending out. The most*
> *difficult question they have to face is, 'Can I go to this*
> *meeting without a tie?' Of course, the Creatives pride*
> *themselves on being the guy who doesn't wear the tie."*
> **- Miriam Jordan-Keane**

Perhaps there is a stage when using your looks is OK, in the lower levels of your career, where any reputational damage you do is unlikely to hang around long enough to inhibit your progress, should you want to be taken seriously. However, if you use your looks or sexuality to gain advantage, you have to realise that you will be defined first and foremost in that context, 'that girl in sales with the lovely hair/legs/breasts'.

> *"Never use sexuality at work"* **- Rebecca Salt**

I was on the Sales and Marketing Executive at Carlsberg-Tetley when this came home to me. We had had an excellent cohort of high calibre graduates join the business in the previous year, and they were firing on all cylinders. The smartest of all the graduates came to the Exec to present her brand plans – a brand which was the most profitable in the portfolio of that division of the company. So what she presented was very important and contained innovative, progressive ideas that would deliver more growth. I was one of two women on this Exec, with six men. This brand manager was about 23 and she was wearing a white blouse through which her white lacy bra was visible, and as her skirt was very short, her long slim legs were clearly visible. Looking round at my colleagues it was clear that they weren't listening, they had their minds elsewhere. Her excellent work was wasted. She hadn't been trying to be provocative. She wanted to be heard and to gain support for all the recommendations that she had worked so hard to develop. Unfortunately, she just didn't know that what she was wearing created an enormous barrier to communication.

> *"If you're talking to someone, they will hear about*
> *4% of what you say, but notice, and remember,*
> *about 38% of how you look. Remember, for many*
> *men, sexual cues are visual, not auditory. Bear*

that in mind when you dress for work. Retain your femininity with careful neutrality.

Lipstick is, oddly enough, a sign of authority, not sexuality.

You must dress for the job you want, not the job you've got."

– Barbara Follett

Double Bind is the term given to 'damned if you do, damned if you don't' scenarios. It describes impasse situations in which there appear to be no route to a positive outcome. It's been used to describe the situation women encounter in traditionally male roles, levels and functions where some women adopt a more masculine style to try and fit in. And other women retain their authentic femininity. Either way, they struggle to be recognised, engaged with and valued equally.

Research has identified a set of characteristics typically associated with men which are summed-up by the word 'agentic', which encapsulates characteristics such as action-orientation, independent-thinking, decisiveness and drive. Women, on the other hand are considered 'communal', a term which draws on the domestic connotations of caring, gentleness, putting others first, listening to others and being quietly spoken. Hence roles considered to be delivered best or delivered primarily by men are associated with these agentic characteristics – with communal characteristics as their antithesis.

Presenting oneself as the embodiment of the opposite of agentic – albeit in the eyes of the beholder – is problematic. And the more you emphasise your femininity or femaleness the more you trigger subconscious associations which say '*she's female therefore she doesn't have the right innate capabilities*' for the role.

Unfortunately, consciously or subconsciously adopting a more masculine style creates barriers of its own, as this has the consequence of reducing 'likeability'. Likeability is significant because people prefer to work with people they like. So, when teams get put together or people make choices about projects, or even who they want to chat to informally about work stuff, they are drawn to those they like.

Hence, women can be 'damned' i.e., held back, if they maintain their natural femininity as they don't fit the mental profile of stereotypically male roles; and they are damned if they are more masculine in their style because they risk peers and superiors preferring to work with others.

> *"I did think that my immediate boss was a man who flirted with women and talked about sport with the boys. I have often wondered whether when I came out he couldn't face me, because I didn't fit in either box properly. I did get the distinct sense that he didn't quite know what to do with me." -*
> **Sarah Brooke**

It's a tricky balance to pull off and there are plenty of women who feel that they should damn well wear what they like. But, emphasising female 'assets' adds another barrier to credibility and progression. Managing your personal presentation thoughtfully is a smart strategy to smooth progress.

The insights from the women I interviewed were that if you want to get on you need to dress for the next job up, not as if you are going to a party.

> *"I think dress is important, in the sense of presenting something that is relatively neutral but screams authority. There is nothing prescriptive about that. The look must be right for the age of the person, the nature of the work environment. Probably the little frilly frocks are not going to get us taken seriously.*
>
> *It is about what looks right and what fits other people's perceptions about what that look is saying. Now I am more comfortable about being a little frillier. I think it is a combination of age and seniority. You have established yourself as a senior woman who is capable of doing the job, and now you can let a little bit of colour in.*

> *It is the adaptation in the early stage. People do probably find it a little hard. They come out of university as graduates where it has been very free and suddenly there are these expectations. There won't necessarily have been any written rules but if you want to be taken seriously you need to conform"*
> **- Marion Cowden.**

So, be warned, if you think it's a good idea to play on your feminine good looks, you're likely to score an own goal. You may trade a short-term win for longer-term losses.

Making it happen:

What has this discussion brought to mind for you?

Myth 9.   Queen Bees pull up the drawbridge when they reach the top.

Men are more likely to appoint other men (S. Thorne and D, 2020) – and specifically other men of their social profile (known as recruiting in their own image) which is partly driven by the 'homo-social reproductive tendency' (HRT). This is a form of in-group loyalty which shows itself as the tendency to recreate and sustain the social profile of an existing group, while women are more likely to involve a wider range of profiles since they are less likely to be members of teams dominated and defined by social profiles matching their own. This doesn't equate to women in leadership excluding other women from the top, there are simply fewer women in the pipeline.

It's clear that female leaders often have an unspoken, additional set of criteria that they are measured against. They are expected to meet all the standard success criteria for that level of role, but in addition there is an unspoken expectation that they will be more listening, caring and supportive. Failure to deliver against this additional set of success criteria can result in loss of the support and respect they merit, and even quite Machiavellian behaviour seeking to bring down this 'failing' woman. It is another frustrating reality that senior women in particular have to be very deliberate about how they are seen to deliver their roles, and about the transparency of the thought-process and analysis behind their decision-making.

> *"I think if you get a bad female boss, it is more damaging than if you get a bad male boss for some reason. We are more forgiving of the male ones because it is expected, but when it is a female one, it really does go down rather badly."* **- Sharon Kerr**

Women know that progress up the ladder can be hindered by doing anything interpreted as waving the feminist flag. It can result in the reputational damage of being branded as 'trouble' and / or being 'a difficult woman'. Consequently, many women will avoid that association – only the bravest attach it to themselves. The #MeToo movement generated the courage to speak out about abuses of power, but the security of this movement and the 'sisterhood' doesn't extend into most workplaces. This reality doesn't go away when you get into leadership. It is actually magnified as women become fewer in number and are more closely scrutinised. So, women leaders tread carefully around overtly adding 'championing women' to their agenda. However, many will be besieged with formal, informal and implied requests from more junior women looking for advice, support and mentoring. Inevitably they have to turn down some requests for support: they've got to consistently perform well and, just like their male counterparts, will only have limited time to give to others. This is not unreasonable; it's survival. It's not pulling the drawbridge up behind them. The perception of doing so is simply a result of there being fewer women at the top to help the many women lower down, and it's just not possible to help them all. The number of other women you can help without detracting from your own performance is limited.

As a woman, I believe we must be fairer to our sex and not prolong this myth. I've heard too many women describe this 'Queen Bee' scenario – whereby senior women treat women at lower levels more harshly than men – but it simply doesn't exist when you look at the reality. Being a leader means making tough decisions and sometimes the support we hope we'd get from senior women isn't forthcoming – but the reasons are not personal.

We want women leaders, as they are fundamental to changing the culture, attitudes and processes that enable many more to fulfil their career potential. If you bring them down by unjustly criticising their leadership; if you undermine their reputation by complaining about the 'deficits' of their style to others, you will do harm to other women, as well as the poor individual that you are criticising. If you haven't been close to the situation then don't try and second guess how and why decisions were made, or what the full reality of the situation was. As Stephen Covey said in *Seven Habits*: "seek first to understand" (Covey, 2004). What is more, if you come across this situation, you must dare to stand up for her, especially when she is not there to defend herself. Don't let the myth persist. Dare to stop it: one intervention, one explanation of these facts, and you set off a new cascade of understanding that can reach far and benefit many.

Making it happen:

Has this exploration of the Queen Bee myth given you a new perspective?

Is there anything you know you want to do, or want to do differently?

What benefits will this have and to whom?

Myth 10.   There's no problem now.

It's true, most of the time there isn't a problem. However, those few moments when the subconscious 'default-to-male' tips the balance can have huge consequences:

- They can mean the difference between getting a job, a promotion, an assignment and not getting it.
- They can mean the difference between being heard and being passed over.
- They can mean the difference between being engaged, energised and committed and feeling disengaged and dejected.
- They can mean the difference in believing that you're good enough to go for it and doubting that you're ready, so holding back.

These decision-points, when women can be less visible and less valued (both by others and by themselves) result in slower and fewer promotions; less support by way of sponsors and mentors; fewer high status projects; and lower pay and bonuses.

Actually, the problem is far greater when you measure it from a different angle. Most governments and global economic welfare organisations are very clear that gender inequalities are a significant problem which hold back economic potential. The World Economic Forum has identified four dimensions of gender parity that are the most fundamental to economic potential attainment. The dimensions are:

1. Educational attainment
2. Health and survival
3. Political empowerment
4. Economic participation and opportunity. Comprising participation (the number of men and women in the labour force); remuneration; and advancement

Figure 6: The Global Gender Gap Index of Gender
Parity Measures 2020. Percentage of the Gender
Gaps Closed to 2020 (World Economic Forum, 2020)

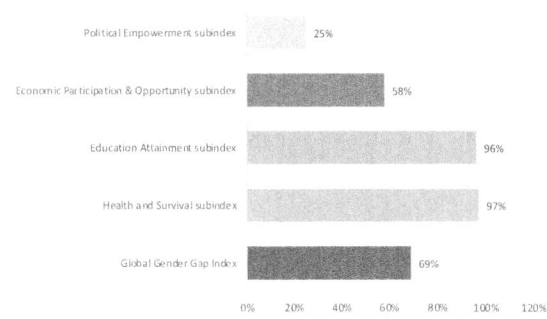

The top 10 countries have closed 80% of the Economic Participation
& Opportunity Gap, while the bottom 10 have only closed 40%.
That represents a vast opportunity cost for every country, aside
from what it means to the individual women who are losing out.

> 'The most important determinant of a country's
> competitiveness is its human talent – the skills
> and productivity of its workforce. Similarly, an
> organisation's performance is determined by the
> human capital that it possesses and its ability to
> use this resource efficiently. Ensuring the healthy
> development and appropriate use of half of the
> world's available talent pool thus has a vast bearing
> on how competitive a country may become or how
> efficient a company may be.
>
> Gender parity has a fundamental bearing on
> whether or not economies and societies thrive.
> Developing and deploying one-half of the world's
> available talent has a huge bearing on the growth,

competitiveness and future-readiness of economies and businesses worldwide.

Companies leading their geography and industry for diversity, equity, inclusion and belonging perform better than their market average across a wide range of key performance metrics:

Profitability: 25%-36% more likely to outperform on profitability

Innovation: Up to 20% higher rate of innovation and 19% higher innovation revenue

Decision-making: Up to 30% greater ability of spotting and reducing business risks

Employee engagement: Statistically significant causal relationship with engagement and retention, for all employees

Conversely, companies that fall behind their regional and industry peers in diversity, equity, inclusion and belonging see a competitiveness penalty, being 29% less likely to achieve above-average profitability than their market mean.

All of these factors are becoming ever more crucial for success in the 'new normal' workplace and economy of the future."

(World Economic Forum, 2020)

McKinsey data in 2015 (J. Woetzel, 2015) showed that if countries matched the best performing on gender parity, then the impact would be to add $12 trillion to the global economy by 2025. That's equal to the combined Gross Domestic Product (GDP) of UK, Germany and Japan! Moreover, full gender participation in the global workforce would deliver $28 trillion to the global economy by 2025 (J. Woetzel, 2015).

So, there is a still a huge problem and it's not just a problem for individual women who don't fulfil their potential or ambitions. It's a problem for employers who don't achieve their performance and bottom-line potential. It's a problem for countries, regions and the world, in terms of economics; in terms of welfare; and in terms of being fit to meet the challenges of the future.

Making it happen:

Reflecting on these myths and mantras, what overall thoughts or ideas do you have?

What specific actions do you want to take, or changes do you want to make? What difference will these make, and to whom?

PART 3

YOUR DNA
FOR SUCCESS

When we are born, we are already unique. The settings of our life journey and our life experiences are also a unique patchwork. These determine what matters and why, our values, what we believe in, and what we want. Even identical twins brought up in the same home and attending the same school have different relationships, perspectives and responses. One of the characteristics that many of the women I interviewed had in common was great clarity on their personal values, what they wanted from work and where their boundaries lay.

The expression *'it's about the journey, not the destination'* is a cliché for good reason. After all, it seems that when we reach what we thought was our ultimate destination, we pat ourselves on the back and set a new goal to aim for. A destination turns out to be a direction, not an end point. The experiences and feelings we have on the way are what really matter.

Unfortunately, our culture currently has fairly narrow definitions of what work-life success means, and it tends to focus on the milestones as destination points: job role and title, salary level, symbols of status.

Knowing who you are, what you want and what you need enables you to be much clearer about the type of work, culture, hierarchy, support systems, location, working hours, and so on that will combine to give you the best career experience. These insights will enable you to know what to look for in an organisation, boss and role – along with what to avoid.

> *"For me it is more about women defining what their measure of success is and not letting others define it for you. Then being very clear about what you are willing to do and not do to get there. Recognising that that can evolve over time. What you thought were your aspirations when you were 25 are not necessarily the same aspirations you have at 50. You can still define what success means for you at that point in time."* –
> **Peggy Montana**

The first real challenge is to read your own DNA for success – to get under your own skin and articulate what your values, beliefs, attitudes and motivations really are. We can think we know these things, but by using the appropriate assessment tools people are often very surprised and even relieved to reconsider their perspectives.

Chapter 7

Define what you really want and why

One of my first jobs was selling drinks vending machines. Not a glamorous job, but pivotal in getting my career on the best long-term track, as the company was part of the prestigious Mars Group. My job was straightforward. I had a range of hot and cold drinks vending machines to sell to small businesses in three Midlands counties. Each month I had a target for the individual steps of the selling process – for cold calls, appointments, vending machine demonstrations, second appointments and the value of my sales. Each month one of our team had to make a presentation at the region's sales meeting and when my turn came round it coincided with a visit by the Sales Director. It also followed the announcement of the year's biggest sales incentive: a trip to Rome for the top salespeople.

I themed my presentation 'The Road to Rome' and laid out what it would take for me to achieve that winning level of sales. It wasn't anything clever, simply the maths of how many cold calls, first appointments and so on I needed to do across those three months to sell enough machines. Then I broke that down to what that meant I needed to do every day. I'd never been that disciplined before, which was probably why my sales had never set the world on fire. But that quarter went on to be my biggest ever and the next time I saw the Sales Director it was in Rome.

I am someone who detests the smart little phrases that some people love. But in this instance the phrase *'No one plans to fail; they just fail to plan'* sums up perfectly what this simple story illustrates. I had bimbled along doing OK. Drifting from one month to the next being as uninspired as you might imagine by driving around industrial estates in the back of beyond trying to wheedle my way into companies to sell them a coffee machine. When my mind became focused by this specific opportunity to travel to Rome and the need to do a good presentation in front of a big boss, it galvanised my thinking and directed my efforts. The outcome was success. I put myself on the radar of the business and I found out for myself what I really could do if I put enough planning time into directing my efforts.

You have to stop and think, and do the homework in order to identify what you really want from each stage of your career (or working life) and why. Rather than stages of the selling process, you need to think about the components of your DNA of success. The most fundamental ones are covered in the following chapters.

Chapter 8

What do you value?

"My working life is driven by my personal views, standards and targets rather than what everybody else thinks." - **Gill Adams**

Values are the foundation to build a life that's true to what really matters to you. When things are in harmony with your values, all is generally calm, and you can get on with life without reference to them at all. However, values are of such fundamental importance that when your values are – or seem to be – compromised, it causes internal conflict which can distract your focus and make you call into question what you are doing. Your values are the foundations of the 'house of you'. When they are shaken, the house shakes. It might only be low-level conflict which, like the minor earth tremors that happen everywhere, will go unnoticed. If the values conflict gets bigger your senses become alert to something going on, although you might not be able to pinpoint it easily. When things happen in direct conflict with your values, the structure starts to break down – and you are forced into tough decisions about taking action, including getting out.

One of the women I interviewed had just resigned, having been offered her biggest ever job, and it was also the first time this huge company had ever offered a woman a main board role. She turned down the job and left because she couldn't align herself with the way her new peer group colleagues treated employees. There was a fundamental clash of values that was so big that she had to walk away. She was, and is, an incredibly strong woman, but it was not a fight she felt able to take on. She subsequently set up her own business where she defines what behaviours are appropriate, based on her own values.

Values derive from many sources, change over time and should inform what you do, who you do it for or with, and how you do it. Identifying your own values is therefore very significant to guide you to make positive personal and professional development choices: choices about employer, choices about the type of work, choices about the working environment and level of commitment you give.

Articulating your values is one of the set of inputs in your control that enables you to pursue the right opportunities and avoid the wrong ones. And given that securing your best career is likely to be tougher as a woman, you really do not want the negative drag of trying to make progress in work that grates away at you because you don't like your employer's behaviour.

> *"I think women always have a different view. They have a much more balanced view of the world and life. Home and social and things like that are a part of our consideration of what makes our world tick and what is important, what we value in life. We try and compete with men in the business world, but we have this whole other view of the world, and our values are perhaps different.*
>
> *When I first came to this country [from New Zealand] I didn't have a permanent job, but I have never gone back, because I realised that that is not the model that I operate best in. That was great because that gave me power. It was not a case of thinking that I had to have power and how was I going to get it. I think I was just naturally very conscious that if I was able to be my own person and set my own terms and conditions (within reason) that gave me some inner power and some confidence to say 'no' to things, to make my own decisions around projects.*

Women do need to be courageous.

They do. They need to be aware as well. You need to be strong in knowing what your personal values and principles are. It sounds like a mantra for life really, but that is what I'm saying. This conversation about work can never be just about work. It is about life. If you know what your personal values and principles are, that gives you strength to bring those into the workplace and to know what that work place represents for you as well as the work you are doing. There are some who use work as a means to get their monthly pay cheque. They will put in a good day's work, but they are clearly raising their three children. There are women who are confused and are trying to get ahead but don't quite know what is happening. There are women who are quite isolated. Some isolate themselves, sometimes by their own attitude and behaviour.

I guess that is what courage is. To know what you want, what you stand for and to go for what you want." - **Charmaine Stewart**

"One of the most important things in my life is my marriage. Our careers are just how we earn money. We support each other, and encourage each other to do a good job, but at the end of the day it is about us. If the job goes, we are still there together. I think that is why I have such a chequered career, if I didn't like doing something I changed my role. I have a loose career plan which has stage gates of what I wanted to achieve by certain times, but it didn't mean I would and it didn't mean I wouldn't. I was always ambitious; it was just that I could see no reason for being miserable in a job. You only live once, so you really want to make the most of it.

I had the advantage that money didn't matter, my husband is the same. We both have the same threat over our employers, we don't need to work. Mind you if we stopped working at the same time it might be a bit of a problem. We don't have any children either, so I was never torn apart: having children and having to look at their needs and my career.

By the time I hit 45, I realised that you spend a lot of time at work, therefore developed the motto, 'I've got to have fun, because if it isn't fun there is no point doing it.'

Don't compromise what you want. Go for what you want but be true to yourself. If you want to have a good work-life balance, make sure you keep it. You don't have to give it up. Be true to yourself. Don't worry what everybody else thinks, at the end of the day it doesn't matter. It is not important what other people think. What is important is what you want and what you want to achieve. You need to be comfortable with yourself, because if you are not comfortable with yourself you will be very unhappy." – Lin Phillips

When you are facing the prospect of a change that will mean a new organisation, team, role, boss or responsibilities, you can look for evidence to identify where there is compatibility or conflict with your values to help you make choices that will sit comfortably. However, it's important to bear in mind that what is presented as we go into a new organisation or role isn't necessarily the truth.

But when things do rub against your values, you have to decide whether or not you can live with it. Does the situation deliver other benefits that make it worth enduring? Or, if it continues, will it de-stabilise and distract you from delivering your role successfully? If you can't live with it, what are your options?

"It is important to take opportunities when they come along. In saying that, one does have to make sure there is an alignment with what is important,

with your own values. Just because a job is offering promotion, you need to see very clearly how that matches and if the company is something you want to be part of. I'm not saying don't do it, because there might be all other sorts of factors involved, but if there is dissonance having found themselves in a position, it is important to start thinking about where next and why it isn't working. And then get out while they still feel good." **- Marion Cowden**

Given your values are likely to change as you go through different stages and experiences in your life, it is wise to reassess them when you enter a new stage or encounter a significant new experience – new qualifications, kids, divorce, pandemic, winning the lottery!

"Ultimately I think where people are truly successful is where you have that complete synergy between the personal values that they have and what they are trying to do in their role. Where you get a disconnect, you are missing an opportunity almost to be somewhere else where there is that connection. I think that is why philosophically I have come to a better point at which I can rationalise that. Where else might I achieve more if there was that connection?" **- Maggie Stilwell**

Make a start now by assessing and articulating what is important for you. You can review and modify it in the years to come. You can download your free values assessment on https://womenssatnav. co.uk/tools and identify your priority values.

Once you've identified and prioritised your values, then the next key step is to identify the implications for working in harmony with them.

- When there is a good match in your workplace with what you feel is important, it's like the feeling in a great friendship – you operate from a secure and certain place and can get on with doing great work.
- Where there is conflict, it gets in the way of everything

else. These issues occupy your thoughts and create a set of negative emotions that can result in disillusionment, disengagement and depression.

- When there are changes or you have new opportunities, you can assess them against these values to decide on the degree of fit.

Chapter 9

Challenge any limiting beliefs

'I'm just not good at selling.'

'I'm not a natural presenter, so I'll never be very good at it.'

'Numbers and analysis have never been my thing.'

These are some examples of the sort of specific beliefs people have about their capabilities – or limits on them. They are known as 'limiting beliefs, and one of their main features is that they are often baseless, with no direct evidence to justify them.

The reality in the first example is likely to be that the person who has branded herself as not good at selling has actually successfully 'sold' plenty of concepts or ideas, but hasn't recognised these as relevant examples. With the second case, in reality there is typically an absence of negative feedback or freezing during presentation delivery which indicates that this is an expression of standard presenter nerves, which don't make themselves patent to an audience and which diminish with practice. The third example may be more complex given the ground we covered in *Myth 5: Women aren't good at IT, maths or science.* However, as with the truth about women and maths overall, there will be evidence of competence if not confidence.

> *"Assume there are no problems until you actually find them. Believe in yourself – why should others believe in you otherwise? If others don't, or if you hit unreasonable obstacles or prejudices (yes, they*

> *still exist!), go and work for organisations or choose*
> *departments where you can see successful female*
> *leaders."* **– Maggie Stilwell**

When people have specific limiting beliefs, they often act upon them by avoiding the things that they feel that they're not good at or that they feel won't work for them. And the more you avoid the task, the more you build the narrative to support this specific limiting belief, so it becomes a bigger issue. If you don't challenge limiting beliefs, the consequence can be that you close down avenues, walk away from opportunities, and limit your career potential.

One of my big things is dancing: Ballroom, Latin and Tap. I've gone to classes for years. Most of the students would be kicked off 'Strictly Come Dancing' before the cameras even started rolling, but we have a great laugh, experience the unique joy of dancing, and marvel at what we manage to learn and do in one hour. We come out on a high after every class. As a single woman, I've relied on the availability of single men to partner with me in these classes. However, there have been years at a time when I haven't had dance partners because men seem to feel that they have to be able to dance already. They feel a pressure to know how already, which I guess is partly due to men having to lead in these forms of dance, but also stemming from a culture that has the unfair expectations of men that they will know how to do anything they are confronted with. Sadly, those men forego the opportunity to experience the joy and laughter, missing the key fact that these are lessons. We are all there to learn. People who are more advanced go to more advanced classes. So, nobody is going to be looking and judging – we're all concentrating on trying to work out what is needed from different bits of our bodies and to get them to do it at the right time and in the right order!

Learning is something we seem to think we leave behind at school. But it's actually there in everyday life; we just tend not to notice it. Embracing it is a route to thriving – as evidenced by many of the women I interviewed, who very deliberately place learning at the heart of their approach to leadership.

There is also extensive evidence of more generalised limiting beliefs in women. An example is an issue which the media face, trying to find experts for commentary and analysis. They struggle to find women because few women are prepared to put themselves into the category of 'expert', despite compelling evidence that would more than justify that title to others. At another level, this persistent issue is more relentless and more damaging, but perhaps less obvious unless you look for it, and then it is ubiquitous.

Women frequently apologise for what they are going to say and how they are going to say it, for the work not being as good as it could have been or how other people are probably better placed to talk about it. They apologise for the font, the format; for opening their mouths in the first place! Listen carefully the next time you are in a formal or informal meeting involving another woman. Listen to her words and listen to your words. Are they interspersed with apologies?

'I probably haven't looked far enough into this but...'
'Sorry, but could I just say...'
'You probably know more about this than me but...'
'This presentation would have been better if...'
'Sorry, I'm not sure if this is relevant but...'

As we've discussed, women grow up surrounded by subtle messages that they are not as good, as worthy and as valuable compared to men. They absorb these messages, so it becomes an embedded belief. In the work environment these are often in the form of the micro-inequities (pages 96 to 97) that can undermine women's subconscious belief systems as they are fed by the real evidence of being overlooked, not heard, asked to make the coffee rather than lead the team – these contribute to the development of limiting beliefs. Vitally, these are NOT founded on the reality of who you are, what you have done and achieved, nor do they predict what you can go on to do.

The *Contribution to Value Gap* data I shared on pages 98 to 99 measures the scale of this evidence in the difference in extent to which women's contributions are valued, compared to the extent that they contribute. The average gap between 2017 and 2020 has been 20 percentage points: 70% of women consistently contribute and only 50% of women have their contributions consistently valued. That means only 5 in 10 women have evidence that their contributions are consistently valuable. Sadly, this drops to 3 in 10 for women working part-time.

This is tangible evidence that women subconsciously process, and it is inevitable that one set of outcomes is that they feel they know that they're not as good. Hence, they habitually preface what they are about to say or do with an acknowledgement that it is not going to be as good as it could be, implying that it could be better if done or said by someone else.

Is this you too? How often do you apologise for and therefore undermine what you are about to say – verbally or in writing? Do you recognise it in the communications of other women, in or out of work? If you talk to other women about it, you will start to spot examples in a myriad of different situations and with astonishing frequency. You'll probably laugh about it as you point out each other's apologies, and yet this is a really serious issue. If you are constantly suggesting that what you say (or don't say) or do (or don't do) is something to be sorry for – that it's wrong or substandard – this message will get through, and you will suppress your credibility with others. It tells people to expect that what you say or do will not be good, and so this is the lens through which they view what you say or do. They will look for the weaknesses that you said would be there, rather than focusing on what actually matters, and is good, great or even exceptional. If your organisation has client, customer, media or patient facing work, how will your organisation feel about putting you in front of these people if you come across as not sure that what you are doing or saying is right or as good as it could be?

Much like people who say 'umm' as they pause for thought as they speak, you are unlikely to be aware that you do this at all, let alone the number of times you do it. A positive and safe way to become aware is to have a meeting with other women and discuss this topic as a prelude to look for these apologies – in you and in each other.

At a keynote speech I gave for an International Women's Day event, I asked that everyone in the audience should be given a red piece of card, in the style of the ones used by referees in football matches to signal to a player that they are being sent off. I told the audience to raise their card if I apologised for anything – any aspect at all – by way of demonstrating this point. I had rather hoped that I would have learnt my own lesson. But in a half hour speech, I managed to raise red cards twice. Point made!

This is a hard habit to break and one you may have to revisit in future, because not only is it a habit, but the micro-messages continue, although this may reduce as your projection of confidence provides a counter to gendered assumptions. And, when you start to become aware of it, you can start to train yourself out of doing it. Keep reminding yourself to **separate the truth about the reality of how good you are as an individual from the generalised perceptions of the 'limitations' of your gender.**

Another problematic consequence of holding these limiting beliefs – expressed by the little voice that creeps into your head that tells you you're not as good as others – is that you may avoid the situations where you fear that the little voice was actually correct. These are pivotal situations, the outcomes of which reflect your value, potential and the esteem in which you are held. They include promotions, special projects, special assignments, salary increases and bonuses – all of which require you to put yourself forward. If you don't step up to what you are capable of, you don't just damage yourself in these cases; you also damage your reputation. *'Perhaps she's not as good as we thought; perhaps she's just not interested or not ambitious enough'.* It can mean that you won't be on the radar for such opportunities in future. So you'll be left behind doing less interesting, less stimulating and less demanding work than you should be doing. You won't secure the roles, recognition, support and rewards which will enable you to thrive. It can become a self-sustaining, self-esteem-draining cycle, driven by baseless limiting beliefs.

There was a recent survey that got in one of the UK's serious newspapers, which was reported to conclude that female leaders can't be funny and shouldn't use humour. But the research appeared to have missed a critical factor – the subject matter of the humour being criticised. Women's limiting beliefs often make themselves apparent through self-deprecating humour. It's another unconscious strategy to lighten the weight of the anticipated criticism or faint praise. But when you are a leader, perhaps more than ever, you have to inspire confidence by being confident, sure, decisive and clear.

While it's important be open to other views, don't project doubt about your capability, even if you have to act. It's just not funny to say that your work isn't good, or you have specific areas of weakness, when you're a leader in control of and responsible for the prospects of an organisation. Definitely use humour, but don't be the butt of your own jokes.

> *"There is a difference between being positively aware and unconsciously aware. I think what you need in a workplace is that unconscious awareness that you are worthy, and you have a place."* – Gill Adams

Table 1: Challenging limiting beliefs

Limiting belief	Factual evidence supporting this belief	If it's true: *Does it stop you doing anything that matters to you?*	If it matters: *What steps can you take to address it?*	Factual evidence in opposition to this limiting belief	The belief is unfounded: *What can you now do that you 'couldn't' before?*

From limiting to empowering

Beliefs can change quite rapidly and for good. Limiting beliefs can be exposed as inaccurate by pushing to find any real evidence for their basis. This is often a liberating realisation which can become a career turning point.

One of the key principles of 'Growth Mindsets' – which is increasing being taught in schools – is that our capabilities are not fixed at birth; we can and do learn everything. So, if you feel there's something you can't do, or that you're not good at currently, the fact is that you can learn, improve and master anything with information, practice and feedback.

Table 1: Challenging limiting beliefs, is a simple framework to help you identify any limiting beliefs that might be holding you back, to dismantle them, and to find the evidence which leads you to the truth. This will help you re-set your beliefs on the firm foundation of reality, and then move on to learn and practise that task or behaviour until you become confident with the proof of your positive capability.

The secret saboteur's chess game

Sometimes we stop ourselves taking the first step along a path because we fear some aspect of the latter stages of the journey or the final destination. For example:

'If I lead the presentation of the results of the strategy I created, it may lead to being asked to head up a much bigger team because the impact was so significant to the business. If that happens, it will lead to new challenges including dealing with very senior people and I really don't think I can do that.'

This psychological defence mechanism is hidden so deeply that most people are utterly unaware it's even in motion. It acts like embarking on a game of chess, but envisaging every move all the way through to finding yourself in checkmate, and losing the whole game. So, you don't move the first piece.

With chess, as with life, there are many moves in every game, and each move has multiple options. You have choices at each step along the way. There are many possible courses and outcomes. In the reality of life, your experience and capability are growing all the time, so what you can't envisage being able to do now, you'll be well equipped to stride up to and take on successfully when you actually reach that point. If you push yourself to complete each component of the challenging limiting beliefs framework it may help to not only address any limiting belief, but also to flush out and address any secret saboteurs.

There are practical steps you can take to maintain a positive, empowering belief system and to provide the evidence to undermine any limiting beliefs that try to emerge in future, which I develop in Chapter 14.

A starter idea which requires a little discipline, and the parking of your modesty, is to build a fact file of the evidence of what you've done and do well. It could be a broad range of things relevant to your role now and roles in the future. The evidence can include a wide range of sources, such as:

- Positive feedback you receive, written or verbal and formal or informal.
- Appraisals.
- Results and achievements.
- Recommendations and testimonials.
- Requests for your help or advice.

The more granular and specific you can be, the stronger and more powerful that evidence will be to buoy up your confidence should it flag at the prospect of slightly scary stuff in future. It will also form a great source of content for your CV. *How about using this opportunity to start it NOW?*

Chapter 10

Harness and hold on to what drives you

> *"I have two driving forces.*
>
> *My children. They are my purpose and my strength, and ultimately, I know they will find their purpose.*
>
> *My company, in two ways: firstly, on a purely practical level I had to keep a roof over our heads and provide for my children's education. Secondly, Aerial Camera Systems was my late husband's passion, keeping it alive was a way to honour his life along with living a full life ourselves. He had a devoted team, some of whom had given him years of commitment straight from university. I felt a responsibility to them all, and the pain certainly taught me who I was and how to apply those responsibilities."* – **Suzie Allwork**

Motivation. Drive. Buzz. Role-Satisfaction. These are some of the headline dynamics that define what you need to get out of work. The specific details you define under these titles are those that provide the positive reasons for doing the type of work you do, in the organisations you chose to work for.

I use the term 'role-satisfaction' to encompass a wide range of aspects beyond the content of your job description. It includes the context: the people, the pace, the environment, the culture. It's this breadth of consideration that makes the biggest difference to making the best choices.

Can you articulate the set of things that would come together to enable you to say that your work is really satisfying? Do you know what really motivates you? Do you know what sort of work, people and style of management?

> *"The day I don't jump out of bed in the morning, passionate about going to work, is the day I give up."* **- Fiona Kendrick**

When you understand what makes up a really rewarding working experience, you can make much better choices about the sort of work you do, the type of organisation (from macro – the whole organisation, to micro – your specific team, unit or function) and the type of culture. It will also mean you can weed out the options that won't deliver. And at relevant points you can check on your current working situation to see if it's still delivering what you want or whether it has the potential to deliver into the foreseeable future.

Articulating the content and priorities of what things make up your best work experience and potential is not easy to do in isolation.

> *"I did need a lot of motivation in the end to get through the partnership process.*
>
> Me: From other people?
>
> *I needed some support, but I needed to find the thing that lit me up about the whole thing. In the end there was a gang plank mentality; it was either I have to do this or I go. What happens in this kind of organisation is that people start talking about who is on the partnership track. It is like being a pressure cooker. In a way there was no alternative; you do have to submit yourself to this process. I couldn't see a future for me in the organisation without doing that.*

Increasingly I felt like I developed my own voice and feelings about how I wanted to shape things within our department and you need to be a partner to do that. I do have a sense of wanting to show other women that you can do it. That does drive me." – **Maggie Stilwell**

You can download a free Career Motivations and Drivers Self-assessment tool on https://womenssatnav.co.uk/tools that will enable you to tease apart and prioritise what matters most to you, from a set of nine common primary drivers. These are:

- Material Rewards – seeking possession, wealth and a high standard of living.
- Power / Influence – seeking to be in control of people and resources.
- Searching for Meaning – seeking to do things which are believed to be valuable for their own sake.
- Expertise – seeking a high level of achievement in a specialist field.
- Creativity – seeking to innovate and to be identified with original input.
- Affiliation – seeking nourishing and rewarding relationships with others at work.
- Autonomy – seeking to be independent and to make decisions for oneself.
- Security – seeking a solid and predictable future.
- Status – seeking to be recognised and respected by other people.

While this is a robust set for the general working population, it may not capture dimensions which are unique to your situation. So, you can expand it to include all the important options for you.

"I'm single-minded, driven and focused. I always enjoyed the adrenaline of working outside my comfort zone. I like a good argument – standing up in court.

I found that I loved criminal law – it was such fun."–
Beverly Bell

Assessments can be interesting but fairly worthless exercises unless you push yourself to answer the '*so what?*' question. In other words, what do these insights about your career drivers mean you should do, and should avoid? Hence, a final critical step is to identify your top three drivers and to invest the time to explore and articulate what needs to happen to ensure that these are a significant feature of your working life. In doing so, you can also identify what to minimise or avoid and the things that are getting in the way.

Knowing what will make you jump out of bed gives you the opportunity to manufacture more of it. Whether thinking about your next day, month or the next five years, you can plan how to ensure you get what you need.

> "*I wasn't sitting there thinking, 'I want to be head of a supply chain.' I had a plan that said, 'I want to do the best that I can.' That is when I realised that I have quite a competitive streak. I didn't think I had. I thought it was just self-motivation. I started with a basic team and I wanted to do well, and I wanted my team to do well. I wanted to prove that we could make a difference. Making a difference in terms of performance. Some of the guys just wanted to carry on as they were, keep their heads below ground. They were quite happy carrying on and doing what they did. I'd be saying, 'What can we do better?'*" - **Gill Adams**

Use your insights to course-correct. If some aspect of your work-life is bringing it down, review your driver priorities to pinpoint the problem and then explore options to bring in more of what you need and do what you can to address the cause of dissonance. That might mean confronting an issue which would require a bit of courage, but the outcome may make a massive difference to your overall happiness!

> "*I wasn't driven to be promoted. I was driven to do big jobs. I was seeking that satisfaction. I was seeking that challenge.*" - **Sharon Kerr**

Using the understanding of your drivers and your values on a medium- or long-term basis enables you to select your best-fit career opportunities. At career crossroads, it's wise to develop or refresh your **best career profile**, covering as many dimensions as are important to you. It's a challenging task if you want to get to a comprehensive picture. So, this is where a mentor, coach, sponsor, or an objective, agenda-free friend or peer can make huge difference. They can help you explore things about your working life that you may take for granted but may benefit from thinking about afresh.

Conversely, if you are not doing work that 'feeds' you sufficiently, apart from enjoying your working life less than you could, you are also likely to be less engaged with your work which could undermine your performance and outlook, and therefore your access to better-fit opportunities.

Keeping your drivers in mind gives you the chance to consistently make positive, informed choices which keep closer to the 'thrive' rather than the 'survive' end of the spectrum. And this final point made by Maggie Stilwell is huge:

> *"No matter what industry you are in, unless you really enjoy what you do, you won't ever be really good at it and succeed in your environment. That has to be the starting point. Discretionary effort, which is often what is required to distinguish yourself, is also exhausting otherwise."* – **Maggie Stilwell**

Doing what you love, in a place that you thrive in, is the best formula for you to be able to excel, and it is also therefore your most powerful springboard to the rest of your best career. On the following pages you can read examples of the driving forces behind my interviewees. They will give you a flavour of the diversity of drivers and to see why they can be so important.

Examples of the drivers of the Understand: Dare: Thrive interviewees

It's taken yonks for me to get to know how I work. Maybe it is possible to attain that a little faster with a better grounding. My personality would have been shaped by knocks and opportunities along the way. I was pretty naïve and not very self-aware for most of the first half of my life and a good bit of the second. It's not that hard to understand one's drivers or to get a bit of academic input on reasons why you might feel a certain way. Perhaps that is what your book is going to try and tackle.

I just want to be doing stuff that is interesting, entertaining and stretching. I don't want to be the head of a thing."
– Fiona Hagdrup

"Not to be able to make decisions. For me that is a killer. That is a slow death. I have no problem being fired for my decisions, but just let me go on and make some." - **Karen Guerra**

"There is lots of stretch and there is lots of future and possibilities. That gets me out of bed. And there is also enormous emotional engagement, which I need in my job. I couldn't come into work if I wasn't emotionally engaged with the people and the outcomes that I am accountable to deliver." - **Sarah Lewis**

"As a child I was quite driven. I don't remember even thinking as a teenager about what I could or couldn't do. I was always quite ambitious in terms of wanting to do well and be the best I could. If I set my mind to something, then I would want to take control of my own destiny and make it happen. Whether that was something sporty or wanting to achieve something academically. I think I have always been self-motivating. Equally I was quite rubbish at things if

I wasn't interested or didn't really want to do them."
- **Claire Walters**

"I instantly loved construction and everything about it. I loved the fact that you can see a physical manifestation of your work coming up out of the ground on a daily basis. You can touch it and feel it. After the accounting it was a godsend. I loved the crazy fraternity boy party atmosphere. They worked like crazy, but boy did they know how to play. They were all slightly on the verge of nuttiness, but mostly in a fun way. There were a few of them who were seriously wacko, but for the most part there was just this great camaraderie." - **Sara Fox**

"I am resourceful and independent. Give me a company that is in a mess or something needs sorting out and I'm your man, I'm in there. I can't just flick around with a duster for three hours."
- *Barbara Harris* "*I was never interested in just counting the beans and managing a steady staid business. I was interested in adding value and growth by doing things differently."*
- **Collette Dunkley**

"In some ways I have never been very ambitious, which I am sure is all very female. Somehow, I landed up here, which I have used as a base to have a great deal of fun really." - **Prof. Dot Griffiths**

"I am an accidental career woman. I never saw myself as, or intended to be, a career woman. I never saw myself as a career woman.

Enjoying what you are doing is really important. If I don't enjoy what I'm doing I can't see any point in doing it. Having fun and challenging myself get my adrenaline going. I love to see people developing, opening their wings and flying, not holding themselves back and being fearless. I get a great deal of enjoyment in coaching and mentoring people to the point where they are confident in themselves. Money is not my main motivator; I prefer to be seen as an expert in my field and the respect it gives.

I understand that respect can't be bought, it has to be earned. Being a thought leader, and influencer and seen as a person who can be a catalyst for change. You know you've gained it when people seek out your opinion. Although I always expect to be challenged when I give it." - **Lin Phillips**

"What motivated me were big organisational problems." - **Anon**

"I find it difficult to explain this to some of my women friends who gave up long ago. They don't believe that I can be so passionate about it. This is my practice. I'm building something. These are my clients. Making money is obviously extremely nice, but it is actually the achievement that appeals.

I like being independent. I like having my own money. These all sound narcissistic. I like being Clare Maurice. I like saying 'I'm Clare Maurice'. I hope that doesn't come back to haunt me. I feel a great sense of personal achievement. I've worked really hard, and I've really enjoyed it.

I sometimes ask myself if I'd do it again, and it's always 'yes'." - **Clare Maurice**

"I had decided around this time that I was going to do Egyptology and that I was going to Oxford to study it. At the same time, I was told by the English teacher that I had to get a grip, that I was in a comprehensive school and I didn't have a chance of going to Oxford. By the age of 11 I was determined that was what I was going to do. That was the time when I set myself a target and that has featured in my personality ever since then. I get to a point and then think, 'Where do I need to get

to now?' So, my career hasn't been in a straight line, but it has always been a question of getting something more. For me, the two motivators are authority and having my own autonomy and financial security. We weren't poor, we were just working class. So, I don't have a history of being without, but I like money. I'm not extravagant, but I like to have my financial security. Financial security drives me forward and that autonomy drives me forward.

I have a short attention span. However, I know men with shorter attention spans that result in aggression. My short attention span results in going out and having to encounter something that is going to extend me." **- Sharon Thomas**

"Before the thought of university, I'd intended to be a hairdresser, until I worked out how many heads of hair I was going to cut over 40 years. I realised that I'd be bored to death! When I decided to do a degree in business, there was nobody to advise me on courses. So, I went through the UCAS book (no internet then), to find out where I could even apply. I went through this tome page by page.

I found the business drivers employed to make money interesting. I was interested in wealth creation. I'm not just talking about for myself, but the process of how a business makes a £1." **- Karen Guerra**

"My MBA was on top of full-time work. It was really tough actually. I worked so hard for that. My son was a young child at the time. I was working all week and working weekends. I was quite driven on that.

It was so fulfilling in terms of personal development. We used to go once every four weeks to Bradford University for a Friday. We would go up on a Thursday night and go out for dinner together. Then we would spend the day going through what we had learnt and questioning and challenging it. I just found learning other people's insights into things and their contribution to helping me think about things differently was absolutely brilliant.

I was excited by the learning, that is what drove me. It kept me going. I loved the group of people that I was working with. I did well at it. I got a distinction. It was all a bit of a competition. I was quite pleased that I came top out of all of them.

The thesis I did was on this organisation. I did a thesis on organisational culture in Transport for London. I did quite a lot of analysis on the questionnaires and interviews that I had done. It was fascinating because I had done all of that learning and then I could actually apply it to where I worked. That was when I really started to realise that my favourite part of all of this is really the psychology bit; why people behave the way they do." - **Dana Skelley**

Making it happen:

So what?

What are the implications of the new insights you have gained?

Are there any changes you want to make to bring your working life experience closer to the best it should be?

PART 4

INNER
MOMENTUM:
YOUR BRAKES &
ACCELERATORS

Chapter 11

Confidence: a little word with a colossal impact on your career

'Confidence' may only be made up of ten little letters but together they create a word representing a concept of the most massive and fundamental significance to women.

> *"If you can't convince yourself, you can't convince others."*
> **- Gill Adams**

With confidence, you can speak up and say what you believe is the case, what should be done, what shouldn't be done. You can make that presentation or proposal. You can take on or challenge people who have a different view. You can put yourself forward for a better / bigger / different job or role. You can make that journey. You can hold that meeting. You can instil confidence in those around you so that you will gain agreement to your point, your request for extra funds, for an additional training course, or your rationale for that pay rise, promotion or special project.

The critical point is that if you do not at least appear to have confidence in what you say, do, suggest or recommend, why should anyone else? Don't be surprised if you don't get support or get overlooked if you are tentative or are the first to put forward reasons why you might be wrong.

For the reasons we have explored earlier in the book women can be tentative about speaking up for themselves or putting themselves forward. And yet they will walk over hot coals to defend a member of their team or to get them what they believe they deserve. But that's different. It's not personal. Women can take on Goliath to fight for another person's recognition or reward, but all too often it's just far too scary, too risky, and too damn close to home to speak out decisively for themselves.

> *"Women are competent but not confident. Men are confident but not competent."* **– Too many interviewees to list!**

Printed indelibly in my memory is a classic example of how this lack of confidence can play out. It was an appraisal I did for one of my team. She was a woman who had travelled round the world in her capacity as a senior researcher for the management consultancy we worked for. She regularly presented to boards and diverse commercial teams from well-respected companies. But when she sat in front of me and I asked her to tell me her strengths, what she wanted next in her career and why, her bottom lip began to tremble. She couldn't look me in the eye. Her dialogue became filled with words like "maybe", "a bit", "sometimes", "sort of" and "quite". And when she did manage to say something positive about herself, she back-filled with a torrent of limitations around it – why the positive was actually overridden by other issues I should be aware of. This conversation was so hard for her. Tears came to her eyes as I tried to persuade her to go on. The trauma I saw playing out in front of my eyes spoke of something so deep and so difficult, and I know now it is also virtually ubiquitous among women.

> *"I wonder what would have happened if I had the amount of confidence I have now at the start...like so many women, I didn't need more than a teaspoon to measure my confidence."* **– Prof. Dot Griffiths**

Even the women I interviewed – women who had made it to the top – described how they had lacked internal confidence for a significant proportion of their career. The vast majority of these immensely capable, intelligent and articulate women had lacked the confidence to negotiate pay increases that their male colleagues would have consistently gone for. The majority of these women waited to be offered opportunities, or didn't go for key roles because they thought they weren't ready.

> *"Confidence is born of assumptions. It is not so profoundly born of any one action in any given moment.*
>
> *I am working with a woman in a major position of political power, and she is very, very well embraced by her constituency, yet every day she cannot get up without a huge crisis of confidence. It is based on the assumption that she isn't actually good enough, she is not political enough, she is not cute enough [i.e. strategic enough] and that there is something that just isn't enough about her. The assumptions that drive our lack of confidence need to be addressed systematically. This is not, in my view, a one stop journey; this is a very big ongoing journey. So this component probably needs a deeper look at it.*
>
> *The other thing I think helps is for women (just as with children) to understand what the gender conditioned messages are, even when it is supposed to be an area free of problems of sexism. It is not an area free of sexism. If they can see that and understand that some of their confidence issues stem from the embedded messages of sexism about women that they carry and can strangle them, and that men carry the converse ones for men. It is out there, and it is happening, and it is not a mystery, nor is it usefully considered to be hormonal or genetic."* –
> **Nancy Kline**

We know that on a daily basis, girls are exposed to messages and images reinforcing culturally embedded perceptions of gender value differences. Hence, they grow up with an internalised sense of lower value and less capability, relative to boys and men. Figure 7, overleaf, shows the scale of this damage, persisting into management and leadership. It illustrates the significant differences between the proportions of men and women who report projecting strong outer confidence and proportions with strong inner belief in their capability.

Figure 7: Proportions of men and women with strong outer confidence and inner belief in capability. (Sat Nav to Success Research Survey 2020)

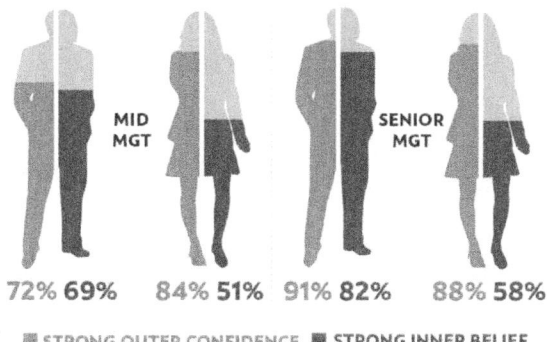

72% 69%   84% 51%   91% 82%   88% 58%

■ STRONG OUTER CONFIDENCE ■ STRONG INNER BELIEF

This isn't just about the big moments when confidence, or a lack of it, affects what comes your way at work. It's also about how we come across on a day-to-day basis, and unfortunately (as we saw in the last chapter), women's communications are littered with apologies. What the hell is going on? Why is it so hard for women to have confidence in themselves? What makes this all so acutely painful?

As you know, I took a degree in psychology after doing all these interviews because I needed to find the real, root cause of this huge and widespread issue. Where does this doubt come from and why does it persist? And more importantly, how can this fundamental impediment be permanently removed?

To change things, you have to address the cause, not the symptoms. So far we've examined a range of causes of the lack of self-esteem and self-belief that in turn make themselves apparent as a lack of self-confidence. I've demonstrated that these issues are caused by external factors which eclipse the truth about individual women's capabilities and potential.

Making it happen:

Do you relate to any of these descriptions? If so, what impact, if any, does this have on you?

What benefits could you gain with more confidence to speak up for opportunities big or small with strength, purpose and conviction?

The 'defend and build' strategy for sustained inner confidence growth

This strategic combination will help you develop and maintain inner confidence in your capabilities. In doing so, this will fuel your ability to secure what you want throughout your working life. It includes:

- Anticipating the situations and people that can chip away at or undermine your self-belief. You've already gained a good insight into this from Parts 2 and 3.
- Having a range of options to build on a deeper sense of self-belief.
- Creating robust scaffolding to self-confidence to maintain it under pressure.

And the great news is that when you apply these strategies in specific situations with your confidence intact, two hugely important things are achieved:

1. You've witnessed yourself do it, and this will, in itself, boost your confidence. You have proven your capability to do it. Now you *know* you can. So, when you enter this situation again, you will enter it with greater certainty of your ability and stronger self-confidence, creating momentum in your virtuous cycle. Recording your successes in the capability fact file I recommended previously will give you an instant source of this confidence-boosting evidence.
2. The people involved in that situation will have encountered a confident person which in turn inspires their confidence in you. They will then respond with greater belief and respect for what you bring, and this will provide more fuel to maintain the momentum of your confidence.

The more you are able to interact with confidence – even when it's pretence – the more this will feed your real, internal confidence. The challenge is to dare to be confident.

Fake it till you feel it.

There are two types of confidence, internal and external. Internal confidence – true, authentic confidence driven by real self-belief - is a powerful source of confidence that you externalise without effort. Internal confidence comes from solid, positive self-belief in who you are, in the salience and potency of your knowledge and experiences, in your capabilities and potential. With internal confidence comes the external confidence which is far less vulnerable to situational factors.

> *"Pretend to be confident, even if you're not – learn to act."* **- Victoria Mountain**

However, external confidence can be very convincingly faked as a stop gap. And, as we've seen from Figure 7, many women are doing just this.

> *"Years ago, early in my career, I had some fantastic leadership training from a psychologist and ex-trading director at IBM. He did some great work. One of the tips he gave me was that, especially if you are a woman (and he hated saying that), dress for the next job and not the one you are in. I thought that was really interesting. Men have their uniform, their corporate suit and tie. It is more difficult to navigate as a woman. Once you get to a place where you actually feel confident enough about your role, then I think you can relax that dress code, but on the way up I think it is important."* **- Miriam Jordan-Keane**

External confidence is the ability to come across as confident to other people to the extent that they automatically accept that you are fully competent in what you are doing and saying and have the wherewithal to demand their respect and attention. When you instil confidence in others through what you say and do, there will be starkly different responses compared to when people lack confidence in you. People will be more likely to accept what you say; to agree to your recommendations; to ask for your advice; to suggest others seek you out for your expertise; to follow your lead; to listen to you; to trust you and your judgement.

> *"It's something I've struggled with, but I know I have to portray confidence. I found it was key to portray confidence, even if I felt uncertain.*
>
> *Half the time I didn't quite know what I was saying, but I said it confidently and it seemed to work. Inside I would be thinking 'they are all agreeing! So, it did work!' I would almost experiment in these meetings with myself and how I should come across. Trying to do the right things in the right way and get the right balance. Not being too dominating, so they didn't think 'for God's sake, who does she think she is?' Or the other way, where they thought I was a walkover. Even if I am not confident, I will look it in meetings. Adding something if I haven't contributed for a while.*
>
> *Portraying confidence really does work and creates peace of mind, strength and security for co-workers."*
>
> **- Suzie Allwork**

On the next page you will find the first of a series of simple self-assessment tools which will help you identify where you are now, and then where you feel you would ideally like to be in order to achieve your goals. If there is a gap between the two states, this will be the focus of your planning.

Figure 8: Internal and external confidence status self-assessment

Q. 1. At crunch points, what is your level of external confidence? Do you manage to make the contributions you need with conviction and clarity, even though you may feel doubtful inside?

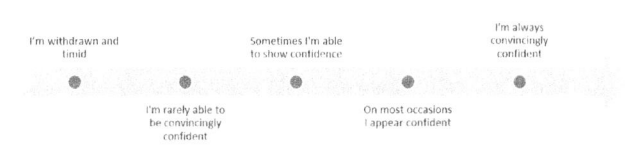

Q. 2. What is your ongoing level of internal confidence? Do you have unwavering belief that you can handle your normal role and any ad hoc challenges that may come your way, or do you worry that you really don't have what it takes to do what is required of you at work?

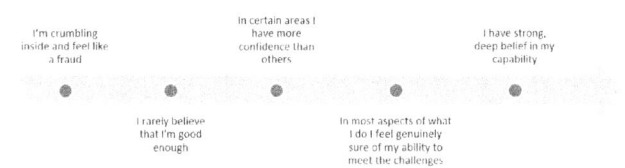

Figure 9: Maslow's model of the four stages of learning.

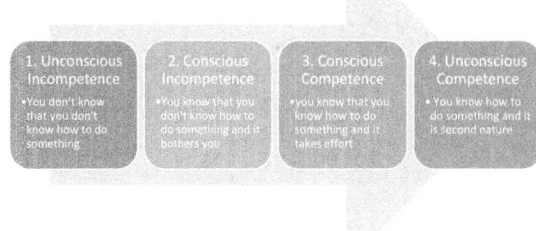

You may be familiar with Maslow and his famous Hierarchy of Needs, but he also created this model of the four stages of learning. Let me use the process of learning to drive to bring it to life. The model shows that people start from a position of unconscious incompetence, i.e., not knowing what they don't know. As a non-driver, you sit in a car driven by someone else and it all looks very straightforward and simple. Then comes the crunch when you have your first lesson and experience the uncomfortable realisation of what you don't know – you are consciously incompetent. You then embark on the process of learning to reach a point when, with intense concentration, you can successfully apply what you have learnt and perhaps pass your driving test. As all drivers know, with practice, you reach a point when you don't need to think about how to drive at all, you just do it – you become unconsciously competent.

Moving back to the focus on confidence in workplace capability, many women would place themselves at Level 2, known as 'conscious incompetence'. Not because they've failed to learn successfully and therefore stay at that level, but because they struggle to recognise or hold onto the truth of what they know and can successfully achieve with this knowledge. The journey to owning the insight, attitude and beliefs that represent conscious competence often takes far longer, and yo-yos back and forth with Level 2. In this ambiguous zone, confidence can be fragile, and it can just take an indirect reminder that you are a woman to temporarily knock you back down to a perception that you're only at Level 2. An indirect reminder can be as simple as being asked to make coffee for a meeting that you are taking part in. This type of micro-message communicates that as you are female, there are different and lower level contribution and role expectations of you.

The period between reaching Level 3 and actually believing that you have is a vulnerable period when opportunities, recognition, support and rewards you merit can go elsewhere. It is not until one reaches Level 4, 'unconscious competence', that you achieve real inner confidence.

> "A couple of things that really resonated for me with your model [the strategic enablers of success that this book takes you through] was when I provide mentoring and advice, I really focus on this confidence thing. I think it is real for me in terms of knowing the times that I have either put myself in or been put into different circumstances that were really a stretch and a test for me. The first couple of times I think I really struggled with confidence. I wondered if I was really going to be able to do it. You start that self-talk and everything seems like a direct reflection of your capability, when in fact it is a series of circumstances that you have to navigate your way through. I remember when I initially started running part of the refinery, we had a lot of reliability problems and the units would shut down a lot. I used to wear that as a reflection of my personal capability for leadership, when actually reliability in a refinery is a combination of many years of leaders and work. It was really about my ability to deal with that situation and to deal with it successfully. You can't look at your job as a two-week event; you have to look at whether you leave it

in a better place than where you picked it up. You have to have a little bit of confidence, but until you get that it can really undermine your whole view of what you are doing and how well you are doing it.

When I took all of these jobs ultimately I was very successful, but then in 2004, very late in my career, I was actually asked what job I wanted. I said, 'I want that one', thinking it was not going to be too big a stretch. Oh man, it was horrible. I really struggled to get it and understand it. I even went back to my boss after six months in the mid-year review and said 'I know I'm not doing as well as I want. Can you give me some advice?' I got nothing. At the end of the year I went to an HR guy and said 'You've got to help me out. You've got to give me some coaching.' He just looked at me as if to say, 'What are you talking about?' Nobody saw it apparently, but I felt it. Over the course of the next six months to a year I got on my feet. It took me a lot longer than I was used to taking. I really started to perform. I just was so surprised, after 30 years, and having so many different types of assignments, going into an assignment where I wasn't successful. It was such a huge stretch. Apparently it was only me who felt that way.

That actually threw me back to the early days of my career, where I really felt ill at ease, not capable. It was mostly that, to a large extent, at least in the early days, what I perceived as personal failure was just a problem that needed to be worked through. I think that is the thing with men versus women, we take it much more personally and much more as a sign of something we have failed to do." - **Peggy Montana**

Locate your pinch points.

For greatest efficiency and to make the most significant positive progress, your development efforts should be targeted at the places where you have most to gain (and equally, most to lose). Reflecting on your confidence levels in different situations will give you an indication of your beliefs about your capabilities and enable you to identify if different situations affect your levels of confidence more or less. For example, you may feel more comfortable and confident in certain capabilities with your team or peers, but less so with more senior people or external people. This will tell you that it is the situation that affects your beliefs about your capability, while your capability remains constant. So, the opportunity is to find ways to think differently or behave differently that enable you to hold on to the certainty of your capability through situations that feel like they challenge it. We'll come onto the range of strategies to help you do that.

But first you should take this opportunity to reflect in order to identify your priority pinch points, using the following questions so that you can focus your thinking and efforts where they'll have the biggest benefits.

Making it happen:

Start by reflecting on your choice of 'scoring' in your internal and external confidence status self-assessment (Figure 8). What situations came to mind that led you to select your status?

Now, give yourself some space and time to think through these questions and to make notes of your responses.

- What are the situations in which you have deep inner confidence?

- What, if any, are the situations and circumstances in which your confidence is lower, more fragile or not yet developed?

- Are there circumstances that chip through your outer layer of confidence? Certain meetings or groups of people? Calls you have to make, or presentations you have to give? New situations?

- What are the components of these situations: people, place, subject matter, your role, the audience etc?

  - And of these, which are the components that represent significant threats to your confidence?

    - And which of these components have a material impact?

    - And which have the most significant impact?

    - What type of impact?

Getting to the truth about yourself.

External factors undermining women's estimation of their abilities and potential are rarely legitimate about the individual. But given the weight of their impact, it's important to find sources of evidence that can re-calibrate the scales.

Interestingly, the one consistent source of confidence I identified in the women I interviewed was their academic record. These qualifications are incontrovertible, unbiased, objective, non-negotiable, universally respected and lasting. Qualifications are a powerful, reliable and consistent source of reassurance and self-belief which can resist the cognitive bias effects and so shore up self-belief and self-confidence. I believe this is one of the key reasons women take opportunities to gain respected qualifications, and work damn hard to achieve the best possible results.

> *"I think there were a lot of times when I was reassured by knowing I was smart, when everything else around me was not clear. When I was looking at a man and thinking, 'Why on earth is he getting that promotion?' I found comfort in thinking, 'But I am smart. I'll find a way.'"* **- Miriam Jordan-Keane**

One method described earlier was to build an ongoing fact file of multiple sources of evidence of our levels of capability and their value. Given the lesson about professional qualifications, it suggests that we need to draw in sources of evidence of our capability that we respect for being objective and robust.

Making it happen:

What are the sources of evidence that you respect?

· Qualifications – which ones?

· Annual appraisals?

· 360-degree feedback?

· Line management feedback?

· Sponsor / mentor feedback?

· Client / customer / patient feedback

· Offers of opportunities.

What other sources of feedback do you have either inside work or beyond?

What do peers say? If you dismiss their positive feedback, consider why that is and whether in the light of why you dismiss it, there is anything you can still take from that feedback.

What do people encourage you to do (currently, or in the past) that maybe you've been resisting, and what does that say about what they think you're good at or have the potential to pursue?

Countering the impact of limiting expectations.

There is a large and growing body of research exploring the issues triggered by the threat of stereotype-driven limiting expectations. The situations where this 'stereotype threat' can occur are common and relate back to the in-group / out-group dynamics introduced in 'Gain a psychological advantage'.

The response is triggered in situations where there is a perceived risk of being treated differently with negative consequences because of the 'activation' of a stereotype. There may be no real threat as the people in the situation may not consciously or unconsciously hold the belief in question. Whether the stereotype threat is real or imagined there can be a response when a member of the stereotyped group carries out a task in which they are considered less capable, in the presence of a member, or members, of the stereotyping group. They become anxious to perform well in order to ensure that the stereotype is not proved correct. They then have to try to manage their anxiety to stop it getting in the way of the task, but this actually diverts cognitive capability away from the task in hand and, as a result, performance is lowered.

This is clearly highly relevant when women work in functions, professions, management levels or encounter situations that may be considered masculine domains. Performance is 'threatened' by the presence of or involvement by people who might consider women to be less likely to be as capable as members of their group. And this is particularly acute at 'skills frontiers' – when you are stepping up to a new challenge that brings the stereotype into acute focus (Steele, 2010). Here are the strategies that the most recent research and my direct work with women over the last 13 years have identified that work in terms of addressing the anxiety and enabling self-confidence to be maintained so performance is unaffected:

1. Re-frame the task.

Sometimes we use labels for tasks or situations that make them appear to be more intimidating than they are. By changing the label or our description of the context or purpose, we can change how we feel about that forthcoming situation. For example, we might refer to a salary as a 'negotiation' and that might bring to mind two opposing parties who have to try to out-wit or out-scheme each other in order for one to win. Another way to think about it (i.e., to re-frame it) is in terms of generously giving your manager the opportunity to understand your value better, to give him or her the opportunity to keep you and the benefits you deliver in the team (and the organisation) and to understand what options they have to make that happen. Here you are being thoughtful about the vulnerable situation they are in and giving them the information to help them make an easy and excellent decision. This has worked many times for my clients.

Another example I shared earlier was the concept of 'selling', which can be a terrifying concept for non-salespeople, bringing to mind all sorts of situations and behaviours with which many people feel desperately uncomfortable. Re-framing 'selling' as simply helping people by exploring problems they face and matching them up with a solution sounds very different and much more comfortable.

Networking is another example – one which many women have seen as intimidating and operating on the premise that you manipulate relationships for personal gain. This off-putting perception is overcome by re-framing it as an opportunity to create new, authentic relationships in which the goal is to learn about the other person and see if you can be of help to them (see Chapter 23: *Network with integrity*).

"That confidence thing is a combination of how hard you see the obstacles (if you imagine an athlete) and how fast can I run, how trained am I, am I a good jumper. Because however good a runner or a jumper you are, if you see a hurdle that is that high and you can't see any other women doing it, your inference is that it's a really hard thing for a woman to do.

That will affect your whole performance. Whereas if you not only think you are quite a good runner and the hurdles look ok and you can see others who have navigated them, that affects your confidence." –
Maggie Stilwell

2. Bring to mind evidence that counters the stereotype.

As an example, let's consider your situation within male-dominated meetings you may attend or chair: a solution to maintaining your strength and confidence is to bring to mind images of women successfully contributing to or running such situations. This might be by thinking of powerful women you've seen in the media, news or politics, online or, even better, in your own sector or profession. You should also bring to mind when *you* have managed these situations successfully and the feedback you received and / or the outcome you secured (perhaps these examples are in your fact file already).

3. Self-affirmation.

This is a powerful technique whereby you do more than remind yourself of all your important values, skills, capabilities and outcomes that you have delivered. Evidence shows that expressing out loud the key strengths you have works, and it works because it is forming new pathways of association (firing and re-wiring). Constructing the association of you and your specific strengths forms a new belief system that becomes more robust through repetition, which is especially valuable ahead of situations which you've identified as being challenging to your confidence.

"Success breeds success. When you succeed you enjoy

it more and then you become even better at it. Then you can transfer those skills into other areas. I've always enjoyed working outside my comfort zone – having the adrenaline flowing." - **Beverley Bell**

4. Recognise your high standards of achievement.

This is where your fact file comes in. Remind yourself of your qualifications (academic record, professional qualifications, training programmes). Then build on those with the facts about what you have achieved – this might include promotions, meeting or exceeding objectives (what exactly were the targets, and what did you deliver, and why was this significant to the team / function / organisation?) and feedback from stakeholders in your organisation.

What else is on your list?

"Civil engineering contracting is a completely male world. You've got all these established companies and they are all run by men, they are all family companies. They are all there to make money. They happen to do it by digging holes in the road and employing navvies. That is quite a tough world because you do have to actually confront them sometimes. You have to be quite tough. I think that is one of the things that I learnt the most. You have to really talk to them on their level and show them that you know what you are talking about, but not in a cocky way. One of the ways I learnt this was just by being out on the job and chatting to the guys and learning from them and gathering some practical knowledge before I could start challenging with a base of theoretical and academic knowledge and understanding." - **Dana Skelley**

5. A Growth Mindset: we get better with practice.

We are not born with a fixed and predetermined set of capabilities. Our abilities are developed through application and hard work – our intellect and attitude are just the starting point.

If you consider and apply these fundamental truths, not only will it stimulate or boost a love of learning, but it will also enable you to see challenges and knockbacks through this lens which will increase your resilience and keep you moving forward to achieve your ambitions. History shows that virtually all great people demonstrate these qualities, as did every one of the women I interviewed – they all had a love of learning and a continual thirst to learn.

One watch-out is that women tend to get less feedback on their work than men, which makes it harder to know how to improve. To counter this, you will need to dare a little and ask for evidence-based feedback to help you learn and grow. Bear in mind improving your performance benefits your peers, your leaders and your stakeholders so seeking this feedback is an unselfish request.

"I think that one of the turning moments of my childhood, that really affected how I looked at being a woman in business, was when I came home from school one day and I was crying because the kids were making fun of how I looked, the way my eyes looked different. I remember my mother saying, 'You are a girl and you're Chinese and you are going to have to work twice as hard to get what everybody else gets.' She told me that if I worked twice as hard I would learn twice as much. That really planted a seed in my brain that said, 'There are some things you do that nobody will ever be able to take away from you.' That is that if you learn you take that with

you wherever you go. I was never afraid of being the one who put in the longer hours or spending more time learning something, when other people might have breezed through things. I always knew there would be a benefit. These things gave me strength to navigate some of these rougher waters. That was a lesson learned that was big." - **Anna Catalano.**

6. Check whether you respect the source of your angst.

Anxiety is reduced when we realise that we don't actually respect, rate or value the source of concern, be that a specific person or a particular meeting, a function in the organisation, or a client. So, it is worth re-connecting with what you value in your work and the purpose of your work, to assess whether this source of your concern actually measures up to your standards and views on what matters. When you find that you don't rate or respect their opinion / approach / role, this will make their input much less relevant to you, so they will cease to be a source of anxiety and your self-esteem will rise and your confidence will remain intact. This revelation can be immensely liberating!

7. Putting change into practice. Daring!

We feel at our most confident doing what we love, what we have the most experience in and in the most familiar surroundings with people who we feel are on our side. Conversely, we can feel least confident if we feel we don't know something well and / or if we are in unfamiliar settings with potentially challenging people. Unfortunately, it is often the latter situation when our confidence is most critical to making the right impression and impact and to support our progression towards our goals. Such things as being asked to present in a meeting you've never attended before to senior people that you don't really know; kicking off a new project with a team that's looking to you to guide them to success; selling to a big client; being assessed as you deliver critical tasks; asking for more money at the annual appraisal; going for a job interview. This means that we have to step up to the challenge and dare to do the things in which our confidence is tested.

[Talking about his approach with his two daughters]

"We always preached to them, have a go. I even used to tell them a cricket story, because I like cricket hugely (not this bash about stuff they are doing now). I was only about 20 and there was a very famous West Indian cricketer called Vivian Richards.

He played at Lords that day. It was a five day test match and after about 40 minutes they were 20 for 3 which is a disastrous beginning. He had come in against our main fast bowler and had a look for a couple of overs and then he had hit him for 24 runs in an over. It is all right later on but not on the first morning at Lords. You are supposed to plod along. He got about 150 or something.

In the evening they interviewed him; a very droll guy. They gave him a couple of easy questions and then they said, 'Why on earth did you do that? You could have got out and it would have been a disaster.' He just said, 'I've always wondered if I could, so I tried.' I thought what a fantastic answer. I always told my girls that, 'Don't wonder if you could, try.' That is what they've done. My older daughter is working in a very specialist pharmaceutical research company. She has a PhD in immunology and all sorts of long words I can't understand. The other one is earning three times as much in the bank." - **Simon Hughes**

In terms of building your confidence, you don't need to start with the scariest situations. In fact, you probably shouldn't. It's more effective in the long term to start with smaller, less intimidating situations, so you can gradually step up to bigger situations with your confidence growing in-step with the demands on it. (You'll read more about how to do this in Chapter 19 on self-promotion.)

"I suppose you get confidence through good experiences. Success helps you to become confident. You need evidence that you have those abilities. If you feel something has gone well, then it gives you the confidence to carry on. You build blocks." - **Lavinia Carey**

Bear in mind that when people are in a negative place, they tend to be drawn to the negatives – they see more downsides, issues and reasons 'why not to' than when they are in a positive frame of mind. So, at the early stage of turning confidence around, belief in capability is likely to be low, and people are more likely to be drawn to things that suggest that they are not as good. This is the point at which a challenge must be made: 'is our perception reality?' Where and what is the evidence that we've ignored or decided to rule out, in favour of stuff that confirms our detrimental perception?

Women who have talked about having a mentor have described how having a secure and mature male mentor or sponsor helps them see and really understand the reasons they should be confident. This profile of supporter has nothing to prove, and no reason to provide sycophantic or misplaced praise and no need for the limelight, so they gently but firmly push their mentee into situations that are outside of their comfort zone, knowing that they can handle it, even when they might think otherwise. This allows them to find that they really can do far more than they thought they could, far sooner than imagined (see Chapter 24: *Get a mentor to navigate your role. Get a senior sponsor to get on*).

In Chapter 6 we did a whole load of myth busting and it's important to hold onto those new facts at times when your confidence may be ebbing or when you are likely to be dealing with people who may believe the old-school fiction.

You may have your own set of myths that exist in your industry, profession or function. So, it can only be helpful to do your own research to identify and document the truth so that you use it to power yourself up in the face of challenge – whether that's internal (i.e., your own beliefs) or external. Keep those positive truths available and accessible and even be prepared to share them. There are likely to be many other women who would welcome those insights. And for those that might represent a push-back, be reassured that many people, when furnished with new, credible and widely beneficial facts, are often delighted to change their minds, and can also become powerful new champions of the truth.

Making it happen:

What do you want to do differently, and what will be the benefits?

What will be the evidence of success? Are there milestones along the way that you can identify?

What resources, if any, do you think would support or speed your progress? People, technology, time? How can you secure these resources?

In what way(s) will you celebrate your successes?

Chapter 12

Life is tough – so deal with it by building resilience

Resilience is the ability to stay on your course despite things going wrong. It's the ability to stay steady and stable when you feel you've had a knock-back. While these are generally big things that feel like fundamental setbacks, sometimes it can be a build-up of smaller things which come together to make you feel you are fighting an unwinnable war.

> *"Everybody in life has things that happen to them, not good things, that is life. Somebody said to me once, 'It is not what happens to you in life, it is the attitude you take towards what happens to you.' It is a mantra that I really believe in. Bad things happen and it is about how we deal with those things. That is buying into the, 'This has happened, and I've got to dust myself off and pick myself up' attitude. It is the richness of life experience.*
>
> *Someone says 'no' to us, so I think, 'What other way can we achieve what we need to achieve?' I think we could do this, or this, or this, or we could do all those things in parallel. There are always lots of things going on in one's mind; you are pursuing things in parallel."* – **Charmaine Stewart**

"Resilience is ordinary, not extraordinary" (APA).

The American Psychological Association (APA) defines resilience as "the process of adapting well in the face of adversity, trauma, tragedy, threats or significant sources of stress – such as family and relationship problems, serious health problems or workplace and financial stressors. It means 'bouncing back' from difficult experiences." The APA makes clear that we can all learn resilience and be resilient.

Resilience is also the one characteristic displayed by all the women I interviewed. It is certainly possible that they would not have achieved all they had accomplished if they had been 'beaten' by setbacks. But they weren't, and they prove that the strategies and outlooks that enable us to get up and get going again are critical and worth it!

> *"Females will get knocked back more than men. The biggest element is self-belief, in what you can do and the value you can add and determination to find a way around any issue. Pick yourself up, dust yourself down, learn from it and be stronger for it."*
> **- Fiona Kendrick**

So, in this chapter I'll share with you the insights about the development of resilience gained from analysing the transcripts of all the winning women I interviewed. It's powerful to note that they mirror the APA's categorisation of the most potent perspectives, actions, strategies and behaviours to build resilience and shows that these women's strategies are robust.

Resilience, self-belief and confidence are inextricably linked, and together form the bedrock from which you can build everything else you need in order to have a fulfilling career across every stage. As Dame Fiona Kendrick points out, women have to be better equipped to ride the waves, to hold onto their dreams and to keep pushing forward. But male or female, life can be tough and the clear message from my interviewees was that you need to face this reality. Working life, like the rest of life, has no guarantees of being fair.

"But I also think that some people can be totally wet. They will cave in, moan and complain and want counselling or want to be analysed. You just have to deal with stuff and if you can't you are not really going to get very far.

There are far too many people who go, 'Oh I couldn't get in [to the office this morning].' Or they will ring up and say, 'I've got a cold. I've got a hangover.' Well bollocks, nobody told you to get a hangover, just get on with it. Or, 'Oh my cat died.' Get a grip! It's not about being completely unsympathetic. It's about saying, 'OK let's deal with this. Make a bit of effort. Don't give up.'

If you are feeling mouldy, moping around at home is not going to help you. Getting stuck into doing a good job takes your mind off breaking up with your boyfriend. If something really traumatic happens that may be different, but don't make a big thing out of it." **- Lavinia Carey**

Life and work have no invisible driving force that makes it either fair or unfair, and if you accept that, as the going-in premise, you will be stronger and better able to cope with setbacks. They're not personal, they're just life.

"Resilience is critical. I would say it's one of the most critical elements. I think about my life and I've constantly had to draw deeply on many things but I think resilience is the one thing that's carried me through.

I've been through many adverse things that I don't think many men would have got through. I've thought, I could sink, or strive and go forward.

My father was dying and was in hospital at Kings. I was carrying Lucas at the time and his twin. I lost his twin. Four weeks after having him by caesarean,

I was asked to go for promotion and to go for Chief Superintendent, so I had my own Borough of Command. I had all of this going on and I thought I could either sink in all that was going on at the time or I could strive and keep moving forward. I decided to strive and move forward. When Lucas was seven weeks old and my stitches hadn't even healed, I was sitting in front of an interview panel having done all my preparation. I passed it. I think he was ten or eleven weeks old when I became the Borough Commander at Greenwich.

The thing is you can make it as hard or as easy as you want. This is the point of my tale. I could have been a Chief Superintendent and taken any other job that I desired. I was told that by my all-male senior team. They said 'Sharon, you are really pushing yourself. You don't have to take these boroughs. We would like you to have this job because we think you are the right fit for it and you have the right skills, but you have just had a baby (or whatever it was). You can be promoted but you don't have to take a big job. You can take a much smaller job and get paid the same money and do your rounds to suit yourself.' I never took the easy path, ever. Something within me, this striving to do it. I think that resilience is very much linked to ambition and the more driven you are." – **Sharon Kerr**

Why resilience matters.

Resilience matters because it stops knockbacks becoming knockdowns or knock outs. It stops detours becoming dead-ends, and it enables you to continue on your planned path or to adapt to a new route that works for the new situation and for you. It enables you to keep hold of the ingredients for your best career even if you have to change the nature of what you make with them. Not giving up or giving in enables you to see what happened from beyond the situation and learn from it.

Resilience strategies help stop you getting into a negative cycle or outlook, in which you see things as being against you personally, and they allow you to focus on the things that you need to get on with, to survive and thrive. Resilience matters because it stops you making decisions in haste that may mean that you will step away from the things that you really wanted, making them even harder to get, or even further away in time.

> *"And I think it is nice that it is sitting next to confidence in your model. I think to the extent that we can increase and implement our internal confidence and shift the assumptions that destroy our confidence, we have more resilience. Resilience comes also from assumptions, but usually assumptions about our future. If we can assume that we can recover from something, re-strategise and move forward, we effectively are resilient. That future perspective would come to a certain extent from the confidence that we have. I guess I also think that resilience comes from knowing that what I am doing is entirely derived and spawned from what matters most to me, without which I would wither and after which, when I die I will be proud. So when I am attacked or undermined or cut down and my confidence wanes and I feel that moment of deciding how to be resilient - I think resilience is a decision – I am in some way clear that if it turns out that The Thinking Environment becomes bludgeoned by some frightening societal shift towards obedience or something, I will know that what mattered to me got expressed through my life. The structures that can destroy us don't matter to me. I think that women should keep rethinking until they are moving to the place that matters most to them and that is how they increase resilience."* **– Nancy Kline**

"I think I am naturally quite robust. I would describe myself as quite strong person, and I know my friends do. I also think that over the years I have developed mechanisms for dealing with things. As a female I do listen to any criticism. I worry about it briefly, and then there is a logic piece that kicks in and moves me onto solving the issue rather than wasting energy stressing. Then I get on with whatever needs doing. But I do always go away and think about it afterwards." **- Claire Walters**

Figure 10: Resilience to knockbacks self-assessment

Answer the question below to ascertain if this is a strategic development area for you – identify your current level of resilience and compare this with where you would ideally like it to be.

Q. If something rocks your foundations at work – you receive negative feedback or pushback (real or perceived) about something of importance to you, – typically, what is the scale of the impact on you?

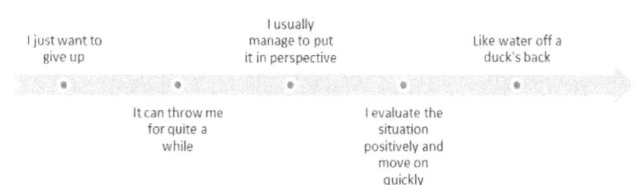

Making it happen:

Try and think in detail about the times that test your resilience so that you can profile your resilience pinch points and target your work on either changing these situations, or changing your response by building your resilience.

Can you articulate what these situations look like – the who, what, where and when?

What does this information tell you about the most significant situations and the value of reducing their impact?

Keep your assessment in mind as you read through the following sections on *building resilience* and make notes to build your plan to address any gap between your current reality and your ideal level of resilience.

> *"There have been some really bad moments but overall I have really enjoyed my career. I would still recommend it as a career for younger women. But when I say that to women I always say that resilience is part of the deal. You have to really have a strategy for coping with all this stuff that will land on you. There has to be a way of managing it. You can't just wander into logistics and hope for the best, you have to have a plan of how you are going to make it work for you.*
>
> *I guess I am fortunate enough to be a naturally resilient person. I think that is partly to do with my brother being severely handicapped. You grow up feeling that if bad things happen to you they are never going to be as bad as what has happened to him. You are naturally grateful for normal life. I do feel grateful for normal life. I get up in the morning and I am pleased to be alive. I do live my life like I could be dead tomorrow. I just think that is a positive outlook on life that you can be blessed with. You can cultivate it, but I have just got it. That does give you resilience. I also have learned (and this is something I have taught myself), but I used to take things very much to heart, I used to worry about things, and I have got better at dealing with that simply by hard work. I have learned not to worry about things so much, but that has been a hard slog through life coaching and the rest of it. But you can learn to be more resilient, it is not just a natural gift."* - **Ruth Waring**

Strategies for building resilience

1. Stay clear on why you are doing what you are doing.

Given that resilience is about getting through the tough stuff, it's important to firmly connect yourself to your goal – your reason why you are doing what you are doing.

It is akin to through mud with water up to your waist like a cadet on an assault course, holding on to the rope that's suspended above you, connecting the entry point to the exit point keeps your head up, and a clear line of view of the best way through. It keeps your arms free to pull you through when your legs are being dragged back and weighed down. Your clarity on what you want out of your current project or role is your way to get you across tough terrain.

> *"What I have always loved about logistics and still do is that it is a very exciting and inspirational industry to work in, in that it is constantly challenging you and things are always changing. I got that buzz from it straight away. So there was a balancing out of those factors. It wasn't that I thought, 'This is awful but I've got to stick at it,' it was, 'Gosh some of the elements of this are going to be really tough, but I think it is going to be a price worth paying because I love the industry.' I knew that very early on."* - **Ruth Waring**

If you are able to be really clear on what your direction is and why it's so important to you, it will help you keep your onward momentum through those tough patches and challenging moments and keep you from changing course or giving up.

"I would probably have given up on it a lot sooner, and there were those who would dearly have loved to see me gone, because what I wanted wasn't going along with the general behaviours. Something outside of the organisation was keeping me in London and it was an amazingly effective secret weapon. I could say to myself, 'I'm staying here. I am choosing to stay in the job because I have chosen to do this and that is important to me.' So whilst the job had reached a stage where I could take it or leave it, other things outside of work were incredibly important and provided that backbone for the resilience that was needed." - **Marion Cowden**

Making it happen:

Can you articulate why you are doing the work you are doing and are you able to say where it fits in your wider plan?

When things do start feeling shaky, the APA recommends you "move toward your goals" by which they mean taking some positive action that moves you forward along that metaphorical rope. It need not be big, but it needs to be recognisable as a positive step forward. By looking ahead and taking action on what matters to you, it enables you to get through the quagmire.

> *"One of my role models was the female CEO of Ogilvy. She always used to say that women asked her a lot about how she had succeeded and how she managed the whole work-life balance thing. She used to say 'You sure as hell need to love your job, because if you don't you will never be good at it and you will never have work-life balance.' She is absolutely right. What gives you the confidence and the resilience at the end of the day is just sheer enjoyment of the job. If you don't love the job, move. Don't sit there and whine, go find a job you do love. Because otherwise you will never be confident about it and you will never get the work-life balance thing right. The work-life balance thing recedes if you are doing something you are passionate about and you love. Somehow you make it all work. If you are doing a job that you resent, that makes you unhappy, that thing will get completely out of proportion in your mind."* –
Mandy Pooler

2. Know your sources of self-belief and confidence.

The last couple of chapters looked at confidence and self-belief because these are fundamental to everything else. At times when the going gets tough and you might start to question yourself, you need to have easy access to the evidence of your portfolio of strengths and how you've drawn on these resources in the past to overcome challenges. I've suggested building a fact file, but it needn't be that literal; the key is to remind yourself of who you are and what you've done that's enabled you to get where you are today.

When you've got through a tough patch, try to take the time to reflect on it and consider what lessons to take from the situation.

Making it happen:

What made it tough and what was it that you did to make it out the other side?

What resources – attitudes, knowledge, belief, behaviours, people, approaches – did you apply?

What made these things deliver for you?

Recognising and logging this information along with the other evidence of your capability, adaptability and potential will shore you up so that next time you will be even stronger and more confident.

3. Stay in the positive – assume you can manage.

Your attitude towards workplace challenges has a significant effect on your ability to grasp the situation, and your ability to get through it. It also affects the response of others along a spectrum of positively piling-in and supporting you, and / or defending the space and time you need, to steering clear and / or enforcing problematic deadlines.

Trying to stay in the positive will keep your brain open to the positive possibilities, whereas having a negative outlook will draw you to focus on the downsides and give more weight to them, thus making the process of getting through the challenge harder and longer. Have confidence in your ability to solve problems and trust in your choices of how to manage situations for the best outcome.

Again, use the evidence of your capability to overcome obstacles and create solutions (for yourself or for others) to reassure yourself that you can and will handle this. You know that challenges come and go and what seems huge now will seem very much smaller when you look back on it in a few months. And if you've temporarily lost sight of this evidence, ask people that won't have, and who will readily share that evidence and their justification for it.

"My experience of women becoming successful was that you really had to depend on yourself quite a lot. Of course, the network of friends is very important, but when it came to it you had to be able to find the resources within yourself. To have the strength to just keep going.

I worked with a wonderful creative lady, Barbara Nokes, who has been one of the most senior and celebrated female Creatives in the industry. She told me that very early on in her career in the tough creative industry she learned to whistle, because you can't cry and whistle at the same time." - **Miriam Jordan-Keane**

4.   Look for the learning.

I said at the start of this chapter that resilience was the one characteristic that all the winning women demonstrated, but the truth is that there is a second supporting characteristic: a life-long lust for learning. It's an attitude to life that may be driven by personality type, but even if that's not you, it is helpful to be deliberate and develop this as a strategic approach to apply in situations that demand resilience. Learning from challenges enables you to identify what aspects of the situation made it challenging, and this puts you in a position to prepare ahead of similar situations. And reflecting on what you drew on and how you successfully negotiated those challenges enables you to keep those resources in mind and consider what additional or alternative resources may be better in dealing effectively with future scenarios.

> *"My partner and I were talking about this at the weekend. I was saying that my most prized possession was my education. I had the benefit of a classical British education and I see that as being of huge benefit to me professionally and personally. It has implanted a desire always to learn. That came from my parents; my education was facilitated through my parents. When I was 40 I remember looking at the £2 coin and it said, 'Standing on the shoulders of giants.' I asked my dad, 'Why does it say that?' He said, 'I think Isaac Newton said that. Let's go and Google it.' My dad aged 70 something was still learning. So the desire to learn all the time*

was very important. Perhaps that was from my parents, but I see my education as part of that. It gave me a great platform for learning. I have a broad knowledge. I can speak two languages as well as English and I can talk about books. I am mathematically capable. I can express myself on paper as well as verbally. It sounds like I'm showing off into your machine, but I can hold a conversation about something that is probably interesting to many people. It has given me a belief that I can learn and achieve things. Leadership is a learnt skill. You learn things every day." – **Morag Blazey**

When you adopt a position towards new and potentially challenging situations by seeing them as learning opportunities you will naturally be looking for the positives that you can take from them. And in learning about how to manage challenges, people also learn more about themselves. This can include a greater sense of strength even while feeling vulnerable, an increased sense of self-worth, and heightened appreciation for what they've achieved, what they do and why it matters.

5. Was it real or did I imagine it?

"My mantra is 'it's not personal'." – **Rebecca Salt**

S**t happens, and sometimes, when it seems to happen too often to be a coincidence, it feels personal, and it makes you feel that your aspirations are just not worth it because it's all just too damn hard.

Making it happen:

So, the first challenge with workplace knockbacks is to get really clear on the answer to the question:

- 'Was this about me, or could it have happened to anyone in my shoes?'

Then there is a second check-question to help put things in perspective:

- Was it really a setback? i.e. did this have a material impact on my work or my plans?'

And, thirdly, if you found that you had read more into the situation in question:

- What are the assumptions I made that gave rise to my interpretation of the situation and could these assumptions be wrong?'

"I learned really early on, through pain more than anything else, that what male colleagues say to you at work is business, it is nothing to do with you personally, it has nothing to do with your personality, it is purely business. I've had many discussions with female colleagues in Asia and Europe on this subject. I share with them a piece of advice I was given to me by my husband, put your virtual suit of armour on when you go into work, it is your protection; whatever hits the suit of armour, you will be protected. This is about being a businesswoman; it is not about the person inside the armour. Don't take it personally. Men don't think it's personal, it's part of the business game. It took me a long time to learn that, through real despair, at times. It has not always been an easy journey." - **Lin Phillips**

However, it's also clear from the evidence of women's slower promotion, lower pay and bonuses and fewer mentors and sponsors that women do experience more knockbacks – or 'hazards' as researchers call them – which could therefore be interpreted as personal. Indeed, the more they happen while you see others around you getting on, the more compelling it is to interpret it as personal. However, it's clear that if these 'others' are men, then the dynamics are more likely to be around your gender than about you as an individual.

Hence, it's not because, I, Diana Parkes, am considered to be less suitable for an opportunity than Daniel Parkes. It's because his gender is considered more suitable. So, I can take action to help people make better decisions by helping them see the truth about me, my strengths, my potential and their relevance and their value. Right here, right now.

If you start to move into a negative space and develop a narrative which says, 'it's about me', then you are liable to misinterpret other messages, gestures and outcomes that will inevitably fit this narrative.

For example, when an update for a project you're leading is overlooked in a management meeting, then it can be read as it being seen as of no interest to them. However, it could alternatively be that people are so confident in your work on this project that they deem that it doesn't need to be regularly reviewed. Or, when you are giving a presentation and someone is looking out of the window, this could just be their way of mulling over and digesting the powerful content you are providing.

I learnt this type of lesson recently, in a meeting with a high-tech global company at their swanky City of London offices. The guy that set up and championed the meeting spent the whole of my presentation and the discussion time tapping away onto his smart phone. I got quietly angrier and angrier as it went on. However, at the salient point of the meeting, he looked up and summarised all the key points that had been discussed and agreed, including the proposed next steps to drive the initiative forward. He had been taking copious notes and determining the best actions to secure progress while the key people were in the room. Oops! As Steven Covey says in his book, *Seven Habits of Highly Successful People*, 'seek first to understand' – don't assume, and don't assume the worst!

6.   'Don't just do something, stand there.'

This was a wonderful quote shared by Morag Blazey. Her point was that it is very easy to be carried away with the sense that you have to take action in the moment when things kick off. However, when you do take the time to breathe and think and review, what may have seemed like a huge issue then shrinks as it slots into perspective and the radical actions that might have seemed appropriate in the instant can be viewed as a knee-jerk reaction.

> "I think increasingly as I've got older my resilience has improved in the sense that I can see a bigger picture. I attach less significance to the outcome of any particular one event than I used to. That is probably how my thinking changed about the assessment centre and partnership. I started to think differently about what would happen if I didn't get through. Those weren't doomsday scenarios. I viewed the whole thing as a learning and development journey and whatever the outcome I was going to learn and develop somehow. That has improved my resilience to many things, I think. I am also more comfortable about crying, which in my experience tends to be more likely for women than for men, who are more likely to get angry. The emotion sitting behind the behaviour is exactly the same for each gender. I recognise that when things get really stressful and tough I may cry at some point and will probably feel better afterwards. It doesn't mean the world is falling apart. If that is the way you deal with things, then be accepting. But as with anger, it's not something that should be on display generally, and so get good at recognising the warning signs and take pre-emptive action like having a walk round the block or grabbing a cup of coffee." – **Maggie Stilwell**

7.   How significant was it really?

A few years ago, I was stressed out of my brain and getting intensely irritated by a guy who was taking up my time when I desperately needed to get on with my work. He was a very laid-back guy who seemed to have masses of time on his hands and not a problem in the world, though I found out later my work-life problems paled into insignificance versus his very real home-life ones. "Ask yourself", he said, "in one or five years' time, how much of an issue would you see in this situation? Given what it'll look like, looking back from that viewpoint, is it something to react to as you are now, or to step over and forget about?" I feel sure that I bit his head off as he made various attempts to help me calm down. But funnily enough, I didn't implode like I thought I would, and as I sit here and try to recollect that time, I have absolutely no idea what it was that was the huge issue. I just recollect what he said. It was powerful advice which I apply when I'm getting myself wound up into a frenzy and becoming an unbearable person to be around. It enables me to keep things in perspective and proportion, to calm down, clear my head and carry on.

8.   Don't just stand there, do something – take action.

Having just described the benefits of staying still and not acting in haste, I'm now going to look at the merits of taking action. This is because it is important to actively confront challenges to prevent them growing in your perception or, indeed, in reality. You need to take the sting out of them before they start to impact your work, your focus and your mental state.

Taking that first step can be the hardest, but it also brings the massive relief of having grasped the nettle and the joy of finding that it didn't hurt after all. Have you had that experience? Have you put off confronting a challenge only to find that it wasn't anything like the huge hurdle you thought it was?

Take decisive actions, rather than distancing yourself from problems and perhaps just hoping they will go away. Meet challenges by daring to take that slightly scary first step. Reflect on and log your before and after experience, to help you take the first step sooner next time, with less angst and with less trepidation. After that first step, the rest are much easier.

> "I think of myself as not a very resilient person, but if you ask anybody who knows me, they'd probably say that I am. I'm a bit overly stoic. You've got to deal with it. Life is what you make of it. Don't wait for somebody to deal with things for you and don't wait for an opportunity to come along. I didn't learn that from my parents. I learnt that from hard work." - **Morag Blazey**

9. Pick your battles.

Unless you are really coasting (and you wouldn't be reading this book if you were) you probably need all the energy you have to make the things you want to happen, and to keep your head above water when the going gets rough. So, don't dissipate or dilute that energy by fighting every battle. When something winds you up, you have to decide whether the cost and implications of engaging in a fight are sufficiently outweighed by the benefits of winning.

> "I found that the best thing was not to react every time I got a knock. Yes it hurt and yes I didn't like it. But if I reacted to that in the way I wanted to at the time, such as letters to the Vice Chancellor etc, that wasn't the way to go forward. The way to go forward was to say, 'I have had that knock. That is the boundary they have set, so I am going to meet it.' It is

how I ended up getting the Chair [Head of the Faculty]. It was then such a compelling case and I'd met every goal I'd been set, and at that point you start to bring people around. At the next point they start to say, 'Didn't they make a good decision promoting you.' At that point you almost have them on your side, because they see it as something they have done. But at any point, if I'd have fought the system, which I could have done, and had put a lot of my energies into doing that, it would have made them more determined not to promote me. I think that is where the resilience comes in. There were times when I went home and cried, but it is about coming back and saying, 'I'm not going to let them say that I can't do it. They have told me I have to do this. I will do that and a bit more.'" –
Prof. Karen Kirkby

[After the tragic death of her BAFTA winning husband, Suzie Allwork went from Office Manager and mother of a 7 and a 9-year-old to Chief Executive Officer of his company.]

"I couldn't even think about following in his footsteps, but I said I could bring my own strengths to the company. I said they were very different. It has been a battle, but I am patient. I suppose it was all about balance. I thought if I started really putting my foot down was it just cutting off my nose to spite my face. You have got to learn to let go of certain things. If they are big, important things you have to stand up for them – if I don't, that is not going to help myself or the company. But with smaller things I have learnt to keep quiet. You have to look at the big picture constantly. You have to let little things go; even though they might hurt personally. You walk

around quietly but use a big stick when you need to." - **Suzie Allwork**

"*Part of the difficulty for women in this environment is knowing which battles to fight. There is a fine line for women between being a bitch and a bimbo. I discovered that, especially in the male dominated industry that I was in. You have to really walk a wire. Because if you fight every single battle you get the reputation of being someone that nobody gets along with. You have to balance that out with being walked all over.*" - **Anna Catalano**

10. Recognise when you need help and ask for it.

There can be a concern that if you ask for help it will be perceived as a sign of weakness, and you may try to avoid being perceived as being weak at all costs. However, it can be argued that asking for help is a sign of strength. It shows self-awareness and an understanding of the range of resources and the ability to use them to find the most efficient and effective route to making progress. Asking for help can also be an opportunity to build relationships that may provide even greater support longer term.

If you don't ask for help when you are unsure of how to do something, you miss the opportunity to learn from someone else who may have experience in something similar and may have a great solution. You may have easy access to an expert who is willing and even grateful to be involved and to become an ongoing ally. Or you may miss the opportunity to talk through the situation, when, in many cases, just saying it out loud enables a solution to spring out from your subconscious. Talking it through with someone else enables them to ask questions about the situation from their fresh perspective, which in turn enables you to see a new angle or critical insight to a solution.

In one memorable coaching session, my client was discussing a problem that had been weighing her down for a long time. It had been preying on her mind, dominating her thinking and planning time. I was able to ask her a simple question which changed everything. "Whose problem is this?" It turned out that it wasn't hers! In a nanosecond the problem evaporated.

> *"Never underestimate the fact that you could run into difficulties at work.*
>
> *You've got to be able to face up to mistakes. I always say to the young ones, 'What sorts the sheep from the goats is if you can tell me there's a problem. Because if you tell me there's a problem then I might be able to fix it, but if you bury it I won't be able to.'"* - Clare Maurice

11. Know who your friends and supporters are and talk to them.

In 1624, English author John Donne wrote "No man is an island", meaning that human beings are dependent on one another. No one is completely self-sufficient, and everyone relies on others. Many women are great at supporting others – going to great lengths to champion their cause and bring them to a good outcome. But ironically, they are not so good at letting others help them. The previous section was about asking for help in work, and this is about using sources beyond the walls of your immediate workplace.

There are two sets of people. Firstly, those people you can call upon who will provide you with unconditional support, the absolute believers in you. These are likely to be friends and family. And secondly, those people whose opinion you really respect, those people who understand something more about the challenges of your type of role and workplace environment. These are likely to be people in your professional network that you know reasonably well and may have comparable experiences or who may be motivated to help by sharing the challenge of being a rare female in a certain sphere of work. These sets of people are ones that will be positively inclined to listen to you and to want to give you their time to provide support for you. Evidence shows that helping others in need is beneficial to both the giver and receiver. There's more on how to develop these relationships and networks in the chapter ahead.

"I have got good female friends who have been through a lot. Four or five female friends. Not in this business, they are in marketing, HR and logistics. I talk with them. And my parents. My partner now, we talk all of the time. We don't have a television and all we do is talk.

One of the things that seems to be terribly important is having love and support.

I think it is. I had it from my parents before, my girlfriends, and now I've got it in a relationship better still. There is that need for resilience. Without that something would happen, some other route would be taken.

I think men might suffer on the resilience side because they don't talk as much as women." - **Dana Skelley**

12. Be open to adapting your plans.

Changes happen at every level and every day. Many people these days will experience redundancy, but changes can be much bigger, as we all know, having experienced the seismic impact of Covid-19. However, a new family, divorce, moving house and death of a relative or friend are challenges that many of us will deal with. And sometimes these mean that you just have to review what you want or what you can have from the next stage of your life. Dealing with the adjustment or total change can be really hard, and this is when you have to revisit your analysis of what matters most to you, and it's when you need to focus on what you can do and can make happen that is positive and of value to you.

It's easy to assume that what is presented about a new job or new organisation is true. But often reality is somewhat different. The question is what can you make of the reality you find, and if you can't adapt it to meet your needs, nor adapt your needs to fit the reality you find, then you have to look for a different route.

> *"It is years of practice. I wasn't always like this. But I live for today. If I go home at the end of today and get run over by a bus, I want to know that I've done a good job at work and it's been a great day in my life as well. I don't know when I actually came across that. I think it is playing golf that has helped; if you don't live the shot, you will never hit it. There is no point planning too far ahead, because plans change. It's about living in the present."* – Lin Phillips

At a much lower level, there are all sorts of elements that change and affect your everyday plans, but the more easily you can roll with these changes as the natural ebb and flow of life, the less they are a drain on your resilience. So, it's important to embrace change positively and look at what you can do, not what you can't. Mindfulness is a great approach to supporting your development with strategy, as it embraces, at its core, the fundamental concept of impermanence i.e., that everything is constantly changing, in our minds, in our bodies and in the world.

13. Stay healthy – balance in everything.

Everywhere we look in today's society, health and well-being are being pitched to us, a constant call of programmes, events and approaches to improve ourselves. But this can just leave us feeling worse about the situation by leaving us feeling unable to make progress. This is compounded by how fast modern life has become, with the increasing hours people work and the many complex and competing demands on our lives. These things can be obvious, but they remain aspirations that go unfulfilled, and end up becoming perennial entries on our New Year's Resolution lists. The reality is that it's hard to achieve a balance in all these areas. However, when this balance is out of kilter you can feel physically and mentally sluggish and everything gets harder. Taking the time to adapt your work-life to achieve a better balance will put you in a stronger place to deal with the turbulence of working life.

Baby steps build habits better than giant leaps. So, just look to build in a little better balance in the key areas and don't beat yourself up if you don't hit your daily aspirations.

Examples include:

- Try to make sure you eat sensibly.
- Drink enough water and not too much alcohol.
- Get enough sleep (being without a few hours' sleep has an impact likened to reducing your IQ).
- Take regular exercise. This is proven to improve your sense of well-being and therefore your positivity, so

squeezing a little in will enable you to handle challenges more successfully. It will give you time, not take it.

- And breathe! The stress hormone, cortisol, builds up in our bodies if we don't disperse it by pumping oxygen round our system. The effects of the build-up can be small, or make you feel very unwell. Sedentary working lives are not helpful in this regard. A simple way to do this is through a non-intrusive regime that takes just three minutes, ideally three times a day, to quietly focus on slow, deep breathing to boost your oxygen input. The magic formula appears to be deeply breathing in for 5.5 seconds and out for 5.5 seconds. This will do the job of reducing your cortisol levels, making you feel instantly calmer and reducing its impact on your mental and physical health over time.

Look after your mental well-being too. That means being aware if you start to feel that you can't cope, and pressures are getting too much. This is the time to stop and evaluate what is going on, and to go and get help in prioritising and managing your workload. Try to put clear boundaries in place that enable you to do the things you need to do and keep them firmly in place.

If times are tough, and the overall trend in how work is making you feel is downward, then perhaps you should consider whether you need to find alternative work options (reporting into someone else, doing a different role, working in a different organisation) for the sake of your mental well-being. While it's important not to react to a short-term blip and hold on to your bigger purpose, putting up with persistent negativity, disappointment, pushbacks, poor management, or a toxic culture over a prolonged period can be damaging. It can also materially affect your prospects of securing something more appropriate for your talent, experience and potential to shine, because it affects your sense of self-worth and therefore your confidence. So, sometimes you have to say that on balance, it is best to find something or somewhere healthier for your mental well-being.

> *"Finally, I have woken up to the fact that resilience isn't about ploughing on when you are not fit or mentally in the right place to do it. Sometimes we have to acknowledge that we haven't got the resilience at certain times in our lives to carry us through. I have never been mature enough to accept that. I have carried on regardless. I have another fifteen years to work and I'm not going to do that now. If I'm ill and I've got problems, then I will look after myself. I have changed my mindset around that."* **- Sharon Kerr**

Making it happen:

What are the key strategies that you have identified through this chapter that will help you build your resilience, particularly to address any pinch points?

How will you make these come to fruition?

Chapter 13

Loving support keeps you going when the going gets tough

What have love and support got to do with career fulfilment? They're not topics that you come across on management and leadership courses or in other career development books. Well, support – the unconditional type – came out as being a vital and active presence in the life of almost every interviewee.

> *"You cannot do it on your own, I am very lucky to have a very supportive husband. There are very few very successful men who haven't got a wife, mother, sister or a boyfriend or somebody behind them."* – Lin Phillips

This support makes such a significant difference when you experience a knockback that feels like a brick wall, or series of frustrations. It soothes away the pain, provides a different perspective and reconnects with why we were doing it in the first place. When the journey is harder and slower than you want it to be, your motivation, energy and drive run low, so you want someone there to prop you up and remind you of what is great about you and why you have to keep going. A true believer can re-kindle self-belief and restore confidence. Having this support is also important for the many women who are still relatively isolated at work and don't have access to peers who recognise the additional challenges they face.

This support outside the workplace can make all the difference. Someone is an absolute believer in you; someone who will support you and encourage you in your times of doubt and even despondency; and who will be there to help celebrate the highs and let you know how very, very proud they are of what you have done.

The reason for defining this as *loving* support is that this type of support cannot come from someone who places conditions on providing support. This type of support comes from people who care deeply and give their time, energy and attention because of that love.

> "Loving support is paramount – even though my family were based in Kenya, they were part of my anchor, along with my children. They were not always there to fix things, but they provided a trusting shoulder to lean on or had an important ear to listen. My mother was a strong constant for my children and I, along with my brother and sister's loving support.
>
> My father was a great sounding board being an astute businessman. He taught me not to take business so personally and told me to 'pull my socks up' on many an occasion because he believed in me, which in turn made me stand up and believe in myself.
>
> My children became great teachers to me and we developed into a small executive team bouncing ideas off each other – I wasn't afraid to show them my vulnerability which ironically gave them a strength – we were in this together.
>
> And, I thank Matthew for the beautiful gift of positivity and the incredible growth journey adversity took me on." – **Suzie Allwork**

To be clear, this is a positive supporter, as distinct from someone who represents your reason for ploughing on. It's not the person or people you do things for – feed the family, pay for schooling, provide a role model. This is the positive support that's there when you need it, and sometimes whether you realise you need it or not. While both things (motivation and support) can come from the same source, they are very distinct and different in terms of the role they play for you. So, it's important to explore what support you have and where it comes from. If there is a gap, you can work on filling it.

> *"There were times when I went home and cried, but it is about coming back and saying, 'I'm not going to let them say that I can't do it. They have told me I have to do this. I will do that and a bit more.*
>
> *Me: Talk to me about how you coped with that.*
>
> *I talked to my husband. He is very good at listening. It does upset him at times because he doesn't like to see me upset. But I am someone who needs to talk things through. He will pull me up at times and say, 'I think there is some merit in what they are actually saying there,' which is very brave of him.*
>
> *He is very good. I do need someone I can talk things through with. I have some friends I can talk things through with who are also quite objective. But the most important thing is having someone to listen."* –
> **Prof. Karen Kirkby**

Figure 11: Unconditional support self-assessment

Read through the question below and then identify which point of the scale best reflects your current situation. Then consider where on the scale you would ideally like to be. If there is a difference between the current and ideal position, then this is the gap that you can plan to close to move you to a more robust position to support you in the achievement of your goals.

Q. Do you have clarity on your source(s) of support? The person or people who prop you up when you need that extra bit of reassurance to believe in yourself and / or in what you are doing?

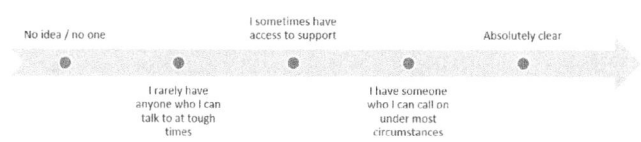

No idea / no one   I sometimes have access to support   Absolutely clear

I rarely have anyone who I can talk to at tough times   I have someone who I can call on under most circumstances

"I couldn't have done it without him. In the same way as I hope I've been a huge support to him. I don't know how you cope as a single mother. For me there was somebody to share these things. He has always been hugely proud. He's also been a good sounding board. He has never ever suggested that this was the wrong thing to do. He told my mother that if I wasn't working he knows he'd have a very unhappy and frustrated wife. He has been fantastic. In those four o'clock in the morning moments when I've been saying, 'Oh my God what am I going to do about...!' He has been very helpful." **- Claire Maurice**

Look carefully to identify your true supporters – they may not be obvious or where you expect.

Sources of support may include a partner, intimate friends or family members. They could be women in similar types of roles who can empathise with your challenges and recognise your capability and potential, and therefore the need for you to continue on your path. However, it's rare to have the level of connection that this special relationship depends on (but I come back to these key people in Chapter 23). There are many sources, but they will be characterised by that person believing in you even when you don't, and being able to tell you why.

"It doesn't have to be a life partner; it can be a child, or it can also be a friend." **- Nancy Kline**

Isolating the fundamental importance of having someone who delivers this role in your life was actually quite a revelation to me. I cast my mind around and could see no one that I felt able to lean on, who I could be really honest with about my self-doubts, never mind anyone who could prop me back up when I was sliding down the walls. So, I felt this was my Achilles Heel, both in terms of my vulnerability when things were hard going, but also a missing source of ongoing strength from a constant, real believer in me.

Then, on one low, low day, when I was feeling like it was time to give up, and I could feel the tears coming to my eyes as I drove towards my mother's house with my daughter in the car, I did the rare thing of telling her I was actually feeling quite down, because I didn't think I was going to make my business work after all, and so it might be time to give up and find a normal job. Her little voice said, "But Mummy, you know that the person who invented the light bulb tried and failed two thousand times before succeeding. And where would we be if he gave up along the way? Don't give up Mummy." My daughter was 11 years old when she said that. In that moment I recognised my rock and my constant believer. She is my most vigorous and steadfast supporter. And I am utterly in awe of the difference she has made to me. Thank you, Gracie.

So, while your steadfast supporter may be obvious, for some it's not so immediately apparent.

For some people, another very powerful source of additional support is a paid professional coach. The reason why I'd include a fully qualified coach here, is that the underpinning philosophy that this type of coach signs up to has a clear parallel with unconditional loving support:

- Confidence in the client's ability to achieve their goals is without question.
- Each client has unlimited potential.

As a coach, this is what you truly believe of each client, and you give your professional support on that basis. You may want to check that this is in the code of ethics that your coach has signed up to, if this is a route you chose to pursue.

"Have a leadership coach." - **Rebecca Salt**

Making it happen:

What are your reflections having read this section?

Are there any actions you want to take as a result?

Chapter 14

Know your strengths and where they have the potential to take you

This is about identifying your strengths and the range of places they can take you – not necessarily just in a straight line to the next role in your functional or technical specialism, but also into new fields and functions. And, as Sara Fox shows in the next case study, to enable you to be open to the potential of an off-the-wall opportunity if it crosses your path or your mind.

To understand your personal potential and its implications for your future you need to understand both what you can and could do, based on:

- What you have done and how you've performed (to identify your strengths).
- What you've experienced, enjoyed and learnt to this point (to help you focus on a good direction).
- And what your attitude, interest and motivations indicate you could thrive in or at in the future.

"I got a message from Carla telling me to send them [Olympia & York Canary Wharf, Property Development] my CV. I said I didn't have a background in architecture, design, construction, engineering, leasing, financing or property

development –s what am I missing? She said, 'You don't understand. We have people who can do all of those things. We've got experts in those things. What we haven't got is good general managers, who know how to manage a project and can make things happen.' So I sent her my CV. Two weeks later I got a call from the office of the Chief Executive and the next thing I know I am going along for an interview with the guy who is the senior vice president of construction who has the responsibility for the whole of the construction of the whole of Canary Wharf.

I learned about the construction and property development business literally by osmosis by sitting at the feet of somebody who had been doing it for 20 years. It was great fun.

[Then further down the line...] Heidi [Sara's boss at the time] and I met at The River Cafe and at the end of lunch she said that Swiss Re in New York had approved the construction of a new headquarters. She said, 'How would you like to build a new building?' I left the lunch with my head spinning and called Richard, who had been my boss at Canary Wharf. I said, 'Richard, Heidi wants me to build a building. I can't build a building can I?' He said, 'Of course you can build a building.' At least I asked the question, rather than just saying I couldn't do it. I just called somebody to validate. Actually I knew what he'd say.

By the time I had finished building the building in New York, the building in London was getting very close to getting planning permission. I got a call from the UK CEO who said, 'Want to build another building?'" – **Sara Fox**

Sara didn't have a goal to build one of the most iconic contemporary buildings in the UK. She had moved between finance and process management and consultancy before moving into the construction industry. She knew nothing about the functional components of construction, but what she had demonstrated were the qualities and capabilities to successfully manage massive projects. That potential was recognised by the right person at the right time to connect her with an industry and role she fell in love with, and networks that connected her with the opportunity to make a mark like no other.

The critical features of Sara's story and her career are threefold. Firstly, she sought out the opinion of people whom she respected. Secondly, she was open to their views about her potential to move in a new direction and a new scale of challenge. And thirdly, she went for it. She sought to *understand* the reality of her potential and *dared* to stretch across into new fields and to embrace new challenges. From her language, there is no doubt that this enabled her to *thrive* in a new environment and in work she would never have actively sought out independently.

We've looked at the factors that can cause women to feel less confident about their range and level of strengths which can affect their view of where their potential can take them. This limits their own prospects and potential to thrive. The same causes can result in a perception that you have to be able to perform at 100% from day one when you start a new role. Hence women can struggle to see what they're good at now, let alone what else they could excel at through developing within that next step up.

> "I never saw my potential. I have always gone one step at a time. Instead of having a big goal at the end, which many of my male colleagues have, I have just sort of got where I've got because I have been good at every stage. People have helped and encouraged me.
>
> Me: What would you say to other women about that?
>
> I'd say have a bit more of a strategy. I could have done with some guidance in helping me understand my potential. I didn't have any plan. I just bumbled along. I think I would have got a lot further a lot

quicker though I am quite happy with the way things have worked out." - **Sharon Kerr**

You leave yourself at a disadvantage if you don't have a clear, evidence-based view of your potential and it's implications, for three main reasons:

1. You can't spot, research or target suitable opportunities if you haven't defined 'suitable'. And maybe you don't just want 'suitable'; you want something exciting, challenging and fulfilling.

2. You can't explain why you are the right candidate for a new role / new project nor persuade people that you have the potential to be a great asset.

3. You've already seen that research shows that men are assumed to have the potential needed, while women need to provide proof. So, to be successful in securing the work you want, you are likely to have a harder job to convince interviewers or panels.

"I think it is not just a case of how women approach it; I think it is a case of how women are perceived. I think that men are promoted based on potential and women are promoted based on performance. I've seen many years of that. I think it has to do with the selection committee. When you are choosing somebody to be in a job you have a tendency to try to envision somebody in that position because they resemble you. If the selection committee is made up mostly of men, they are more likely to take a chance on a guy who hasn't done it, but seems to have all the ingredients that they had when they might have been in that position. So they are more willing to take a chance, or it is less of a risk. When it comes to anyone who is different, whether it is a man of colour or a woman of colour or someone from a different country, they tend to go back to, 'What has this person actually accomplished?' From the selection side I think that bias is there.

As a result, as one of the few women who might be considered for a job, if you don't have many role models there who look like you, you are going to want to make sure that you are successful. Because once again you are representing not only yourself, but you are carrying a flag for the whole gender. So we have a tendency to question our abilities and our potential for being successful to a fault. Our greatest fear is to go into a job and not be successful, because that not only lets us down, it lets all women down. Therefore, before I put my hand up for this job I want to make sure I can really do it. Because I can't afford to fail. This whole notion of not being able to fail is what causes women to be more reluctant to self-promote or even believe that they have the potential, because they want to make sure they are not going to fail.

One of the things I have always been a proponent of is examining selection committees to see if there is a current bias in the makeup of the selection committees. I think that is very important. I think it is important for women to be more aware of these self-conscious gender biases that we hold. We are as guilty of the biases as men are. I think we should be more self-aware. I always say to people, 'I want an equal chance to fail. I want an equal chance to fail as the men have.' That is actually what we should be asking for. Not an equal chance to succeed, but an equal chance to fail. Because what happens is we don't get the breaks that they do. So we don't have an equal chance to fail." **- Anna Catalano**

Figure 12: Personal potential self-assessment

Against the following two questions, identify where you are now and where you would ideally like to be. Does this indicate that assessing your strengths and identifying your personal potential is a strategic development need for you, or can you move straight to the next chapter?

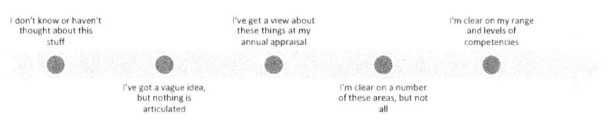

Q.1. Do you have clarity on your range of functional* (or technical*) and general* competencies* and the level they currently reach? *[definitions are available at the end of the chapter]

I don't know or haven't thought about this stuff

I've got a vague idea, but nothing is articulated

I've get a view about these things at my annual appraisal

I'm clear on a number of these areas, but not all

I'm clear on my range and levels of competencies

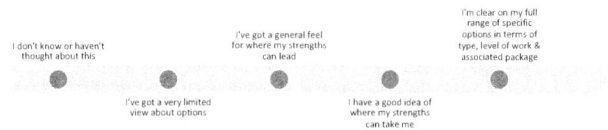

Q.2. Have you identified where these strengths can take you?

I don't know or haven't thought about this

I've got a very limited view about options

I've got a general feel for where my strengths can lead

I have a good idea of where my strengths can take me

I'm clear on my full range of specific options in terms of type, level of work & associated package

This goes beyond your CV. Your strengths and potential need to be articulated and, ideally, rehearsed.

Your strengths and potential go beyond what is included in a typical CV, but it can provide a start point. However, I know writing a CV is a painful prospect and task for many women; it confronts our undermined belief in our capabilities with the need to demonstrate evidence of comprehensive and compelling proficiency. I've found that many women are inclined to describe their work – which is clearly of truly strategic and step-changing significance (for their team, customers, department, function, organisation, shareholders) – as something "anyone would have done in my shoes". They miss the vital point that no one else did!! In the case of your CV or any other form of applications, if you don't package and appropriately communicate what you did, what it says about you – your strengths and potential – and its value significance, it will be your loss.

What are strengths?

The conventional HR perspective is that workplace strengths are defined in terms of competencies which might be technical (specifically required to be successful at your functional or technical specialism, e.g., IT, Marketing, Finance) or general, such as leadership, problem solving or teamwork. I rather like David Parnell's dynamic definition (author of *In-House: A Lawyer's Guide to Getting a Corporate Legal Position* (Parnell, 2013)): "A workplace strength is any ability that is enjoyable, applicable, and that you are better at than most of your colleagues." Here, the emphasis is brought back to the aspects that you love – the work that is most stimulating and interesting to you – or the parts that you focus on because you feel strongly that they're the most important. The principle is simply that you tend to do best at the things that you are most motivated to do. So, this is not only a great way to identify your strengths, but it also is really powerful in showing you the sort of direction you should pursue, i.e., a direction that delivers lots of what you love and do really well, which is also likely to provide plenty of evidence and enthusiasm to support your case.

However, it's still important to know that bigger organisations often document and measure key competencies (strengths) at role, function and even organisational level, as these will be the factors they believe will bring about their success. So, a source of insight into your portfolio of strengths will be those that your organisation (if it is fairly sophisticated or large) articulates for your role, for your function, and overall. And if you know what the next step or steps are for you, then you can try to identify those strengths considered important for these roles so you can collect evidence of your performance against these competencies to demonstrate your fit and potential.

Terminology in all of this can be confusing and actually it doesn't really matter that much. Strengths, capabilities, competencies and skills are often used interchangeably. So, it's potentially very confusing – but everyone is confused, including HR and other consultants who are paid to develop these things! The key is to know what you mean by a term or to find out how the relevant organisation defines it. However, I've included the standard key definitions at the end of this chapter.

Questions and frameworks to prompt your thinking.

Given how tricky this is, and how critical it is to articulate a comprehensive picture of your strengths and potential, I'm giving you lots of support over the next few pages. It will prompt your thinking and open it up to some important dimensions that can be pivotal in your future. And it will help you dodge your modesty.

When you look at your achievements - i.e. what you've actually done and delivered, not your job description, which is what you're supposed to do - and you think about the way you went about securing those things, what does it tell you about:

· what you do well

· how you identify what matters

· how you do things to make them go well

From those insights, what does that indicate are the most important aspects which make the difference that you deliver:

· skills

· knowledge

· approach(es)

· attitude, philosophy, values

What's your supporting evidence?

Then considering the key aspects of delivering your role, what are the skills, knowledge, behaviours and competencies required (both technical and general).

Think widely to identify your foundation and drive strengths.

The table on the next page is a simple framework focusing on your strengths in which I make a distinction between 'foundation strengths' and 'drive strengths'. Foundation strengths are the set of factors that would enable someone to successfully deliver your role. Drive strengths are unique to you. They are the things that motivate and stimulate you and that you consider important. You focus on them especially, and perhaps instinctively, to do a great job – or the best you can in the circumstances. Drive strengths are also important as these show your potential: both your potential to build from, and your potential direction.

If you are looking towards leadership roles or advancing in leadership, **reflect carefully on the strategic significance** of these to your part of your organisation, its stakeholders or the organisation overall. Demonstrating strategic understanding, strategic ability and the strategic impact you've delivered are fundamental to success at this level, and they're often missing from women's CVs and interview conversations.

Table 2: Foundation and drive strengths framework

Strengths	Smarts	Technical Role-specific Competencies	General; Managerial or Leadership; and Organisational Competencies
Foundation strengths *(what a person in your role should have)*	Qualifications: academic and professional	The factors that are widely considered to bring about success in your role	Examples: Presentation, interpersonal skills, team working, communication, influencing, managing people, analysis & problem solving, decision-making
Drive strengths *(the strengths you have that make the difference to the work you direct or deliver)*	Further qualifications: academic and professional Attitude to and engagement in learning Emotional intelligence	The factors that you excel at Additional factors that you bring to the role and deliver with energy and commitment – that you see as important and make a positive difference	The factors that you excel at and additional factors that you bring to the role and deliver with energy and commitment. Those that you see as important in making a significant difference. Examples: Thinking beyond the plan, coaching others, strategic thinking, integrity, adaptability, pioneering new ideas.

Struggling? Some more techniques for accessing these important insights.

Read over previous appraisals and 360-degree feedback (if available).

If you haven't already done it, complete the Career Drivers Assessment tool free at https://womensatnav/tools/). This will help you identify what gives you the greatest buzz at work – the aspects that motivate you most, which are likely to be closely linked to your strengths, and help indicate the profile of your future direction.

Reflect on what your colleagues, bosses and other stakeholders seek you out for, or about, and if it's not obvious, go and ask them!

Reflect on the positive feedback you receive. What are the consistent themes?

Ask your boss or sponsor, "If I said I'd be interested in moving to x/y/z role, would you support me? And if so, what would you describe as the reasons why I'd be suitable?"

Find a suitable reason, and ask any of the following people about your strengths and where they could take you:

- workplace sponsor; the person that gave you this job; your mentor (formal or informal); your boss; peers; people you would ask for a reference; external recruitment consultant; family; friends (including old school or university friends)

Ask external stakeholders what they value about what you do and the way you do it. If you combine that with asking about things that they would like to see improved, it can all be positioned as part of your efforts to do the best possible job for them.

Imagine you are your greatest supporter – what would she say about you and why? Women will often – metaphorically speaking – walk over hot coals for members of their team or others they feel need to be championed. So, if you were that woman, how would she champion you?

Work with a coach who will provide a structured, assumption-free approach enabling you to articulate your strengths and potential.

Some check-steps around your professional value proposition.

Take the time to step back and work out if you are selling yourself short, and consider involving someone you trust and respect to review your findings.

Below is a framework to help you check through the critical components of what you can now consider to be your professional value proposition.

Figure 13: Professional value proposition

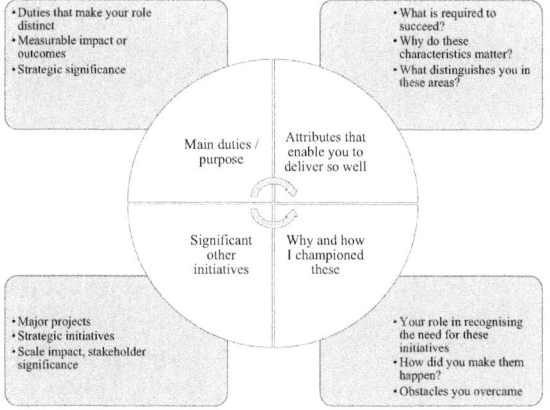

If you fail to recognise, under-state or under-sell your pivotal strengths and their potential, you've created your own career roadblock. So, this is the time to take courage and be brave enough to say, *"Actually, I did that, and it was significant and valuable, and it demonstrates the following characteristics about me which are important because..."*

Also, check back over the work that you've done here to see if there is an emphasis on your technical strengths, at the cost of general ones. I've found that women are more comfortable articulating technical skills specific to their job role. This may be because they are often more easily articulated and objectively measured. This makes them more obvious and easier to access and to have confidence in (as we saw with academic qualifications). However, it is vital to explore and identify strengths and potential in the category of general competencies, as these often open up more transferable opportunities, enabling your career to move further and faster and open up entirely new possibilities as they did for Sara Fox.

> *"Women are not very good about showcasing their achievements, it is seen as boasting, whilst men are brought up to showcase how good they are. I have mentored many women to actually recognise their achievements and to talk about them; if they don't, no one else will!*
>
> *For example, one team of my team doesn't actually see what she has done. She has done some amazing things and achieved a lot, but she can't see she has done that. Whereas if she was a man she would tell me what she had done. I have to sit and say, 'what about this?'. She will say, 'Oh yes, I suppose I've done that.' I said, 'Don't you think that is an amazing achievement?' She said, 'I suppose so, but is just the normal stuff. It is just my job.'"* - Lin Phillips

Have you quantified the impact of what you've done to provide evidence of the scale of your achievements and strengths? I can't emphasise enough the importance and impact of doing so. When I've pushed clients to articulate the numbers, with a question like, 'What was this worth to the business, the client, the economy', they find that the career benefits of discovering the reality of the true scale and impact of their work, their ideas, their vision, their innovation and their perseverance have delivered and multiplied for years. So, I know that doing this work will help you see, believe and own the real significance of what you do and have done. And then you will be strong, clear and compelling when you pursue the opportunities that should be, and will be, yours.

Me: *Personal potential is linked to some of the other areas we have spoken about. Women seem to have some sort of limitation in terms of what they think they can do.*

"I am always doing it. My partner is always saying, 'Of course you could do that. I am absolutely convinced you could do that.' I will be saying, 'No I haven't got this or that or I would need to do that first.' Always.

We think we are not equipped to do it. We have got to be absolutely equipped. I couldn't go for an interview unless I was 100% convinced I wanted the job and 100% convinced that I'd done everything possible to prepare in terms of demonstrating my competence. I have pulled out of jobs before because I've felt I wasn't 100% competent to go for it. I do think that is something that women tend to do. I have had to encourage women to go for jobs that they've felt they couldn't do. I have actually found myself pushing women to apply for promotions when they've thought they weren't up for it. It has been quite clear that they were far more competent than the people around them.

It is a little bit like somebody saying to us, 'That is a lovely jacket' and we say, 'No it's not, its really old.' We are not good at taking compliments and storing them. And that goes for taking on people's compliments about our business skills. There does seem to be a need to help women more than men in enabling them to see what skills they have and how they can utilise them.

That goes back to that example I gave of my boss asking me who he should bring in for the role and me not saying, 'What about me?'

Me: Where have you got your belief from about what you can do?

You have to actually see the results. You need to see evidence that what you have done has been right and successful. And to have feedback as well. It is important for people to tell you it. The technical societies, like the Institution of Civil Engineers and the Institute of Highways and Transportation, there are people there who ask you to do things. So if people come and ask you to do a presentation on something it is a corroboration that they think you know what you are talking about. Those are the sort of things that have given me the idea that I am quite good at things. I do need recognition. When I say recognition, I mean feedback from people telling me I have done something well. The higher up you get the less you get." – Dana Skelley

Mapping a thriving future.

This section is designed to stimulate your thinking about your medium- and long-term future. You can use it to expand your landscape of possibilities. It starts with some blue-sky thinking nudged by my questions and the insights about your values, drivers, strengths and potential that you've identified along this journey with me so far.

To make the most of this opportunity, you'll need to take your time in a suitable space in which you can reflect without immediate pressures to grab at your first thoughts.

By addressing these questions you will be articulating your future career path and developing a plan to get there – building on your drive strengths and gaining the evidence to secure the work that will be most rewarding for you.

Making it happen:

So, let's make a start. Thinking about what you've learnt about yourself (or reminded yourself about), imagine yourself three or five years in the future...

· Of all the dimensions you've considered, which represent the most compelling and fulfilling prospects that you want to ensure are central in your working life?

· What aspects do you want to have left behind?

· What subject matter would you love to be the focus of your work – all practicalities aside?

· What would be the perfect profile of a working environment and / or organisation? Describe as many characteristics and dimensions as you can.

Then consider:

· What would it mean to you if you achieved this / these dream (s)?

· In the light of these ideas and the benefits they deliver:

  ° What would you say if you were your own boss or fiercest supporter?

  ° What would you be pushing yourself to think about / work towards / push for?

  ° What would you say should be the first step you should take tomorrow?

You may have had ideas before reading this book, so you may want time to let the new insights you've developed marinate over a few days to see what else comes to mind. You may also want to look further into the avenues you've now opened up. This could mean having discussions with people in your network or seeking new contacts via your network or social media, to broaden your thinking and knowledge about possibilities for people with your focus, passion and talent. Bear in mind that if the ideal job or role doesn't exist, you can always look at ways of creating it.

> *"My Chairman said, 'Why don't you go for the Managing Director's job?' And I said, 'No, it doesn't appeal at all.' It was really just because I was scared of being out of my depth. Just the idea at that stage of him saying, 'Why don't you apply?' was frightening. I think I'm conscious of my own limitations as well. A man might say, 'I can do anything.' I don't think I can do anything. I don't know what that is, whether it's just being realistic, or overcautious."* – **Lavinia Carey**

If you've done all the thinking and the research that you wanted to do, then the next thing to identify is the gap you need to bridge. What experience, skills, knowledge or relationships do you need to build to move you closer towards securing the future you've scoped. Once you've gained this level of clarity you will need to develop your plan to accrue these things.

Making it happen:

Which roles, projects, support, training, organisations will give you the opportunity to build and demonstrate this portfolio and give you a great experience along the way?

What are your first steps to start making progress?

"I think it is important to take risks in order to succeed.

A couple of times I have taken roles that weren't natural fits and they have allowed me to have a greater impact and have broader choices later on in life about what I choose to do.

There was an important one of those. I was always operational, always in the refinery, and then I went and did some technical work and some research, then I went into corporate doing some technical stuff. I had a sponsor who came to see me. She said, 'I am looking to reorganise and I am thinking about putting you in a position where you are leading sales, marketing and operations.' My first response was 'No I really couldn't schmooze with the customers.' I went home and had a margarita and said to myself 'You are a stupid idiot. You could spend the next twenty years doing the stuff you know how to do. You should go and try this.' So I went back and said, 'If you are still interested, I would be interested in being considered.' But I had to work my way through that. However, I got two promotions in three years." - **Peggy Montana**

A watch-out!

A material issue that affects a significant number of women is making career-limiting decisions based on thoughts about future responsibilities, and which they perceive might take priority over their career ambitions.

"How often do you say, 'If I had no other responsibilities who could I actually be?' I think very few of us give ourselves the opportunity to do that. Whereas I think more men do. They don't

seem to have their decisions as cluttered by their responsibility for others. It is much harder to get to a definition of my personal potential, because I always think about my personal potential as a Venn diagram. I have my personal potential here and attached to it is my responsibilities for everyone else in my world; whether that is parents, brothers and sisters, family. It comes as a package. I think we think about personal potential with those things attached to us, whereas I get the sense that men make their decisions about personal potential differently. They decide what their personal potential is and then think about the impact it is going to have on the people they are responsible for. So, I think most men think about their potential with fewer constraints, which means it's more likely they think bigger and bolder about their careers." - **Sarah Lewis**

A 23-year-old I interviewed during another stream of my research articulated this career-limiting thinking very clearly. She was highly qualified, massively enjoying her work and very ambitious to do bigger, better, more exciting and more challenging stuff. This young woman had recently married a man with the same qualifications; indeed, they'd met while studying the same course at university. This young woman made patently clear to me that she had no interest in having babies, but their respective families had started going on about them. The problem was that when opportunities came up – such as a transfer to the United States – she thought, 'What if we have kids? We'll be in America. It'll be down to me to give up my work to look after them as, it's only logical, he [my husband] is already earning more money. And if we're in America, because I've grabbed this opportunity, I won't have any family around me to support me with childcare'. At 23 and just married, this woman had already passed over opportunities like this one, while her husband had not, which was why he was already earning more money. So, this projection into the future about how things might turn out had become a self-fulfilling prophecy – not pursuing opportunities had cost her salary parity with her husband and, in her view, the option to have a fulfilling career rather than becoming the default carer. This is not an unusual situation. In fact, her example represents a significant proportion of women.

Analysis of the gender pay gap has shown that thoughts of potential childcare responsibilities undermine women's careers because they result in these types of decisions – turning down good opportunities with better remuneration – even before they have a long-term partner or any plans to have children.

Making it happen:

What are the biggest insights about yourself that you've gained from reading this chapter?

How do you want to act on these insights and when will that be?

Some definitions and examples.

A *strength* is "any ability that is enjoyable, applicable, and that you are better at than most of your colleagues." (Parnell, 2013).

A *skill* is an ability or capacity acquired through deliberate, systematic and sustained effort to smoothly and adaptively carry out complex activities or job functions involving ideas (cognitive skills), things (technical skills), and / or people (interpersonal skills) i.e., something learnt in order to be able to do a specific job.

Competencies are identified in relation to an organisation, function or role as those things which are believed to be the factors which will bring about success. They are the portfolio of characteristics that are looked for in certain roles due to the positive specific impact they have and are often graded by level. They are a combination of knowledge, skills, abilities, behaviours, and other characteristics that an individual needs to perform work roles or occupational functions successfully. So, they are more than the skill, and include abilities and behaviours, as well as knowledge that is fundamental to make successful use of that skill.

Functional (or technical) competencies are the things that you need to deliver within a specialist function or technical role successfully.

General (non-technical) competencies are the range of skills, abilities, attitudes, behaviours and knowledge that are needed to operate successfully within the organisation and, where appropriate, with external stakeholder groups (e.g., communication, team working, problem solving).

Chapter 15

To have your best career you have to address your home front strategically

In October 2015, an Ipsos Mori poll for The Thomson Reuters Foundation found that out of 9,500 working women across the G20 countries, their top concern was that having a family would damage their career. And research cited in *Through The Labyrinth* by Eagly and Carli (A. H. Eagly L. C., 2007, p. 55) showed that women have good cause to be concerned. They found that "having children under the age of six reduces women's leisure time by an hour a day and so does marriage. Yet men's leisure is not affected by either. In the USA men have 212 more leisure hours a year, the equivalent of almost five 40-hour working weeks". UK research reported by *The Observer* in February 2016 into couples' domestic activities showed that on average, men did six hours' housework a week while women did an average of fourteen hours (or 70% of all chores). This difference accumulates to 416 hours a year or 43 working days (assuming a 48-hour week). In this research, white men did the least domestic work of all ethnic groups.

But what this really tells us is that we still live in a society that expects, as the norm, for women to carry the burden of responsibility for childcare and to do the lion's share – perhaps we should say, the lioness's share – of domestic work in long-term partnerships and marriage. These are issues that need to be anticipated and agreed early in a relationship so that inequality is minimised. This will enable both you and your partner to keep gaining fulfilment and self-esteem from both your home and working lives.

> *"Ditch the guilt for working and being different to other mothers. What matters are family, friends, balance and confidence.*
>
> *Block out time for key events – treat them as a business commitment. Learn how to say 'no'."* -
> **Beverley Bell**

The drive for equality in the workplace is high profile and being driven as an economic if not a moral imperative by an increasing number of national governments. However, the conversation about domestic equality has only just started.

What focus there is, is on the first year of a child's life. Shared parental leave (the option for parents to share up 50 weeks' leave and up to 37 weeks' pay) was introduced by the UK government in 2015. However, very few employers have promoted it to employees. In fact, 2019 research showed a consistent decline in those four years in the number of eligible men taking their basic paternity leave, with less than a third participating (654,000 women took maternity leave and 203,000 men took paternity leave) and only 2% of fathers took up shared parental leave in 2019. The unequal sharing of domestic responsibilities is a silent crisis, quietly endured by many, many mothers.

Figure 2 (page 73) shares data from the 2020 Sat Nav to Success Research survey which shows that 51% of women with children under 17 reported being solely or mostly responsible for ongoing domestic responsibilities, compared to 14% of men. Only 1.6% of women compared to 27.4% of men said that someone else did it all.

Equal sharing of the responsibilities for a shared home is fundamental to enabling women to really have the opportunity for fulfilling their career ambitions and potential, and to maintaining their economic and mental well-being. Currently most mothers, not fathers, have commitments to their children's care which restrict the hours they can work, the locations they can work in, the flexibility they have to respond to last minute workplace demands or opportunities, the jobs they can go for and the headspace they have to focus on the roles they are trying to deliver. There is a huge toll, mentally and physically, on mums who are left to try and do it all.

> *"I guess I do see socks because I am a retailer and you are trained to pick things up off the floor. Men on the whole are messier and will live with the attitude of, 'We'll do it tomorrow. A bit more dirt. What the hell.' Ladies don't do that. Men are skilful, because they think, 'No need, she'll do it eventually.' It is about the standards of the woman. If she wants it done she will do it, either that or she shouldn't have married him. Early on you need to put your marks down. That is about being true to yourself.*
>
> *Pairs never agree on everything, you have to work it through.*
>
> *It is about setting your stall out, just like when you go into a company. Don't moan about it, just set it out the way you want it. That's what blokes do, why shouldn't you?"* – Simon Hughes

Managing your home life is a fundamental and critical component of the plan that enables you to have your best career, but one that most people don't consider strategically. Women rarely evaluate their options. They rarely negotiate or re-negotiate terms.

While the biggest domestic challenges are for those with a child or children, there are challenges for women in established relationships without children and those living independent lives. This chapter will explore these realities, with the weight of emphasis on women with or considering families.

The silent crisis of 21st century mothers

The 2015 film *Suffrage* is a reminder of the colossal struggle by women a century ago to secure basic rights for women. Since then, we've had a series of eras named to represent the stages of continued struggle for equality, and today we are living in the Fourth Wave of Feminism. And of course, thank god these women had and have the courage to lead the drive for social change. However, what my own research has shown is that this high profile drive for equality inadvertently results in another layer of subconscious expectation that seeps into the reality of modern day's domestic inequality. It creates painful conflict that is difficult to identify, therefore difficult to talk about and address. And, in many ways it has become taboo. So, what am I talking about?

It's now expected that women must strive for the top – to 'make it' in their careers – given all that has gone on before and is currently in place (including specific initiatives with some employers: women's networks, balanced recruitment policies, focus on closing the gender pay gap, and so on). So, the message is 'push forward, be grateful and don't complain. It used to be a lot worse'. Be grateful for this idyllic landscape, the land of opportunity, that's been created for you. But whatever you do, don't mention domestic issues and baby stuff. Work is not the place to talk about, think about or be distracted by domestic logistics or issues. Be committed. So, this creates an environment in which many women must pretend it's all OK. While inside they deal with stress, panic, worry, exhaustion, and frantic planning.

> *"The senior men here, you wouldn't think they had children. You can see that somebody else is filling that gap. They have to be, because they are here from 8am to 7pm, so somebody is magically in the background sorting it out."* – **Anon Interviewee**

So, it's clearly not OK because these duties and responsibilities sit with mum, while her other half breezes along at work blissfully independent of external challenges. For women who are not mothers, but are potentially interested in becoming one, they quickly 'get' the implications of this scenario.

Here, I want to face up to the reality of these issues and help start to change the balance for 21st century women, so that they too can focus on their working day and have the options, freedom and flexibility to pursue meaningful, satisfying and rewarding work. I'm going to share a lot of experiences, approaches and views from the women I interviewed. I'm going to do this for a few reasons. The biggest reason is that there are so many mixed messages, both about what is expected of women when it comes to working, to families, and to feminism (what you should and shouldn't do or be if you align yourself with feminism) and about what the hell you are supposed to do about managing a family once you have one. In countries like the UK and the USA where extended families are rare and childcare is very expensive, it is very hard to find a path through. There is also colossal pressure on women (not men) to be a great parent. Yes, it is shifting a bit, but the shift needs to be seismic in scale. In the media the focus is nearly always on mothers as the sole source of responsibility for the welfare, mental development and happiness of their offspring. It's the mother's fault, never the father's, when children's progress and development doesn't match expectations.

Do it together, your [plural] way.

Sharing the experiences, approaches and views of my interviewees is partly to give you ideas, but it's also mainly to reassure you that **there is no right way, only your way,** and that you must feel positive and confident, rather than guilty, about the arrangements you make based on your values and priorities and your circumstances. Nobody else is you – so you have to get clear on what matters to you both as parents, and create your own path. And if you are a single mum, as I am, it's perhaps even more critical, but luckily with the benefit of less negotiation and compromise.

What is really critical is that if you are half of a couple, then he (or she) has to carry half the responsibilities – which include anticipating, thinking about and planning those duties. **Responding** to 'could you go to the grocers and buy...?' is not sharing the load.

Every year in our research, we see a ten-percentage point difference in the number of men compared to the number of women reporting that they share domestic responsibilities equally (57% of men and 47% of women in 2020) (Parkes, *Sat Nav 2020 Report,* 2020). What the qualitative commentary makes really clear is that more men believe they are sharing equally because they don't recognise the planning and logistics that are required, and believe they share domestic responsibilities equally on the basis of sharing the tasks that are done (once the work to make them possible is complete).

> *"After we had kids, we got to the point where one of them would get sick and we would look at each other and say, 'Who is going to take time off of work?' When I started travelling a lot he said, 'we brought them into the world. I think we are supposed to raise them. Why don't I just quit and stay at home and run the house?' And he did that. He didn't just quit and stay at home; he literally ran the house. He did the cooking, the cleaning, the driving, the ironing, everything. It was wonderful.*
>
> *He said, 'This is a decision that we are making. It is about us. I really don't care what other people think. I'm comfortable with who I am and that is the choice we have made.' Tremendously enlightened and not a big ego, which I think is one of the things that's important. If you are someone who cares a lot about what other people think about you and how other people define success, you are not going to make decisions like that. Joel is very comfortable in his own skin and knows what he wants out of life. I am a very lucky girl.*
>
> *Those are all choices, in terms of division of labour and all of that. I've read a lot about how unfair it is that women have to do all this other stuff and men don't have to do it. I say, stop. The only thing that we absolutely have to do that the men cannot do is give*

birth. That is the only thing that absolutely must only be done by a woman. All other things, whether it's mowing the lawn, running the errands, buying the groceries, those are all conscious choices that a couple makes. It is easy for me to sit here and say this because I happen to be married to Mr Perfect.

Me: A family is a collaborative venture.

I think it is totally unfair and impossible for women to succeed in business, if they have to come home and do everything around the house. It is impossible. You either have to find somebody to help you, or you have to marry someone who is willing to do more than half of what needs to be done. It is impossible. It is unfair for people to say, 'Women can't be successful because they have to do all of this.' That is not right. I would just push back and say, these are choices that are made. If you have chosen to be the only one who can help with homework, then don't complain about it, because that is a choice you have made. Otherwise, you have to have a conversation with the person you are married to.

It seems that the men are not willing to give up. That is the part that is not fair. You can tell I have very strong feelings about this. I think it is extremely unfair for people to say that women can't be successful because they have to do more of the work at home. A lot of people say, that is just the way it is, but I would push back and say, 'No, I think it is a conscious decision people make in terms of how they want to run their lives.' If you want to be the person who is always doing all that other stuff, then you don't get to whine about how tough it is. I mean that in a nice way. You can't set expectations so impossibly high. There are only 24 hours in a day.

I don't mean to sound cold and callous about it. You've got to decide on what is important in your life. You've got to decide what matters the most. It could be that, if you are married to somebody who doesn't care about the kids and doesn't care what the house looks like, isn't supportive of what you are doing, there is part of me that says, 'Why the hell are you with this person?'

If that is something that turns out to matter the most to you, you have to focus on that, make sure it gets done right and then the job thing you need to let go and not kill yourself over it. I am serious. There are women who are getting stressed out physically because they are trying to do everything. They are married to a bum who thinks that everything she does is incremental. I say, if you happen to be married to someone who refuses to have a conversation about this, refuses to budge about it, doesn't see this partnership as truly a partnership, you've got better things to worry about than whether you are getting paid more than 70% of what men are getting paid. I don't think there's an easy fix for this. You cannot blame a corporate environment for this. I do not believe the bar needs to be set lower for women than men, just because women have all this other stuff they have to do. I think the day we say the bar has to be set lower, that is the day we lose the battle.

If this is the case, you don't need corporate counselling, you need marriage counselling. I'm serious. If there is a woman who feels that being in business is very important to her, then it is important to the couple that she is successful in business. They need to sit down and have a conversation about who is doing stuff in the home. It is a huge subject, and it transcends business. You are going into social mores and cultural norms. It is not easy. Men and women are wired very different, which is why a lot of things bother us that don't bother men." - **Anna Catalano**

When I interviewed Anna, I really struggled with what I saw as an idealised view of the world. However, as my research went on and I had more and more conversations and saw the impact of domestic inequality, it became very clear that Anna is absolutely right. However, negotiating an equal sharing of responsibilities can be extremely difficult once the power balance has become habituated and entrenched in a relationship.

"Running a home, particularly when you have children, needs its own strategy. My own view has been to swallow the fact I am going to have to pay for things which, given more time, I would do myself. Rather than waste time arguing about it with whomever you are supposed to share those responsibilities with. That has enabled me to enjoy the time I am not at work more. It means having the right domestic help, getting childcare which suits the demands of your role, planning holidays so you can pace yourself in between. More than anything I have also learned that it is easy to fall into the trap of it all being about work and about home life/family – you also have to plan looking after yourself, which is a separate thing! – **Maggie Stilwell**

What this means to me is that we need to educate girls and women to establish an equitable balance of responsibilities at the earliest possible stage of a relationship. What can start as a romantic gesture can become a ball and chain as women become tied to the continuous tasks (the must-dos like planning what food is needed, shopping, cooking, cleaning, washing, preparing the kids in the morning, taking them to and from school, supervising homework) and men pick up the ad hoc ones (the 'at-some-points', like decorating, mowing the lawn, and cleaning the car). Equally, we need to educate boys to expect, and want to, share these responsibilities.

"Cutting the grass – he mows the lawn and I do the weeding. The weeding is ongoing and the lawn needs doing once a week. That feels like a metaphor for what happens at our home." – **Morag Blazey**

Home life makes demands on your resources: time; energy; mental capacity (head space); money, and physical presence – where you need to be and when. To have a fulfilling work-life these demands need to be strategically managed to enable you to know what you can do, what you can go for and what you can commit to without holding back. Anything less and it's very easy to slip back into gender-stereotyped roles and all the limitations that go with them for women.

Whatever your choice, hold onto the positives and ditch any guilt.

The following extracts from my interviews are here to show you a range of the benefits that the children of full-time, full-on career mothers experience – I share them to help balance the noise and nonsense to the contrary that gets a disproportionate share of airtime.

*"I had fantastic nannies. I had two wonderful girls who got us through the first six years, which made an enormous difference. **Childcare is the most important executive decision you make.** I was lucky that the original nanny happened to come back and she was an enormous support. I also had wonderful secretaries.*

The kids, if you interviewed them, would say that they are so glad that I always worked. They felt that they benefitted enormously because they felt engaged. I always talked to them about work, I used to take them to the office on occasions, they used to love going into agencies and meeting colleagues. I

*remember taking a year out a couple of years later;
technically I retired. It turned out to be a year out,
but that is another story. The kids were horrified
because they saw it as a waste. They have this thing
that you would be crazy not to work mum, you
would go mad, it would drive you crazy, it is such
a waste if you don't. I think they thought that their
lives were much more interesting because I worked.
They never made me feel bad. They have never once
made me feel guilty about being a working mother.*

Me: How did you manage business trips?

*You have to have infrastructure. I had to have a live-
in nanny. There was no other option. I have never
done a job where I could say I'll be home at 6. You
have got to get the right people and you have got to
love them and make them part of your family. Our
nanny is still part of our family and much loved." –*
Mandy Pooler

*"I felt bad for not being there. But they always say,
'It would have been ghastly' and that they wouldn't
want me helicoptering over their lives thank you very
much. They are great supporters of my commercial
life. They've enjoyed the fruits of it. I think I would
have gone potty if I'd stayed at home. But I assume
I'd have done something else and things would have
been different. But it won't get any easier. I had a
nanny. I was fortunate and economically I was able
to afford that. For me that was the key. She lived in.
People used to say, 'How awful having to share your
house with somebody else.' I'd say, 'No, she doesn't
want to be in when we're in.' It was one of the biggest
revelations for us, that our nanny thought we were
really old. We assumed she'd be wanting to sit and
chat over supper. No fear. She looked after our
children all day and the last thing she wanted to do*

was to sit and talk to old people." - **Clare Maurice**

"I have absolutely no guilt whatsoever. My family have a nice lifestyle, we have a nice house, we go abroad, both of the children are at private school, they can do whatever sport they want, my daughter has a horse, my son has a couple of dogs. They all do what they want; they live a very comfortable life because I do what I do. So, I have no guilt at all.

Me: Do they want to see more of Mummy?

They never really see that much of me. It is the rhythm and pattern of our lives.

I am pure and simple career woman. If you met my children, they are both very happy, well grounded, well adjusted. If I am travelling, they will not even turn a hair.

I see them a lot.

I think it is good for my two to have a father as a role model, and it is good for their friends. Lucas is very confident because his daddy is his best friend. Sarah is developing good techniques for dealing with male behaviour because she has to deal with both of them. She does it in her own way. I have never felt guilty. Maybe I should. It's a bit late now isn't it?"
- **Sharon Kerr**

How did these women do it?

There is a vast media industry that thrives on the basis that people want to read about the lives of the rich and famous and find out how they did it – made their money, got famous, got skinny, stayed that beautiful, met their gorgeous partner – as if to find the illusive trick to accessing those things. So, just in case you feel you need to know how the women I interviewed 'did it' in terms of a highly rewarding and fulfilling career and a home life, I will tell you by way of the following chart and excerpts from the interviews. However, there was no easy or obvious simple solution that is available to us all. Each woman's home life developed the way it happened to develop and each one, with or without a partner, found her own path through. So, if you are looking at what the options are for you, you have to remember to make your own choices based on your values and needs at the various stages in your life, your partner's life and your children's life.

Figure 14. Interviewee's domestic set up. (percentages of total group)

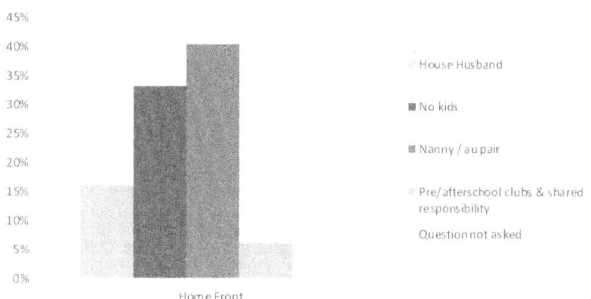

"*I could have accelerated faster, moved international earlier – however, it was a family decision – it's not just about the person who does the job.*

Two people with children are challenged to have the big career – travel, long hours – finally you have to make a decision, a choice. We decided my career was the lead career. We had a nanny for 16 years

and my husband, whilst working, was there on a day-to-day basis. I topped and tailed the day and I never, never missed a single parental event. It was absolutely critical. It's all about prioritisation" –
Fiona Kendrick

"I came back after three months because I was getting to a stage where... I love my children dearly, but I had decided I needed something else other than changing nappies and going to coffee mornings.

I was also coming back as a mother and I had done the most obvious female thing and highlighted that I was a female to those people who had got used to me and almost forgotten that I was female. I have always been very ambitious and in academia you are expected to travel a lot. That is not compatible with small children. I felt dreadfully torn. With Abi I took the decision that I wasn't going to travel for a couple of years. First of all I got very upset when I was away because I missed them all and it was difficult with a baby. I still miss them dreadfully when I'm away, but it is easier now.

I have a wonderful husband. We forgot to have diary meetings sometimes! There was a wonderful occasion when he said, 'Fancy coming to Amsterdam for the weekend?' I looked at my diary and said, 'I'm in Taiwan.' We both said, 'Who's looking after the kids?' He didn't travel as much as I did. He is in academia, but he is not as senior as me. He was good at looking after the kids when I was away. Though he did occasionally get fed up with it.

He did a lot of the school pickups and then I'd cook in the evening. He'd do some work once he got home. I tended to do things like the washing and the ironing, so it evened itself out. School holidays were an absolute nightmare.

What we tried to do was not leave my son to look after his sister, because he would get resentful, and so would she.

We had a great group of friends – mums in my daughter's class – who were wonderful at having her. Every so often I'd have a day off and take the girls out somewhere and do something really nice with them. I think I was very lucky to have a group of friends who'd say, 'Don't feel guilty about it. It is easier for me having two of them here.'

I'd often have to leave the house at 4.30 in the morning.

The government goes on about the childcare they are providing but it's not practical.

What we actually needed at home was a 'wife'. The men who do have wives at home don't want to consider that. The feeling is that when you get home you have everything else that's got to be done.

When I was offered the job in Manchester, he gave up his job so we could move together. It was a huge sacrifice on his part, but he also thought it was the best move for us as a family." - **Prof. Karen Kirkby**

"Then he took what started as a career break and began loving being at home. So now he really carries the majority of home life. But that is a fairly recent occurrence.

Me: What about looking after the kids. How did that work before?

We had a nanny. Then she moved back to Australia and that coincided with his decision to do it for a bit, then to do it long term. It's nice. I like it. I like it, but there are down sides. It's easy to take it for granted. It's definitely given me a view on the typical male role in the family. I've had not much more time off work to have my second baby than a man would have off (maybe 10 weeks). I've slotted back in, in the same way that men do. I probably talk about my children as infrequently as men do on The Floor. Not consciously. It's just the same in that way. And I've got someone back at home who runs our real life. That doesn't seem weird. For Tony it must be a bit odd to be the only bloke on the school steps every day. Not that he minds. But that doesn't seem strange to me either, because it's the norm here. In that one way I feel sexless. I feel I'm the same as them. Maybe it's a hideous sacrifice, but it hasn't felt like that.

I don't know. Maybe I've said that to myself. But you still need to do it really. But something had to go and maybe I felt secure enough to allow that to erode a little in order to focus on things I care a little more about, like my home front." - **Fiona Hagdrup**

"I have a daughter who is nine in the summer and a son who was seven at Christmas. They have a nanny. She is a part-time nanny who has them at the beginning and the end of the day.

Me: You managed to find somebody suitable.

I did, she is lovely. We have really fallen on our feet. She was originally from Slovakia; a highly educated lovely lady, who wants to continue her own personal education. She works for us mornings and evenings and goes to college during the day. She did her first training in teacher training, but her qualifications don't translate over here. She is able to help my children with their homework. She finds English punctuation quite tough, but she has bought herself a book so she can work it out. She is amazing. Ken now works for himself; he has his own business, so a lot of the time he is relatively flexible. We do have the

*odd month or two where he works away. He has been
working in Ireland for the last month and a half and
that has been horrendous."* – **Sarah Lewis**

Mummy isn't best. Consistency of care is.

In the 1950's a psychologist called Bowlby was asked by the government to look at the importance of infant bonding – the impact on a child's development of the presence or absence of a strong secure parental bond. His research only featured the mother as the parent, and it gave rise to the understanding that infants have to have their mothers at home as primary carer till they are at least two or three (ideally older) in order for them to grow up as balanced adults who can operate successfully and be of value in wider society. In the absence of this bonding, the child would become a 'delinquent' (as they used to call teenagers that pushed the boundaries or broke through them), and this would clearly be the fault of the mother. This was a classic example of poor research, exhibiting clear *'confirmation bias'*, i.e., succeeding in confirming what the researcher set out to confirm. What was not tested was other types of carer (as alternative experimental conditions) to test whether the biological-maternal combination was critical to successful development or whether it was other factors that were the key influencer on the outcome. Subsequent research studies have proved that it's the latter. What infants need is consistency of care. The profile of the carer – gender, relationship to the infant, age etc – is of no consequence. Infants simply need to know that their source of care will be there when they need it – when they reach out, arms will be there; when they fall over, they will be picked up and 'there-there'd'; when they cry, they will be understood and responded to with attention, food, love or a clean nappy. So, of course, this could be any caring adult – male or female, related or unrelated. They just have to care and be there, consistently.

Current thinking about the truth behind Bowlby's remit was that his research was instigated as a propaganda tool to get women to go back home and stay at home, to re-instate the pre-war status quo and to resume 'the norm' in terms of gender roles. Men 'needed' their jobs back, but the government were faced with the issue of discontented women who wanted to retain the privileges, enjoyment, self-esteem and growth they'd experienced when they had been workers during the war. 'Proving' that mothers were uniquely made for the critical role of infant bonding was a neat strategy which has created a perception that lasts to this day. However, be reassured if you are a new parent that Dad, Grandad, Nanny, Au Pair, Child Minder, Nursery or Mum are all excellent options so long as they are caring and consistent.

Figure 15: Home front self-assessment (with or planning children)

As with the previous assessments, identify where you are now, and where you ideally want to be in order to identify any gap between the current situation and how you'd really like things to be.

Q. To what degree do you share the responsibility for ongoing* domestic responsibilities?

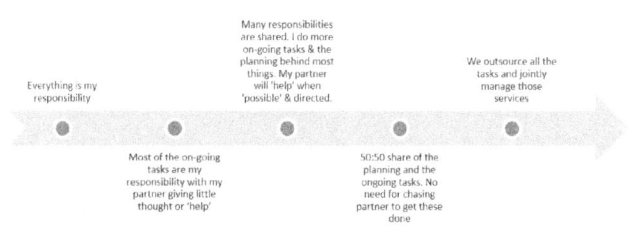

| Everything is my responsibility | | Many responsibilities are shared. I do more on-going tasks & the planning behind most things. My partner will 'help' when 'possible' & directed. | | We outsource all the tasks and jointly manage those services |

Most of the on-going tasks are my responsibility with my partner giving little thought or 'help'.

50:50 share of the planning and the ongoing tasks. No need for chasing partner to get these done.

* 'On-going' includes such things the planning and delivering of tasks such as the food shopping, preparing meals, washing up, cleaning, washing clothes, taking kids to and from school / nursery, supervising homework, talking and listening to child(ren) etc. Tasks that have to be done come what may, or the consequences are significant. This does not include ad hoc things like getting the car serviced, decorating, replacing bulbs etc, which can be fitted in around the core schedule and can be moved, postponed or out-sourced if necessary.

To have your best career, you need to have equality in freedom, flexibility & focus.

These three dimensions make a huge difference to what you are able to achieve within your working day, month and life. These are the things that you need to consciously think about and work through with your partner and your childcare providers (if you have them).

There's a price to pay in many organisational cultures without having strategies to enable degrees of freedom, flexibility and focus on your work-life:

- You could miss out on knowing the important stuff that can make all the difference, stuff that often emerges informally after work or outside work at ad hoc or planned gatherings (see Chapter 22: *Build your social capital*).
- You could miss out on attending pre-planned or impromptu networking opportunities which have a high value for career progression (see Chapter 23: *Network with integrity*).
- You could miss out on informal trust building opportunities with a wide range of people in your organisation, which can open up new connections, raise your profile and provide new work opportunities and exposure.
- In many organisations a lack of flexibility to work later or start earlier to support a team, project or customer priority can result in questions about whether you are really committed. It can also result in being systematically excluded from work that 'requires' this level of presence.

These cultural conditions may well be unfair and odious, but they will exist in many workplaces and types of function. However, you do have choices. You can develop a set up at home that enables you to meet management and peer expectations. Or you can decide that the price you pay for not having the level of presence expected is OK, or you can choose a different working environment – an employer or type of work that provides a better fit.

I'm optimistic that there will be fewer and fewer organisations where you are forced to fit in with this type of regime, and more alternatives to choose from as the new norms defined by the principles of inclusion are brought to bear. But for now, they remain in the majority. In the meantime, both you and your partner should have clarity on the answers to the questions in this section, based on what you jointly agree.

Freedom: this is about having clarity on your degrees of freedom, so you know when and what you are free to choose to do. Then you'll be able to make choices about the work that works for you (given what you both need and want) and within what parameters. Here are some questions to help you start your discussions:

How far away from home can you work? Are you free to travel abroad or do you need to work within half an hour of home?

How long can your days be? What time can they start and finish?

Can you work or attend conferences or training at weekends?

Can you be incommunicado (from home), and if so, for how long, when and under what circumstances?

Flexibility: this is about having clarity on what immediate or short-term changes you can make to your working-home schedule. For example:

Can you stay late or start early if you need to? How much notice do you have to give each other and / or your childcare provider?

Can you go out for impromptu drinks or dinner after work?

Can you attend networking sessions?

*Focus (**or headspace**)*: this refers to your ability to have your mind on your job. If your mind is full of domestic logistics and challenges these will impinge on the amount of focus you can give at work. There can be a significant impact on your quality of contribution if, for example, you are in a late afternoon meeting and sitting there, sweating and thinking, 'is it going to finish on time? How am I going to make it to school / nursery / the child minder...'? Then there are the other brain fillers like:

- Childcare, clubs, food, cleaning, other family members to visit / look after, bills to pay, organising jobs to be done at home, managing tradespeople.
- Filling tummies – 'What are we going to eat for supper? What have we got? What can I get? What about breakfast? What about packed lunches for school tomorrow?'
- 'Alice didn't look very well this morning – what am I going to do if she gets worse when she's at school? When might that happen? What will I be doing? How can I help her if she needs to go home? How do I manage all this work and the deadlines if I have to be at home with her?'

As part of your planning with your partner and / or carers, you have to answer the 'what if' questions – 'what if Alice is ill?'; 'What if school closes because of snow?'; 'What if my train is late?' Always have *joint* contingency plans for when things go wrong.

> *"We never had a family network where we lived. I always tell women that they have to have a plan B. They can't rely on plan A working every day. We were so fortunate to have a nanny come to our house every day. In fourteen years she missed three days of work. That was the backstop. Money was never important to me. I wanted to be safe and secure and to know that everything was cared for. Having them at home for the first couple of years, even if they split their time between home and preschool until age 5, was good. I always worked close to home so I could go to the schools and see their plays. If there was an emergency*

I could be there in five or ten minutes. It would have been the same if I had been at the supermarket. So it is about creating that framework where you know you can handle emergency situations. I was out of town when my husband was at a plant doing a construction job. The plant blew up and killed twenty seven people. He had three hundred men on the site. When he was able, he called home. The nanny said she could stay. When I was in the refinery and there was an emergency I would call up and ask her to come in earlier at six instead of seven. She would say that was OK. You have to have something, whatever it is, because it doesn't always work right. I could not be stressed about that because I have enough stress. Try to take some of the stresses out. I would say 'I'm not going to be the perfect mother. I'm not going to be the perfect employee. I am going to do the best job I can in the whole space and somebody will tell me if I'm not doing it well enough.' This perfection thing is suicidal." **- Peggy Montana**

Negotiate a fair balance.

The previous section described the fact that you need to be able to have the freedom, flexibility and the headspace to focus on work. To make these things possible requires planning, discussion and negotiation.

The start point of any negotiation is to know what you want from maximum (the best possible outcome) to minimum (the least you can live with) and to know what you are prepared to compromise on within that middle ground: the cost of that compromise and what you want to get in return. So, start by identifying what you really want and need in terms of those three Fs (freedom, flexibility and focus) and work from that point to gain an equitable distribution of responsibilities outside of work.

Negotiation between partners can be difficult and you often struggle to remain objective. Any negotiation needs to be thought through, and must seek to avoid ill-founded gender-based clichés, myths and mantras that we explored earlier in the book. Arrangements that have been agreed should be reviewed with a sensible frequency to prevent a drift of tasks in one direction and to provide the opportunity to flex and change things as different demands occur.

Right first time – set it up the way it needs to stay. Gain agreement before making or even thinking 'babies'.

When two people make a baby, those same two people are equally responsible for that baby. Obvious? Those two people should therefore explore their values and ambitions for their children, and for their individual careers, to be really clear on how it's going to work from the outset. The fact that only one of you has breasts and a womb (or only one set of these in use at one time where the parents are both women) is only of momentary significance in the overall scheme of raising a family. Breastfeeding isn't significant in the strategic decisions on carving up how you will flex responsibilities as you bring up your children. In the UK, just 17% of mothers are breastfeeding exclusively by the time the baby is three months old, which means that 83% of mothers are using a mix of methods or not breastfeeding.

Research by Sylvia Ann Hewlett for her book, *Off-Ramps and On-Ramps: Keeping Talented Women on the Road to Success* (Hewlett, 2007) showed that women taking a total of more than two years off lose 18% of their earning power across the remainder of their career. For women taking three years out, this figure soared to 38%. A huge loss to the individual and her family, with many implications. On the other hand, two maternity leaves of six months had little or no effect on a woman's future earnings.

> *"I didn't enter married life until I was 30 and I didn't have children until I was 40, because I didn't want all of that stuff. I knew in my mind that it was going to be a bind, because I'd done three months of au pairing when I was 18. It was such a shock. It shocked me into not wanting to have children for a long time.*
>
> *I said to my husband when we started discussing the possibility of having children that I didn't want to have children until I knew I could afford help. Because even if I hadn't had to work, I didn't want to be stuck at home with nappies at children's tea parties*

with mindless baby talk. I know myself well enough to know that I would be resentful, bad tempered and horrible to live with. So it wasn't an option.

We're much more of a family than a lot of other families are. That is the reason why I wouldn't want to have a commercial job. I like to be able to say, 'No I'm not going to be on the phone doing a conference call with LA at 10 o'clock at night, I'm going to be with my children.' Lower salary, but a lifestyle that suits me as a mother." – **Lavinia Carey**

Gain agreement before making or even thinking babies. This may sound like it's going too far but it's not. Research clearly shows that men in particular, but also a significant proportion of women, assume women will carry the lion's share of childcare responsibilities and domestic tasks and that it is their career that will have to be compromised.

"I would say have children later, but then you increase your risk of being able to have any at all.

If you want to get on, you either have none at all – and the most successful often don't–– and the ones that are fairly successful (and I would put myself in that category) have them late, once they are established, can set their own agenda and manage their own time." – **Karen Guerra**

Continuing to pursue your career is better for a wide range of reasons in the context of parenting:

- Management and leadership positions have more flexibility than more junior positions. The lower down you are, the more your time-keeping and commitments to the standard working day are expected (and measured) and are non-negotiable. Research by Laura Vanderkam, published in her book, *I Know How She Does It* (Vanderkam, 2015), shows that senior women with children have both more flexibility and more money to make childcare easier to manage and to afford. International assignments are very powerful assets on your CV and many parts of the world have far better childcare provision than the UK or the USA.

- You may well be the one who has the greatest potential to be the lead earner and your family would therefore gain the greatest benefit from you pursuing your career potential rather than your partner.

- Your partner may well want to have the opportunity to spend his time with your babies, infants and children. Men are under the same veil of cultural expectations of gender roles, and it will also be hard for them to put themselves forward for this counter-cultural opportunity. So, explore it together and support his inclusion.

- You or your partner may not be able to have children, so why make decisions on the basis of something that may never happen, as sad for some as this may be.

Watch your language. Don't let it reinforce stereotypical gender roles.

"I have a very *understanding* husband" (the words of interviewee Beverley Bell). This is a very common example of how our everyday language can confirm and entrench the model of parenting we have to move away from as a culture – allowing for individual choices within it – if women are also to have truly fulfilling careers.

The way many women describe men's roles makes them sound like an unexpected helper who has no fundamental responsibility for child rearing tasks. Any 'support' being responded to as if it was a sign of their generosity – 'he's very helpful'; 'he's very good'; 'he'll often get involved if I'm stuck'. This language reinforces the status quo and actually excludes men from learning and embracing their fair share as the norm. This is the way most mothers talk – listen at a school gate if you are in any doubt. So, be careful not to use language that makes you the one with full responsibility and gives your partner optional involvement, which will earn him Brownie points for pitching in (while you get none). Choose inclusive language very deliberately that ensures responsibility is shared – from planning to delivery of all the everyday tasks, and ideally from day one.

Another thing to watch out for which will result in an own goal is criticism of the quality of the parenting done by your partner. Just like new mothers, new fathers are nervous and unsure and have to learn and develop as parents. If you undermine his confidence in specific tasks, it will put him off and encourages him to believe that his role must be elsewhere if he can't 'naturally' do the stuff that you seem to do better.

It's a reversal of the experience women have at work, and it can have the same disengaging impact. As with everything, practice makes perfect and making mistakes is just part of learning. So, give your partner space and support to learn and to gain pride in his parenting skills. And try to be open and flexible about any differences in the quality of what he does. Perfection isn't important. Consistency and reliable commitment are.

Parenting demands differ hugely at different stages.

The reality of the needs of children at different ages is not necessarily as you'd expect before you become a parent or at the early stages. In fact, it is probably not until you've been through the full cycle that you can judge how 'hands on' or present you need to be to do your best by your child / children. As the mother of an 8-year-old at the time, it stopped me in my tracks when Karen Guerra said, "Small children graze their knees, big ones break their hearts." I'd assumed that the time to be there was when they were tiny, but teenagers need you in more important ways.

> *"Fiona Miller, Alistair Campbell's partner, wrote in the Telegraph Magazine this weekend, that the teenage years are when you need to be at home. Falling over and scraping your knee and 'Sophie pinched me' is one thing, but 'What am I going to do with my life mum? 'Why won't you let me stay out until 2am?' and 'What A levels should I*

do?' It's finding time for that that's important'". -
Clare Maurice

"I think that small problems with children are big problems to women. Women worry enormously when they first have a baby, as the responsibility feels overwhelming and inevitably the guilt sets in when you return to work. However, help can be hired to manage the under-fives as their needs are fairly simple, unless you have a child with specific problems. Hire the right nanny, don't skimp on what it costs and most of their needs are covered. It may cost you your entire salary in those pre-school years, but don't give up.

However, if you have a troubled teenager, you can't hire the help to fix it. Which is why I was very keen, if I was going to come out of corporate life, that I did so when Oscar was at puberty, rather than at primary school. I've had problem teenagers and you cannot hire to solve the problem. This help doesn't exist. It's consistent parenting, being aligned on the issues and the potential solutions that can help teenagers through the complexity of adolescence.

Me: So, the implication is you have got to put them first.

Sorry to be depressing. An eight year old is the easy bit. The harder part is if they are going off the rails. Then you need to be there. A nanny will not have the tools to deal with those issues. And you can't expect them to. I think if I was advising anyone as to when to take a career break, my advice would be not when your child is a baby, but when it's 13 or 14. Everyone worries about having a baby, but if they are physically well you can get the help." - **Karen Guerra**

Table 3: Parenting considerations by main stage (based on the UK education system)

Nursery stage	It's open every working day and for long hours and there is an army of people qualified to look after and love junior You'd be very hard pushed as one parent to give the care, the stimulus etc that nursery staff can give all day and every day – so relax, they are in the best place
Primary school	Difficult hours (8.45 to 3.30 roughly) but often with breakfast and afterschool clubs A minimum of 10 weeks' school holidays per annum (more if at private school) when children will need full, proper supervision
Senior / secondary school	Difficult school hours with more limited pre- and post-school supervision Less of a parental community to share with Long holidays Homework that really matters Extracurricular activities perhaps in more diverse locations Internet & social media supervision required Mental health vulnerabilities

Making it happen:

If this section has been relevant to your circumstances, what do you plan to do as a result?

What has motivated you to make you want to do those things?

Independent women also need to think clearly about what they want from life outside work to ensure they get it.

> *"One in five professional women don't want children."* –
> **Prof. Dot Griffiths**

Independent women can get a raw deal at work too. Sometimes employers put more demands (stretching into leisure time) onto single women than employees who have families, assuming they have no other priorities or demands on their life outside work. It may therefore be important to consciously and strategically build in that balance as it's easy to just get lost in work and lose sight of your health, friends and family.

> *"I don't have children. It doesn't make my personal life any less important to me than it is to women with children. Some people might think, 'It doesn't matter if Morag goes home late because she's only going home to her partner, her garden and her TV'. It is just as important to me that I have my personal life."* – **Morag Blazey**

> *"I have often joked that I could really do with a wife. I've got a great cleaner and gardeners. A lot of my friends are my age and are in exactly the same sort of situation that I am. They are high in their careers and have made the choice not to have children."* – **Lin Phillips**

Figure 16: Home front self-assessment (living independently)

As with the previous assessments, identify where you are now and where you want to be, to be clear on any gap between the current situation and your desired situation that needs to be closed.

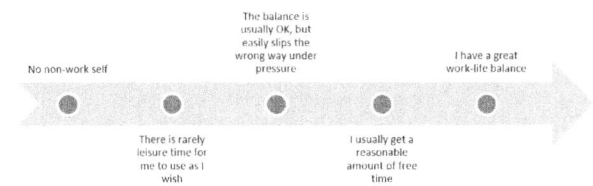

Q. To what extent do you feel that you have time for your non-work self once work and domestic responsibilities have been covered?

If you have found that your assessment indicates that the balance isn't right for you, then it's time to work on putting some boundaries in place. These start with the simplest and most direct option, saying 'No' and if necessary 'I'm afraid I'm not free to work that evening / weekend'. It's very easy to feel you have to provide reasons why and to ensure that they're compelling. But the fact is all you have to do is say that you're not available. Full stop. You don't need to explain what you do with your non-work time! In Chapter 16, there are more techniques for defending your boundaries.

Chapter 16

Select appropriate benchmarks and defend your boundaries

"We've been told we can have it all. What I have learned is that we probably can, but not all at once."
- Marion Cowden

In this chapter we're going to look at the implications of trying to be good, great or perfect at too many things, and at the benefits of focusing on the few that are most important to you at this life and career stage.

Overleaf is a completely made-up graph, based on discussions with delegates at the workshops I've delivered, where I've asked the question – "what's the range of things you want to do really well at this stage in your life? And how well is 'really well'?" Then I've asked, "how would the men you know well answer the same questions?" It's highly unscientific, but it illustrates a picture that many men and women recognise. Women tend to have a larger set of things that they feel they want and need to do, and to achieve a high standard in, while men focus on fewer things that they want to do well, typically career, partner, and following or actively participating in sport.

Figure 17: Women and men's priorities and benchmark standards of success

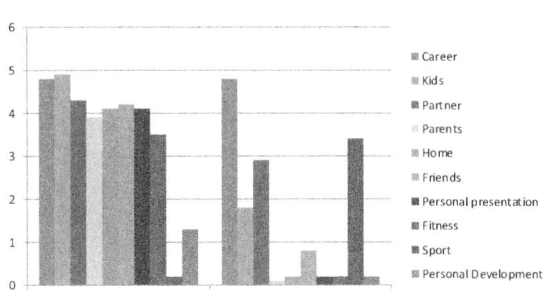

"The way I see it is that it is very difficult to have a conversation about women in business without looking at their lives and the choices they make in their life. Women view the world inherently differently from men, I believe. This is a massive generalisation. But women look at life as a full circle with many facets, with work and business as one (and an important one). Men tend to be pretty well single-focused and consider work to be a major component of their life. As a result they measure their success in life against their success in business. They fill their time with work related activity. I think women always have a different view. They have a much more balanced view of the world and life. Home and social and things like that are a part of our consideration of what makes our world tick and what is important, what we value in life. We try and compete with men in the business world but we have this whole other view of the world, and our values are perhaps different.

Women are very inclusive. We value relationships and we respect others and try to assist them. It is that whole nurturing thing. Men, if they have any

time, will go and play golf or climb a mountain. They will do something for themselves. They won't ring their mother. It is nature versus nurture, the wiring of the brain, what we have been taught." –
Charmaine Stewart

The critical point is that there are only the same number of hours in a man-day as there are in a woman-day – there are only the standard, unisex, 24 hours in a day! And the implication, if you are a woman trying to do all of these things to a high standard, is that you will either be constantly beating yourself up for your underachievement or you'll burn out, and something that may actually be really important may get sacrificed in the meltdown.

"I don't think it was an accident that my marriage broke up. I think my ex-husband, who I have a very good relationship with, very accurately said to me once, 'I was the book that fell off the end of the shelf.' Between the twins and my career, he was the one who lost out." – **Mandy Pooler**

So, when I talk about benchmarks, I mean a couple of things. In this first instance I'm referring to the ***standards*** that you set yourself for the range of things that you regard as important in your life. Clearly, the effect of having high benchmark standards across a lot of things is simply that they take more time than if you have fewer high benchmarks or a more manageable aspiration across the range.

"I left because I'd done 14 years with the agency, I was going to die one day and look back and think 'I did well in agencies. Is that it?' I always dread getting to 50 and thinking 'what did I do?' so I made sure that I learnt something new every year. I scuba dive, I practise yoga, I snowboard and ski, I did my Competent Crew Certificate, so I sail. I try to do stuff so that every year I've achieved something new." – **Morag Blazey**

At this point I recommend that you take a few minutes to reflect on, and capture, the range of things that you currently see as important to be successful in across all aspects of your life, i.e., define your *Success Portfolio*, and then clarify what standard you have set for success in each area. Use the empty bar chart in Figure 18 to capture this. Each bar will represent one area that you have decided is really important for you. So, label the x axis where each bar will be with a name for each priority area. (And while I have given space for a number of bars, you don't need to fill the space, just because it's there!)

Above each label decide on the height of the bar, as this represents your benchmark standard for this area. So, 0 to 10 on the y axis is the scale of your standard of success, where ten would represent 'I want to be perfect'; eight is 'I want to be good at this'; five is 'OK is good enough.'

Figure 18: Your Success Portfolio Profile

When you have completed your Success Portfolio Profile, take some time to consider it carefully. Are you setting yourself up to fail or to succeed? Are you taking on too much, or have you got a sensible but rewarding balance for this life stage, based on your values? Are you setting your standards too high across too many things or have you got clarity on what it matters most to be good at, and what's OK to be OK at? To what extent do *you* need to carry the load for achieving these outcomes?

If you are constantly tired, tending to be irritated by things and lose focus on what you are doing because your mind has moved onto other things, this suggests that you are trying to take on and do too much, so, in very simple terms, you will need to:

- Reduce your number of columns (challenge your priorities).
- And / or reduce your standard for success on some areas to a more manageable level.
- And / or use other resources that are available to you (or should be) to enable your aspirations to be achieved.

It's worth repeating the words of Peggy Montana – a woman who had become the second most senior woman in Shell worldwide by the time I interviewed her:

> *"Try and take some of the stresses out. I'm not going to be a perfect mother or a perfect employee. This perfection thing is suicidal."* **- Peggy Montana**

Making it happen:

In light of those thoughts, what changes do you want to make to that profile?

Do that now! Create the profile that will work for you and deliver what success really means to you. Your thoughts from reading Chapters 7 (Define what you really want and why) and 8 (What do you value?) can help guide you.

Use benchmarks based on role models carefully, and in the context of your reality.

The second type of benchmark standard is based on role models you see as your benchmark of success. There is more emphasis now than ever on role models. We are overwhelmed with 'celebrities' and their lifestyles being presented as aspirational. And there are personal and professional development approaches that emphasise 'modelling' the behaviour of a person or people you consider to be successful.

The problem with both of these is that we tend to only look at the one facet of that person. We tend not to consider the whole person including their context, their resources, their values and the way they act or live to achieve that success. What enables a person to be successful is a whole set of things that lie out of sight. For a celebrity it might be being able to spend five hours a day at the gym, employing a chef and nutritionist and spending vast amounts on tailored clothing, and plastic surgery. For a highly successful businessperson it may be a single-mindedness enabled by a certain mind-set and set of values and team of people doing everything else – from great personal aßssistants, to a domestic set up they don't have to consider and maybe rarely engage with. It may mean a whole set of other elements of their role gets neglected – people poorly managed and led; problems overlooked or tossed to others as the proverbial 'hospital pass'.

The people you admire may have outcomes to their work that you wish to emulate, but you need to consider the rest of their picture first of all. In doing so, you may find that modelling yourself on them is either not possible because of your own context and commitments, or you may find that you actually cannot respect, condone or support the way that they go about achieving their outcomes.

Benchmarking yourself against a role model is fine as a way of helping define your ambitions on the basis that you are able to see what can be possible. And, without doubt, women who 'make it' are incredibly important to show other women that it's worth keeping at it, as it is possible. But be wary of trying to turn yourself into that person to get there. You have to be true to what you believe is important in the way that you work, and the way you interact with other people and within other parts of your life. There is no harm in trying to identify the approaches and techniques used by people that you admire, but be guided in what you adopt by the context of what is right for you.

Making it happen:

What's your position on using aspirational role models? Do you have specific people in your workplace or beyond that you use as a benchmark for certain aspects of approach, behaviour or achievement?

Who are these people? What aspects are you selecting to measure yourself against or aspire to? Looking at this picture of your choices and selections, does this provide a good stretch aspiration? Do these help: in what way? Or hinder: in what way?

Is there a bigger picture to factor into your review of your choices? If you choose to have role models, is there an opportunity to look around for a healthier fit with your values, your context, and your goals, overall?

You need boundaries to focus on what matters to you.

Once you have clarified the range of things that are important at this work-life stage, and what your benchmark standard levels are for these things, you then need to defend those priorities, by putting boundaries in place. This means having a clear idea of what things and at what points you will say *'yes'*, or *'no'* or *'yes, but not until three weeks on Thursday'*.

> *"You should make your boundaries clear from the outset just like anybody else would. Set your rules out. Do it consciously. These are my boundaries. Make conscious choices."* – **Simon Hughes**

My hypothesis is that many women believe that they need to say 'yes' to stuff at work or they risk being exposed as conforming to a stereotype of being unable to handle the pressure. So they accept too much, and struggle to deliver, because it spills over and creates problems across the board.

I've also observed a tendency to take loyalty or a personal sense of responsibility too far. I've seen numerous situations where women take on tasks that they believe just have to be done by someone or there will be some level of consequence, although these are often so small as to be imperceptible to anyone else. So, they pick them up and are so busy doing all these things that they can't apply the necessary focus and time to more visible and valuable work. Someone else gets on and does that.

There are also situations where women stay in a job far too long in the belief that there would be a problem for the organisation (and / or individuals) because stuff they know matters, wouldn't get done, or not done as well as they believe it needs to be. So, women pick up tasks that their sense of integrity makes them feel they should pick up, and sometimes even continue in jobs they should have moved on from due to an exaggerated sense of loyalty – loyalty that is rarely ever matched by the organisation they work for.

Saying *'no,'* or *'yes, but not now'*, means that you can focus on successfully delivering your priorities. Multitasking is not great if nothing actually gets the attention and time it really needs. Tasks that no one will notice, nor benefit or suffer from if neglected, are usually not worth doing. Or they should be flagged up to the next level of management for their ownership.

Saying '*no*' can be a strength as it's a way of communicating your focus and your commitment to an agreed or defined set of priorities. And delegation can be a very good thing for those around and 'below' you as it gives them opportunities to learn, grow and shine.

> *"Trying to juggle children and running the company meant I had to restructure the way I did things – I knew I couldn't do everything 100% personally.*
>
> *I had to rely on them [my team] but I knew they were more than capable of it. I learnt the art of delegation, which I was not accustomed to, but how liberating it was! In turn they stepped up to the plate, realising their full potential and responsibilities. After all my skilled team were the ones delivering, I was there to support and encourage. So, it's not only me that benefitted – they have grown themselves.*
>
> *Having created this bond, they always went the extra mile.*
>
> *Empowering my team became my passion!"* -
> **Suzie Allwork**
>
> *"I admit that I used to go home, have dinner with my family, bath the kids and read to them, and then I would go back to work by turning on my computer or whatever. I admit I didn't draw that line there. I find that so limiting. I find there is a view that says, 'My value and worth is only about how many hours I spend in the office and somebody has to give me permission to draw my own boundaries.' I just don't get that. I would schedule my daughter's basketball games on my schedule. I would go and see them. If there was an issue at the refinery I wouldn't go, but that was rare. I think the workplace is*

very conducive to setting those boundaries. I find the people are so limiting. I really don't get that. Particularly now where it is so virtual, it should be easier creating the space that works for you, whether it be going to the school event or going home every day at the same time.

It is about deciding what is important to you and setting your own limits and boundaries. I always felt that if that wasn't meeting somebody's expectations I would figure it out or they would tell me. Until such a time it happened, I was headed in that direction."
- Peggy Montana

The 'yes-no-yes' sandwich

I have shared this simple technique to great effect, both inside and outside the working environment, as it's a method for projecting your positive and willing image while deflecting a non-priority task. This will keep your workload manageable and enable you to stay focused on what's really important, to and for you. It will also keep people clear that you are committed, focused and well organised.

This is how it works:

When you are approached and asked to take on something that doesn't fit with your priorities your answer to the request is,

'Yes, I can do that. However, I can't fit it in until the latter part of next week, [i.e., yes, I can do it just now]. How do you want to take it forward?'

Here the *'no'* (*'I can't'*) is sandwiched between the positives, so the person goes away feeling that you were open and willing to help, yet clearly busy with a well-planned workload.

If you continue to be under pressure to say yes, what you can also add is a reference to the senior source of the work you are doing, such as *'the Marketing Director has made this a priority, you can check with her if it's OK to pause on this'*. This has the effect of routing the person making the request to this other individual who they will have to get a *'yes'* from if they want to challenge or change your priorities. This often has the effect of making the request go away, as people often try to get away with delegating tasks by going under the radar, because they know they wouldn't be supported if they went via the more formal route.

The other element you may have noticed is: *'How do YOU want to take it forward?'*, which neatly bounces the task off you, and back at them. This ensures you aren't left owning the task. This is really important as people are often inclined to take on ownership of sorting out a solution which isn't actually theirs to sort out.

Making it happen:

How would you summarise any changes you want to make given your thoughts as you've read through this section?

What difference will these changes make, and what makes them important to you?

PART 5

DRIVING

YOUR AGENDA

So far, we have explored the historical and psychological realities you need to understand to successfully navigate the dynamics which can make having your most fulfilling career easier for men than women. We have also exposed the main myths that sustain beliefs about why men are 'naturally' the ones to rise up the career ladder. We then took the time to examine the dimensions that together define what success really means to you at this stage in your working life.

Then we've looked in detail at the strategic aspects affecting your inner momentum. Those aspects might hold you back or be sources of strength and drive to keep you moving forward, collecting the best career experiences all the way: your levels of confidence and inner belief in your capability; your level of resilience; your understanding of your strengths and potential; your domestic responsibilities and degrees of flexibility and freedom. You've had the opportunity to assess your current position with each of these and make decisions about where you would like to be, and then we've worked through how you can make that progress most efficiently and smoothly.

So, you are now in a position where you know what you want, and how to create and sustain your inner momentum. Hence, this next part, Driving your agenda, covers the strategies that are the most potent in moving forward to what you want with the greatest of ease and the least friction along the way. As in the previous sections, you will have the opportunity to assess your position in order to prioritise and focus your plan, based on what is most significant for you in light of your definition and priorities for success.

Chapter 17

Understand the organisation's culture to smooth the path ahead

'Culture' is a term that is used liberally to mean everything and nothing. When it refers to an organisation, 'culture' simply means the accepted way things are done. It's the organisation's unquestioned habits and beliefs. Culture is what that community is happy with or used to and accepts as a norm in terms of the way it works. Examples include how meetings are run; how financial, people, process, policy and functional decisions really get made; what working hours are really expected; what is normal practice in how people are managed; how teams work; what and who is valued, recognised and rewarded; why those that get on in the organisation do so, and why others do not; if and how lessons are learnt. An organisation's culture commonly differs from its written values, approaches and processes (on websites, official communications externally and internally, policy and process documentation, and job descriptions) for how things should be done. Those official rules are often subordinate to the cultural rules, which are the givens for how the organisation really operates – these are the real rules of the game.

So cultural rules are the givens for how the organisation really operates. Organisations, industries, professions, functions and even teams have their own cultures and subcultures. If you don't know the rules of the game, then you can't influence it to secure the best outcomes for you.

"Understanding culture is absolutely essential. I wouldn't have been able to get either of the projects done at Swiss Re [building The Gherkin and the New York headquarters], without totally understanding the inner workings and the culture of the organisation. Where the decisions are really made, what the buttons were for people; people in the post room or the board room. It is absolutely and totally critical to be really plugged in to all the cultural nuances. For me at Swiss Re it was even more complicated because Zurich is the headquarters and the cultural soul of Swiss Re. I had to understand two cultures, in fact three in the end, because I had to understand the American culture of Swiss Re, which is not the same as the Swiss culture. Then I had to learn the British culture of Swiss Re. Also during that time there was a change of CEOs, which again changed the culture. Without having my finger on all of those pulses it would have been like trying to do the job with a pair of handcuffs on.

Me: How do you go about it?

Meeting people, interviewing. I think the second or third week that I was with Swiss Re I flew to Zurich and spent three days talking to people. Then I went to Munich and all I did was talk to people for a day. When I was back in New York I interviewed everybody. It didn't matter whether they were on the board or head of the post room or the receptionist.

Me: When you say 'interview' what do you mean?

Just going to them and saying, 'We are going to build this building. I need to understand how the building needs to work.' This is really a way of saying, I need to understand how the culture works.

Until you understand the existing culture and

> *subsequently understand the goals for the culture,*
> *there is no way you can make a contribution to*
> *either."* – **Sara Fox**

Accepting and working with the reality of the informal way things are done at work often goes against the grain for women. Many women tend to believe, or want to hold onto the belief, that things can and should be done by the book (i.e., as laid down in the articulated rules, processes, policies and procedures) and therefore sometimes struggle with participating in approaches which are a departure from the 'right' way. Women often feel that the 'game' should be unnecessary and should be ignored and that the best outcomes for the organisation (and the individual) will come about by doing it 'properly'. Unfortunately, this puts them at a disadvantage, as they are only operating part of the machinery.

As relative newcomers to the working world, women haven't been handed down, from mother (or father) to daughter, the insights about the mysterious dark art of 'playing the game' and the benefits of applying these techniques, as well as the formal versions, to make things happen! These apparently dark arts are often referred to as workplace 'politics' which are viewed by many as divisive and underhanded, if not positively Machiavellian. However, there are certain aspects of these politics which you ignore at your cost. These costs include limiting the recognition of and engagement with your work and potential, and limiting the profile and network you have in the organisation and sometimes beyond it too. Many women perceive this 'political manoeuvring' as counter to their integrity, and where this truly is the case, then it is a compromise too far. However, it is too easy to dismiss 'politics' out of hand.

Learning about the range of informal cultural behaviours and beliefs can be a huge advantage, starting with the ability to make informed choices about what to engage in, or not, or to what degree.

> *"The trouble with the word politics is that it's got a*
> *span of meanings from very bad to actually being*
> *the way things have to be done. I think you need*
> *to define politics when you talk about it. There are*
> *quite nasty politics that can occur when people will*

> *spot threats and undermine them, but there are other types of politics where two board members go for a beer and say, 'If we are going to get this through then we have got to persuade that person. How do you think we ought to go about it?' That is kind of OK because that is how things get done."* –
> **Simon Hughes**

The word 'politics' actually comes from Ancient Greece, and specifically Aristotle's series of books called *Politika* written around 350BC. They were about governing and governments, and therefore about influencing outcomes where both power and people are involved. Hence, for some, politics conjures up power-plays and jostling for position, while for others it's simply the informal workings of an organisation which are as legitimate and normal to engage in as the formal workings – just the other side of the same coin.

So, really understanding these informal workings of your organisation and selectively applying appropriate approaches is all about oiling the cogs – the important cogs – in the machinery around you, which makes it work more smoothly for you. The machine will work without extra oil but there will be more crunching of gears, more worrying noises and more uncertainty about potential breakdowns, which may happen when you least expect them, and at the most inconvenient times. Breakdowns which mean you have to pull off the road and watch the traffic pass you by as you wait for the rescue truck, only to get going again when you've paid the price of repairs.

It's to your advantage to understand the realities of the culture you operate in and to work with it, to the degree that you decide is appropriate. It can seem like embarking on a far longer and more convoluted process than following the official protocols. And obviously it should be fine just to do things the way the formalised process says it should be done. How straightforward life would be if that was the case! But human beings are very complex creatures with all sorts of vanities, egos, hopes and dreams that they seek to serve, and this drives behaviours that result in this informal culture which is very tough to work against. So, working with these realities should actually speed progress over the medium term and across a wide range of significant dimensions.

However, if you don't involve yourself in this form of influencing of outcomes then you leave yourself open to the impact of those that do. Which may mean, for example, that when you present your recommendation at the correct formal point in the process, someone else may have already secured the relevant budget for it, or a commitment was given to something else which they have taken round informally, and gained support for. So, as great as your work is, it's just arrived at a decision point too late.

> *"I haven't been very good at politics over the years. I'm quite focused on goals and wanting to move forward quickly, and so it doesn't really feel like good use of time when a straight conversation should move things forward easily. As I've got older I've learned to adapt, my earlier style of wanting instant revolutionary change didn't work so well at board level, where you sometimes have to take people on a journey and accept change by degrees. I've learned to adapt my style to what works best with the person I'm dealing with to get to the best outcome and make sure people listen."* – **Claire Walters**

Understanding your organisation's culture gives you more choices.

Once you have gained a working understanding of both the formal published approaches and the informal, but ingrained, modus operandi of your organisation (or your part of it) you are able to make choices about how far you engage with the latter. There are broadly three choices, although these will overlap and maybe dependent on different situations and contexts in which you operate:

- Play 'the game' whole heartedly or to some degree.
- Don't play 'the game' and work by the written rules and policies.
- Use the knowledge to change some of the rules.

Here are what the women I interviewed had to say about the pros and cons of what emerged as these different options:

Option 1: In favour of playing the game wholeheartedly or to some degree.

"To be honest there are a number of women I know who say they are not interested in the politics, but to a certain extent it is part of the job. My feeling is that you can't say, 'I'm not doing that.' In some ways it is undervaluing yourself. It is not nice, and I wouldn't say I enjoy the politics, but if you don't do it, you will be trampled. It is working out how you influence someone and looking at what the problem is. Why does that person feel threatened by you? If you can work out why they are feeling threatened and effectively take that away, that is politics, because you then get what you want."

– Prof. Karen Kirkby

"It takes about a year to do work out the politics of a place, to stumble up against things and learn, to go down a track, get rebuffed, and then try something else that works. I wouldn't ever take a stance against that, if only because of the futility of that noble position. I want to get things done and I want to feel content and that I've achieved. There is usually a way, but it can certainly take time to find it or to appreciate where the landmines are going to be. A year feels

like a reasonable time before you properly know how an institution works." - **Fiona Hagdrup**

I think you operate within a cultural set of norms in any business and if it is not your natural style you have to flex towards it. I just think there are probably more women who have to flex towards it than there are men." - **Sarah Lewis**

Option 2: In favour of NOT playing the game.

"I think the rules of the game in academia are pretty clearly spelt out. You need to win grants; you need to write papers to get published in the very best journals. Those are unambiguous and you can't succeed without those.

Increasingly the college is moving to a view that they will get people to do quality and not quantity. Only publish in the very best journals but publish less. I think in the corporate world those measures are less clear and much more interpreted.

"I think there are formal and informal rules to the game. The formal rules to the game in many organisations are quite often OK; it is the informal rules that aren't OK. We have very clear promotion processes, but I expect the way they are implemented in the informal rules of the game in some departments are not as we would want.

You have to know what the rules of the game are, and you have to make choices when you are doing it your way about which ones you are going to try to obey and which ones you are going to say no to. I think you should stand back and look at it so you can make those choices. Maybe if you are very ambitious that is hard to do. I am not sure if I am qualified to say this. I have just always done it my way for better or worse." - **Prof. Dot Griffiths**

Option 3: In favour of using the knowledge to change some of the rules.

"When you know the rules of the game you can break them, or subtly change them." - **Barbara Follett**

"I had to learn the culture to change the culture. Challenge behaviour in a very pleasant and amusing way. Don't make people feel embarrassed about their behaviour." - **Beverley Bell**

"It is even better than that, you let people think you are playing to the old rules but you are actually putting new ones around them. It sounds incredibly mercenary. I don't actually think like that, but I do think that is what I am doing. You are never going to achieve change by being the maverick. You have to change from within." - **Charmaine Stewart**

"If you are not happy and you are the boss or part of the senior management group, you change what you don't like, and you are quite bold and explicit about that. You don't try to do it subversively.

When I was at one of the boroughs, the uniform response teams were very insular looking. I thought there was an inappropriate culture. It wasn't a male culture, just inappropriate. It was more about them as individuals rather than a group, and serving the public. I used a whole range of data and information to develop a strategy to turn that on its head and for them to become more external focused, more diverse and to behave in a different way. It took me two or three years to accomplish it. I personally went around to every single group, every individual, and every single training day and delivered my message. I said it was non-negotiable and it was the way we were going to be and if they weren't comfortable with it, they could come and see me to arrange a transfer. These are the values I am setting and anyone who isn't comfortable, we can arrange for you to move. People liked that directness, they liked to know where they stood, particularly those that were not comfortable with the culture. It is only a few that make the culture bad. It is not the majority. There are a dominant few. I targeted a few of them and moved two or three on. I broke up the bad network. I gave them important jobs and roles to make them feel differently. I involved them in the change. They lead the change." – **Sharon Kerr**

If you want to learn more about this approach, I recommend a book by Debra Meyerson called *Tempered Radicals*. These are people she describes as those "who want to succeed in their organisations, yet want to live by their values or identities, even if they are somehow at odds with the dominant culture of their organisation. Tempered radicals want to fit in, and they want to retain what makes them different. They want to rock the boat, and they want to stay in it." (Meyerson, 2001)

Can you read the culture?

Here are some questions to prompt your thinking about your understanding of your organisation's culture and what insights you could or should gain. Make notes about any implications for action as you go through.

What do you understand about how decisions are made?

This is the area that has the greatest single impact on you getting the things you want, or need to do, done, and has the greatest single impact on your progression.

So, how are decisions really made? What characteristics are most valued, regularly influencing the outcome of decisions? Who are the people that get listened to and why? Who influences decisions and who really makes the decisions? Where are decisions made? In meetings, in offices, in the pub? What are the implications?

> *"Understand who makes the decisions and be very aware of what will make a difference"* – **Gill Adams**

> *"I think that is one of the most important things, know who the influencers are, quite often you are trying to convince the wrong person"* – **Lin Phillips**

> *"There was nothing I could do as all the key decisions were made or changed after the meetings, in the urinals!"* – **Anon Interviewee**

What do you understand about what is really valued in your organisation?

What types of work have the most recognition, profile, support and gain the most rewards? Can you articulate why? What are the implications for you?

> *"What is the currency? In some organisations people care about how many windows you have in your office, in others it is about what your salary is or your job title.*

The currency in PHD was your brains. That was very refreshing and unusual. I think there are organisations where those things are so visible and organisations where those things are deeply buried.

I couldn't imagine going into an organisation and not taking the time to understand them. To go into an organisation and expect to climb to a leadership position without understanding the culture and values is a real hallmark for failure in my view. Understand the culture and values first and then change and improve them." – **Morag Blazey**

"In certain firms today, it might be changing slightly... but I think the basic principle is that you don't get recognition for the quality of the work you do, the only measure is quantity, the quality is the quantity. You might get somebody who is really good at bringing clients in, that is quantity, so that would work.

The reason I like the job I'm in at the moment is because there is no concept of being judged on or ticking boxes on the hours you have spent doing something. It is all about getting the job done.

So, there is no need to charge me out. It is all about adding value to different things, giving advice to people, nothing about the amount of time you spend in the office." – **Sarah Brooke**

Running meetings – who gets to go to the various types of meeting and who doesn't? Why? What does your organisation have formal meetings about versus informal conversations between specific groups of individuals? What are meetings used for at your place, in your team or your function? Who gets heard and why?

Projects that make progress – what's the difference between those initiatives that succeed and those that wither? What are the foci of successful projects? Who are the official sponsors and unofficial supporters? What is the make-up of successful project teams? What are the measures of success or the type of intended impact that get the most support?

> *"I know who the terrorists are in the organisation and I work very hard on them right from start. There are those who just can't bear change.*
>
> *Identify where your biggest barriers are going to be, and go and engage as often as needs be, and one-to-one. Don't wait for it to be a problem." –*
> **Dana Skelley**

Response to failure – is failure seen as progress towards success, or a lack of ability? Does it depend on the person / the team / the subject matter / the client or beneficiaries / the timing?

Managing people – is there a certain style of people management that is favoured in your organisation? What does it look like? What are the implications for people on the receiving end of this behaviour or the results of this preferred style?

Communicating – is your organisation a real or virtual communicator? Do discussions have to be face-to-face to make real progress or are other forms of communications more / as effective? Which topics and which people get listened to and why? What and who struggles for airtime? What else is significant about communication in your organisation?

Leading – what sort of leadership is dominant and respected? Command and control? Inclusive, collaborative? Is it devolved or very hierarchical? Where does the real power sit? Are leaders strategic and consistent, or does direction change with the wind?

Celebrating success – what types of success are recognised, profiled and rewarded?

Working hours and presenteeism – what is really expected? What is frowned on, by whom and why? Does it matter?

Figure 19: Understanding culture self-assessment

Before moving on to read the rest of this chapter, assess your level of understanding of the culture in your organisation – or your part of it – by identifying where you are on the scale below. Is it where you want to be? If not, which level would be ideal? Use this insight to focus your thoughts on what you might want to do differently as you read on.

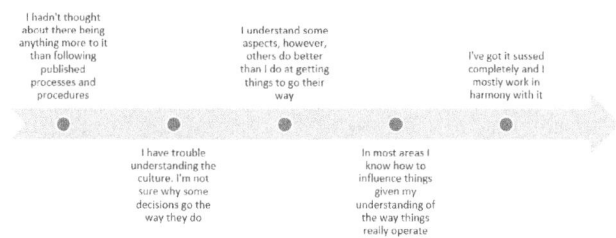

Q. To what degree can you articulate the realities of how your organisation, or your part of the organisation, operates?

I hadn't thought about there being anything more to it than following published processes and procedures

I understand some aspects, however, others do better than I do at getting things to go their way

I've got it sussed completely and I mostly work in harmony with it

I have trouble understanding the culture. I'm not sure why some decisions go the way they do

In most areas I know how to influence things given my understanding of the way things really operate

How do you get to understand how things really work?

It can seem like Sherlock Holmes level detective skills are required to spot the behaviours and activities that make up the informal but all-powerful culture of your organisation. If you are focused on your need-to-know priorities, this will direct your investigative efforts and give you a better chance of making sense of what's around you. Decision-making is one of the most pivotal components that can impact your day-to-day and long-term success, so it makes sense to start by focusing on this priority area.

There are overt and covert approaches to finding out the information you need. Covert approaches are simply about raising your awareness and consciousness of how decisions (in this first case) are influenced and reached, and using your eyes and ears to identify how these things happen. Who is involved? When? Where? If you are able to observe decision-making in action (round a meeting room table for example), what sort of behaviours and language make the process run smoothly? Which people have the most sway in getting decisions agreed in their favour or that they support? Can you work out what aspects about who they are, what they do or the way they communicate and influence, make them successful (what are the common denominators)? This may give you information about what is valued – roles, styles, functions – so you can identify if there are ways to align your contributions to that agenda.

There are distinct styles of communication that develop in every culture. It's worth stepping back and listening to work out what the style is, including what terms and phrases get used, so you can fit them into your communications. This will mean key people can hear you better given they are tuned into that style and vocabulary.

In different situations, different people are listened to. So, which forums, meetings and groups can you identify where your voice needs to be heard? How do people get to participate in these set-ups? Who seem to be the winners in these circumstances and why?

An overt approach means talking to people individually, to ask for their view. While it might feel easier to talk to peers, the key insights rest with senior people involved in significant processes (clearly, these may be your peers). You can position these conversations as seeking to understand things better in order to ensure that you are able to engage with the most relevant people in the best way, for the best outcomes for the team / function / organisation. This may help you feel more comfortable about asking, and the person you ask should also be in the most receptive mode. Then you can ask them how decisions are influenced and made. What's the range of ways? Who do they think does that well and what do they do that stands out? What do they suggest that you do / do differently (if anything)?

Helping people understand what it really takes to make things happen is often a key role for a mentor, given their remit is to help mentees to work successfully with and through the system. Chapter 24 looks at this in detail.

Making it happen:

Which area(s) do you want to understand better and what is your approach going to be to meet this need?

Make your best job-change decisions by reading between the lines about new organisations, line managers and leaders.

Both organisations and individuals can excel at presenting a fabulously attractive and positive proposition to bring about the best recruitment outcomes. I'm sure that many readers of this book will have their stories about what they believed to be the truth about an opportunity given what they read on the organisation's website and the spin presented during the interview process, only to find that when they got into the organisation things were very different. For some, that will have meant turning around and finding the exit door very quickly, and trying to find a way to explain that blip on their CV; for others, it will have meant toughing it out until there was a respectable opportunity to move on. Hopefully very few just put up with it long term.

> *"I've done so many interviews. I love interviews – it is another way of learning, to find out from the other side, what they don't want to tell you, a bit like playing chess."* - Lin Phillips

It's actually very hard to separate the marketing gloss from the truth about an organisation during the application and interview process. This means that you have to go into the process with a clear idea about the sort of culture you want to work in, and then ask the right questions during interview process to find the evidence that will shed light on the truth. For example:

Do they support people's development and progression, through investment in training and development? What programmes are they currently running? Who can access them and when? What examples do they have of responding to individual requests for development support in the part of the organisation you are interviewing for?

How does success get recognised and rewarded? How does this work in the organisation? What examples would they like to showcase?

Are their leadership open to new ideas and innovation? What examples are they most proud of and why? How did these come about – generated from the teams and individuals involved, or in response to a brief from the top? What changes did these ideas bring about in the organisation?

How do they ensure gender balance in their decision-making about opportunities? Can they give examples of recent appointments, projects, etc that have been awarded to women? What are the gender ratios up the organisation and in specialist functions? Does the organisation have key measures in place about gender ratios for internal and external appointments, training provision and leadership?

If this is an organisation that has to publish its gender pay gap data (in the UK, that's any organisation with over 250 people), look it up online to see its gap size and trends, both in salaries and bonuses, and compare this to its competitors. What does it tell you and what might you want to ask in relation to this?

Culture is what you do, not just what you say, and it is set and transmitted from the top, so when there is a change at the top everything below will change to varying degrees. And cultures exist within functions and even within teams, so these will also be greatly affected by a change in who is running that part of an organisation. So, when someone new comes in, or moves across into a role above you, or into a role that has significant influence on you, it is wise to understand what their values and beliefs are and how they translate into what they favour and support as well as those that they don't. From these insights you can develop a view about how compatible this new context and influence will be with your ideas, ambitions and modus operandi, and this gives you the opportunity to make better-informed decisions about how you navigate the implications.

> *"John [Browne, BP CEO] and I got along very well. I also knew that John was going to be leaving and I took a look at who was going to be coming up and decided I didn't want to stay."* - **Anna Catalano**

> *"One of the lessons that I learned from that was that when senior management changes, I need to re-evaluate whether I still belong in an organisation. Senior management changing is a shorthand for*

changes that happen in an organisation. The boss will change or your immediate line manager or whatever. There are all sorts of subtle things that will change. Depending on where an individual is within an organisation, that will determine your reaction to whatever happens next. That change may become the opportunity for you to unleash something else and to launch into other opportunities or it can become not as good as it was (as I found myself). What I recognised was that it was time for me to leave. It was no longer the right time for me to be there. Interestingly, from that organisation I took my ideal role.

The other thing can be the fact that when we engage with an organisation and make a hiring or joining decision we are presented with, 'Here is the organisation, here are its values, and this is what we do.' We make that decision to join on the basis of our personal values. Then the journey starts. Often we will find that that fit is not what we first thought it was in all sorts of ways. Again, this is the thing about reading the cultural rules and understanding the organisation. If that distance builds up to too great a level it is another signal to get out, because you are heading for disappointment and bitterness because it hasn't met your expectations. The thing then is to use that experience as a stepping stone to something else. It is important to get out while you still feel good." – **Marion Cowden**

And finally, the good news is that when there is healthy gender balance at the top, the culture change benefits everyone...

"I have to say that it was rather interesting to see, in my last two or three years with the Met I worked in Serious Organised Crime, and for the first time in the whole history of the Metropolitan Police, my

boss was a female and two of my fellow Commanders were females and there were only six Commanders, so 50% of the Commanders were females in Serious Organised Crime. The dynamics in the five years that I worked within that group turned on their head and changed overnight. The informal networks had been when the guys used to go out drinking and they used to do boys' things like going to the rugby...things that I wasn't really interested in. When the girls became a monopoly group the conversations at breakfast meetings changed. It was a broader range of subjects. There was a lot more laughter and freedom because women are very honest. It was a completely different set of conversations and the power base shifted from the male group to the female group because we were the dominant group.

To start with the men found it difficult. And some of them were really liberated by it, particularly those who were more rounded. The interesting thing was that a number of those dominant alpha males also came up to retirement and left and were replaced by a completely different set of individuals who were not alpha males, they were very competent and very experienced, but a different kind of male seemed to be recruited. I don't know if that was because of the different dynamic within the group and some of the males that felt they couldn't get on before because of this alpha male monopoly now saw that there was an opportunity that they would be valued. I think it is interesting when you look at the power base and the way it can shift." – **Sharon Kerr**

Chapter 18

Deliver strategic impact & develop a strategic point of difference

The assumption in this chapter is that you want to progress your career. However, 'progress' can mean many different things. In some fields that might not mean climbing the hierarchical ladder to leadership but working on areas of greater challenge and / or significance.

Whether your ambitions mean you want to rise through the ranks, do more and more interesting, stretching and stimulating work, or gather new experiences, you will need to stand out and be recognised as having the experience, track record and potential to successfully step up to the role that's in your sights. And if you want to be on the right radars for the right opportunities, you have to stand out for the right reasons. To do this you have to know what is valued and respected by those that control the gateways to your future career, so you can provide salient evidence of your capability and potential which puts you in pole position by the time you want to go for it.

> *"Winning the UK Engineer of the Year award demonstrated the big impact I was making was recognised by my peers, which gave the organisation confidence to make me a director. I think the rest of the male world still think putting women up here*

> *is a bit of a gamble and they need to be reassured that it's the right decision and have reasons to have confidence in what they see as a more risky decision than promoting a man. So that they're not ridiculed for appointing a woman. They need more evidence that they are making the right strategic decision." –*
> **Dana Skelley**

There are two dimensions that have become really clear through my research that are of greatest significance for having the career stand-out that will enable you to secure the best opportunities. They are:

1. Delivering strategic impact.
2. Gaining strategically significant experience that differentiates you from your peers.

1. Delivering strategic impact

What do I mean by strategic impact? It's a grand phrase. Essentially, it's about prioritising your delivery (the output or outcomes of your work) on the things that are of greatest significance to your organisation at whatever level you are able to impact. This might be at team level, client level, functional level, total organisational level, or by internal or external stakeholder group. Being able to identify what's really critical to make the most important things happen speaks volumes about a range of salient capabilities.

> *"Men always think about what is in it for them. To be successful in business it is about self and what is in it for me.*
>
> *You should always think about what is right for the business. That is often in direct opposition to what might be right for you personally. That is another thing that really brings people up. They hear you*

say something, and they are expecting you to say it coming from a certain angle because that represents who they are, and when you come in from a different angle you can see them thinking, 'Where is she going with this? What is in it for her?' Then they realise there is nothing in it for me, but it is what is right, and it is for the business. That brings you to their attention." **- Charmaine Stewart**

At more junior levels it can be easy to identify what is of greatest significance because it's what you're measured on, and most specifically, the subset of measures which are prioritised when evaluating your performance in readiness for promotion.

"Because I have been in the public sector for five years now it is completely different. I came on a part-time six-month assignment and just kept getting promoted because it is so easy to get promoted. Because they are not used to people actually delivering.

Me: How do you make an impact in the world of HR?

By actually delivering something. Not many people do. They sit behind closed doors shuffling forms about." **- Barbara Harris**

Ironically, in more senior roles, it can be less clear to see what you need to deliver within the organisation in order to make the most significant positive and strategic impact. As a management consultant I regularly interviewed employees in significant posts across organisations around the world and routinely asked what the organisation's most critical strategies were and how they related to their role. Very, very few were able to provide an answer, even in highly respected global companies. So, strategic imperatives, strategic direction and strategic priorities are not always obvious, and often the information doesn't even exist. This means that you will need to infer what the strategic imperatives are likely to be overall, and decide what they should be for the area you are concerned with. Incidentally, by strategic imperative, I mean the critical things an organisation has to do and do successfully to survive, compete (for resources or customers) and to thrive.

> "I started thinking that I would like to do something that would help me understand everything about running a business: the people, the leadership, the finance side. There was this wonderful MBA opportunity. It was organised by all the engineering institutions: the Civil Engineering Institution, the Mechanical Engineering Institution. So, I sat these initial papers and basically ended up doing an action learning MBA, which was absolutely brilliant for me. That is the way I like learning – reading, synthesising and then talking about it. I have to discuss things. It is about challenging insights. It was perfect because I did it with a group of six people who were all engineers from different disciplines. The range of people was amazing. Between us we were a range of fantastically connected people.

> I started to realise that it was a business that we were running, rather than working for the council. I went onto the consultancy side and worked for a team initially that did the bid. We were bidding as a local authority department against a private sector company. We bid for doing the work as a trading account. We won it. It was very close, but we won it. That was brilliant, working on the bid. I was just part of the team that time around. The second time around I led the whole team and led the whole bid process. That was when I started to understand about business and finance and also about leadership and people. It has changed a lot now, but Investors In People was one of the things we decided we were going to go for as one of our offers as a consultancy. That was very interesting

because I learned the whole thing from scratch. It did help me understand the fullness of what was needed in a business in terms of the people considerations, the development considerations as a whole. It was starting to make me realise what business leadership required and has equipped me now in running the Directorate." - **Dana Skelley**

Figure 20: Strategic impact self-assessment

Looking at the scale below, identify which best fits your current situation. Then identify where your ideal situation would place you on the scale. Is there a gap? If so, will closing this gap make a significant difference to your prospects for success? If it would, you need to make developing strategic impact a priority in your development plans, and follow the rest of the chapter closely as the first step.

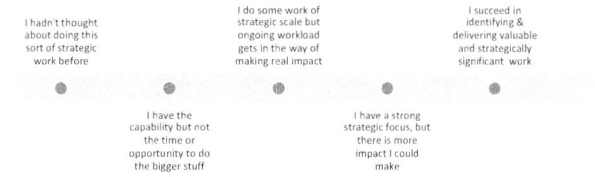

Be diligent, but don't get bogged down in the little stuff.

If you are bogged down crossing t's and dotting i's, you are not likely to have the space to do the stuff that's of greatest value and that gets you noticed by the people that make the crucial decisions that will affect your short-term and long-term future. Nor are you likely to be doing the stuff that will be giving you the biggest buzz or greatest sense of fulfilment.

This is where women's higher levels of integrity and loyalty can be a double-edged sword. This real and measured difference is one of the very few between the genders. While it has enormous upsides, it can mean that women are more likely to get bogged down in the little stuff that they feel has to be done to do the job properly and responsibly. The experience of the interviewees supported these views about women sometimes being too diligent for their own good. Unfortunately, too much time with your head down attending to the detail stops you having time to do the things that get you noticed. You may feel that this very phrase jars with you. However, this is all about balance. It's about being wise to the fact that sometimes you're a bit of a mug for doing the detail, or for doing it to such a high level of finish or perfection.

As a doctor, scientist or programmer, the detail really matters, but in how many other fields do you need to be the one that focuses relentlessly on the minutiae? *'Why would you do more than 51% if that's all that's needed?'* one male businessperson memorably said to me. More savvy workers will spot either who is prepared to pick up the pieces or to say yes to the lower-level tasks, or who they can appropriately delegate to, so they can be available for the more significant and exciting work.

> *"You are going to get the work that people want you to do.*
>
> *I am coaching a lady at the moment on my team. I am telling her, 'Just quit trying to fill in the gaps that you see. Do your job and expect others to do their job.' I stopped her from going to this meeting a couple of weeks ago. I said, 'You're not going. I*

am expecting that guy to do that job. If you go to that meeting, they are going to turn around and give you all of that work. Isn't that right?' She said, 'Yes that's right.' I said, 'Do not go to that meeting.' That plays into your bit about women focusing on making their work very good. That is OK, but is it enough to get you ahead. No, not really. People are just going to give you more work to do because you do it very well. To their credit most women don't say no. They take it all on." – **Peggy Montana**

Focus relentlessly on what really matters and makes a difference.

I'm not suggesting you side-step all tasks which are not beneficial to your profile in the organisation, creating a wake that others drown in. However, you have to put your success agenda towards the front and balance the small with the big and impactful. 'Success' by doing the things that matter most to the success of your organisation should produce wins for others as well, so you should consider the scale of benefits you will bring, if this style of focus initially sits uncomfortably.

"I think when you are in a business you absolutely have to add value and sometimes make big decisions if you are really going to help make these businesses stay ahead and grow. Collaboration is a critical component if you are to get support and buy-in.

However, if you don't put something out there that is big, brave and different you will agree on just moving 2 degrees from where you were. As Steve Jobs famously said, 'You should always try and obsolete your own products before your competitors do.' Nokia learnt this the hard way. Complacent with their market leadership, they tweaked rather than transformed their mobile phones and Apple's innovations left them behind. They didn't challenge themselves. They should have kept their cash cows while simultaneously driving innovation. Where are Nokia now?

Creating the right team is really important. You need collaboration with all kinds of people to stimulate new thinking, big thinking and to challenge yourselves and the status quo. Not just the usual people in the company because this perpetuates 'group think' and continuous support of previous decisions." - **Collette Dunkley**

So, the first step is to identify what is of strategic significance to your organisation, or your part of it, and to get really clear how your work does, or could, contribute to or lead to that. If you formulate what you believe to be strategically or significantly beneficial, it is wise to gain formalised approval from appropriate members of your leadership group.

"It is about important versus urgent. Stop doing all of the urgent and get into the important." - **Jill Caseberry**

Jill Caseberry is referring to another dimension which sucks resources and focus away from delivering outcomes of strategic scale or significance, and that is the stuff that masquerades as urgent: the emails asking for this, that and the other; the requests for meeting the 'could you just?'s. Cutting through to and delivering the bigger stuff is seriously tough these days, with the 24-7 bombardment from every angle and communication device.

Jill is also referring to the neat tool below that helps you assess and prioritise work so that you can keep focused on the stuff that really counts. It can be used on a daily basis instead of a to-do list or, at the other end of the spectrum, you can use it as a strategic planning tool.

Figure 21: The Urgent Important Decision Matrix

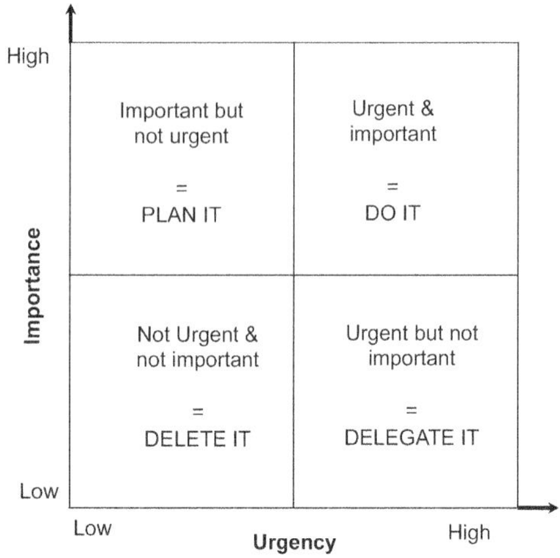

Making it happen:

Reflect back on your last week's activities and those which dominated your time.

Plot them on an urgent: important matrix.

- Where were you operating for the majority of your time? Did you have a predominance in the top two 'high importance' boxes or were your resources drawn down to the 'low importance but high urgency' box?

- What are the insights and implications you draw from this?

You can use this matrix to plot your ideal work balance, to ensure that you are doing work in the top two quadrants, and you can challenge yourself to see what else you could do, or do differently, if you feel that your focus is too much in the lower half.

Depending on your level of seniority, your line manager can be another source of prioritisation. They should also help find solutions to the small stuff dominating your time or give you authority to drop, postpone or reassign it. So, if you are unable to spend enough time on the strategic stuff, you can take the challenge to her / him and say, 'Of all these things, would you agree that these are the most important for me to get done.' You then ensure that they are buying into your focus.

> *"Delegation is the key to success – don't get hung up on the detail. Just look at the big picture with an eye out to spot a flaw [problem]."* **- Beverley Bell**

Balance your daily regime for maximum impact.

It's very easy to let time get eaten by trivia. Getting into the office and working through emails first is a common way of easing yourself into the day or getting the feeling of being in control, but more often than not, these types of tasks are better to be done at another time.

A popular metaphor to explore your approach to time management is the filling of a jar with a set of different sized stones: rocks, pebbles and sand. The jar represents time; the stones represent tasks; their size represents their importance. If you fill your jar with the sand sized bits first, then the pebbles, you'll run out of space for the rocks. You should start with the biggest stones and fit the smaller stones and sand in the spaces around them.

Mornings have been shown to be the most productive time for most people – so unless you really know you are different, use the morning for the bigger, more challenging but most important stuff.

Is it really your responsibility?

It seems obvious to say that you should only focus on work that is your responsibility but sometimes it's easy to drift from that path and this happens for a range of reasons:

- You just want to get involved because it is interesting or exciting.
- You've been asked to do it by someone persuasive or more senior (but perhaps not your direct line manager).
- You get invited as part of a wider group and just didn't question the relevance of your presence (and neither did they).
- You feel that you ought to be seen to be involved.
- You are uncomfortable asking someone else to do it, or just saying no.

> *"If I fill in those gaps, I'm needed, and that makes me feel good. Often I can get mired in the miniscule and I like the security of routine. That is very important to me. I have to consciously stop myself from doing tasks that could perfectly easily be done by somebody else."* –
> **Fiona Hagdrup**

Tell them it was you!

I will talk more about this in the next chapter, however the key point I'd like to make here is that without being known as the person responsible for the strategic impact you deliver, you are limiting the benefits to your future. Putting your name to your great work and communicating may feel uncomfortable, but if you don't, someone else will (and then reap the benefits) or the potential gain will be wasted. There are painless ways of doing it, so read on.

Making it happen:

If the assessment of your level of strategic impact meant that this is a priority development for you, what do you want to do differently to step-change the situation?

2. Gain strategically significant experience that differentiates you from your peers

At the beginning of the chapter I said that there are two dimensions that are of greatest significance for having the career stand-out that will enable you to secure the best opportunities. Gaining strategically significant experience that differentiates you from your peers is the second of these powerful strategies.

When you look around you, you may see people who stand out because they have an additional set of experiences that sets them apart and makes them considered more valuable. They are therefore more respected and sought after for particular tasks, assignments or bigger opportunities. It was clear from my interviews that many of these women gained a distinct advantage through acquiring clear, distinct and valued experiences which enabled them to get further and get further faster.

> *"Moving to Singapore. That was a huge step. I am absolutely certain that I would not have progressed three more levels since that job if I hadn't taken that spot. It really gave me a window into the global Shell, and some of the significant differences in issues that you face in developing countries. It took me to where I felt quite capable of running global distribution, and to now running global supply and distribution. That was a big step."* -
> **Peggy Montana**

In the fields of business and academia and maybe many more, international assignments have been shown to be very significant in creating that distinct and powerful differentiation that catapults people over their colleagues. A great book that looks at this in detail is *Get Ahead by Going Abroad* by Stacie Nevadomski Berdan and C. Perry Yeatman (S. Nevadomski Berdan, 2007).

> *"I had a very standard career until the international piece came in. I told the AMOCO people very early on in my career that if the company ever decided to do anything in China that I would love to be a part of it. I planted a seed very early on and just left it there.*
>
> *In 1994 there was an opportunity to open up an office in China. There were a group of people sitting around a table who were talking about this opportunity. Somebody at the table said, 'What about Anna? Wouldn't she like to go?' Another person at the table said, 'I'm sure she'd like to go but she's pregnant, so she shouldn't go.' And then another person at the table said, 'I think we should ask her.' I was pregnant with my second child at the time and there was an assumption made at the table, that because I was having a baby I would not be interested in taking an overseas assignment. So I am living proof that if the assumptions are allowed to manifest themselves, I would not have been allowed this opportunity. I owe a lot to the men at the table (and they were all men) who intervened and said, 'We should ask her.' As soon as they asked me, I said, 'If my baby is born healthy I will go after three months.' And sure enough I did. My son was born in January and we went in April. That actually was a turning point in my career. Because until that time my career progression looked like everybody else's in my peer group. We'd all gone through these sales and marketing jobs. You get to the point in your career, ten years in, where you say, 'How am I*

going to stand out? How am I going to be different?'
The China thing was what catapulted my career.
Getting an international ticket punched. First of all
it changed my life, personally and professionally.
Secondly, if you compare my professional life with
everybody else's, that is what made a difference." -
Anna Catalano

However, it's not possible for everyone to have or take these opportunities, as Jane Walton points out. Her view was that being a woman is a stand-out, positive differentiator and, in her case, as a business and market analyst she also had a positive differentiation, working with commercial teams dominated by other commercial functions, which needed her insights to make strong commercial decisions.

"The international trail of moving every 2 to 3
years presents a series of not particularly attractive
challenges. It's impractical and difficult for career
couples – male colleagues were rejecting the option too.

I stood out as the only woman and I got away with
behaviours I couldn't have if I was a bloke. I could
do things differently because of that. Maybe also
because I had a specialist role." - **Jane Walton**

For Maggie Stilwell, her strategic expertise was a specific specialisation within her profession that she had identified early in her career might balance any drag on her career progression caused by being female.

"I guess a couple of years in a big insurance
company made me realise that having a degree
wasn't enough to be able to get on. I felt particularly
as a woman, I needed something else to demonstrate
competence and specialism in something. I thought
it could be accounting because I was dealing with
accounting concepts all of the time in what I was
doing. Or I could be an actuary, because I was

working for an insurance company and that was a fairly obvious route.

Then I started to specialise. I became interested in an area of accounting called Forensic Accounting, which is fraud and dispute work. That is what I have specialised in since that time. I moved to Ernst and Young in January 1996 into their litigation support practice, now called Forensic & Integrity Services. Since joining them I have had my three children and went through the ranks, which were executive to manager to senior manager to director and then to partner in 2008." – **Maggie Stilwell**

Making it happen:

How does this question of a strategically significant point of difference measure up in your situation, and your ambitions?

Is it something you have or would benefit from acquiring?

If so, what could you acquire and how could you go about securing that experience?

Would it fit with your values and career drivers?

Chapter 19

You need to self promote, so make it count

'Anathema', that's a word I'd never fully understood, but I instinctively felt that it was the word that describes how the vast majority of women feel about self-promotion. According to the Oxford English Dictionary it means 'Curse, accursed thing'. The Oxford Thesaurus suggests the alternatives 'abomination, abhorrence, aversion, bane, bugbear'. So my instinct was right, self-promotion is anathema for most women across all generations, including those that are yet to join the workforce. And yet, self-promotion is simply taking ownership of making key people aware of your capability, professional interests and potential, and giving them the opportunity to give you the right roles, rewards and recognition at the right time for the mutual benefit of you and the organisation.

What drives such a strong reaction?

We have examined the causes and impact of the insidious and relentless communication of the value and expectations of women compared to men in society. It measurably reduces women's belief in their capability compared to men (Myth 5 and Chapter 11) and undermines their sense of worth in the workplace. In addition to this I've also identified an intense subconscious conflict which, if expressed by an individual, would go along these lines, '*What if the reason women rarely get to the top is that they actually aren't as good as men? That means I'm not as capable as my male peers and I've been kidding myself about what my work is worth and what I can achieve. But, I have to keep pushing forward or I will let down all the women who have fought for and continue to campaign for equal pay, treatment and opportunities for progression.'* This internal turmoil is aggravated further by the distorted and counter-productive dialogue around Imposter Syndrome, with its common attachment to women. The term 'syndrome' infers a medical basis for a feeling of doubt in one's capability, which can lead people to believe that they suffer from an innate, biological medical condition that they are therefore powerless to 'cure'. This is simply not the case. Women's lower level of belief in their capability is a straight-forward, logical cognitive response to external factors – simple cause and effect. Addressing these causes enables us to change our response.

Together these are the reasons why the prospect of asking for a pay rise, a promotion, or even a much smaller opportunity, can be so daunting for many women. It can seem inevitable that the outcome will be the worst possible scenario, striking a direct blow to their fragile confidence and self-belief structure, demolishing it like a house of cards, and bringing untold consequences for their future career and professional identity. While these thoughts rarely consciously reach the surface for us to act on or challenge, our unconscious has done the processing and nudges us away from situations that would potentially be so harmful.

This is why even the highly successful women that I interviewed – with just a couple of notable exceptions – hadn't asked for such things during their careers.

> *"My son at 14 was graded into ski groups. I said to him, 'You'll go into the top group won't you.' He said, 'Well actually mum, all they do is racing and I'm not interested in racing in skiing, so I'm going to go in the second group.' He came home and I said, 'How was it?' He said, 'It was fine. There are only two boys in the [second] group. It is so typical mum. All the girls think they are useless, so they put themselves in the second group and all the boys*

think they are brilliant, so they put themselves in the first group.' He said, 'It's all rubbish because often the girls are much better skiers.' At 14 he has already sussed that women will underestimate their abilities." **– Karen Guerra**

The background messages from society are clearly very different for boys and men, and this is why it is so apparently straightforward and risk-free for them to put themselves forward. They are both expected and encouraged to compete for what they want, and to take the knockbacks 'like a man'. For men, status and power have always been important, and are gained by taking risks and always pushing forward. Boys grow up expecting to be the breadwinner, the provider, and they know they have to tough it out and do what's necessary to get on. They also know it's OK to put themselves forward and ask for what they want from their careers, because it's the norm, and it's been done by men successfully since time immemorial.

Even when dating and finding a partner, boys and men are expected to be the ones that do the asking – the ones that risk humiliation and rejection – and girls and women are still, to a large degree, expected to wait to be asked. So, men are 'trained' to try, and have endless practice at both asking and dealing with the consequences. This is experience that women lack, but can rapidly and safely gain.

"One of the things I have noticed is that women are more tentative. I have noticed that most of the women I have worked with find it much harder to have a conversation about a salary increase or a promotion or something due, than the men I have worked with. The men have no problem coming to me and saying, 'I think I have earned this.' Women kind of say that and stop, and give all the justifications for why. I have taught myself to stop. To just say (even though I am biting my tongue) 'I have earned this.' Rather than giving the 27 reasons why, in case they haven't noticed.

But I certainly found from my own point of view and watching people operating, that men do better at negotiating salaries by saying very little other than, 'I've earned this.'

I am doing a lot of work at the moment exploring women and self-esteem because 90% of our customers around the world are women. I did some work with a behavioural psychologist and we came up with some really interesting statistics. In 24 years of practising as a behavioural psychologist, specialising in eating disorders, she has never met a heterosexual man with an eating disorder. Eating disorders are very linked to low self-esteem. We have done some work in the UK on this whole self-esteem piece. We have been asking women, 'Tell me the last time when you felt really good about yourself.' It sparked off the thought in my head when you were saying about the emotional weight of discussing yourself. When really pushed you get, 'When my son won a prize at school.' It is so hard for them to talk about themselves. The other interesting thing, when you come back to the hardwiring plus stereotyping and what men and women do differently, you ask them, 'What do you like about your body?' The first thing you get back is, 'I hate my legs' or 'I hate my hair.' It always comes back as what they hate. They can't come back and say straightforwardly what they like. I think that is terrible. That is why I love what you are doing. I feel we have a responsibility to do something." - **Miriam Jordan-Keane**

Don't ask compellingly, don't get.

The consequences of not promoting yourself, or not doing so compellingly, are that you exclude yourself from opportunities. Put simply, you are discriminating against yourself. If key people don't know enough about you, or what you do and how well you do it, how can they consider you for things that require those capabilities, that knowledge, that attitude and potential?

If you see other people getting to do the work you would have liked to do and getting the rewards for it (buzz, pay and profile) it can undermine your engagement and your performance, '*what's the point of doing this if nobody ever notices what I do, appreciates it, or rewards me with new opportunities?*'. However, being rewarded for your work is in your control. You need to make it clear to your management or leadership team what you believe you merit – opportunities, rewards, profile, whatever it is that you are after – otherwise someone else will, and it will be them reaping the rewards.

Psychological smoke and mirrors.

A common approach I see in women is putting a different emphasis on what matters to them most about the work they do, positioning money as of less relevance to job satisfaction, or just being able to do the sort of work they 'love'. I'm fairly sure this is a self-protective mechanism, creating a narrative smokescreen to hide behind. It's a way to explain and rationalise avoiding squaring up to 'demand' more or different, that fits neatly into our culture's narrative about the way women are supposed to be – modest and selfless with no unsavoury interest in status, power or influence. So, it goes unchallenged – both by women themselves and by people around them.

> "*It is like the pay rise thing. I have never asked for a pay rise in my life. In fact, I'd never dream of asking for a pay rise because I feel valued in a different way. Recognition, being given more responsibility – that is the way I feel valued.*" **– Dana Skelley**

I'm challenging it because I believe women construct this perspective, or exaggerate its importance, to deflect what they otherwise subconsciously conclude will be an inevitable crushing disappointment, if they dare to pitch higher in terms of roles and rewards. The expectation of ambition (hopes and dreams) being impossible to fulfil is a painful reading of reality. So the strategy of constructing an alternative value set for success is incredibly smart in this one regard.

However, I believe we need to address this issue at its roots, so women can reap the full portfolio of rewards for their hard work, dedication, creativity, drive and talent. Women deserve to be proud of what they do, and the value and significance of their work. Commensurate recognition should be the result which would then spur them on to even greater things.

> *"I know for a fact that I haven't been as good, and I haven't earned as much as same grade men who earned substantially more. Men are more focused on their value recognition while women tend to accept what they're given. If it mattered to me more, I'd have done more."* – **Jane Walton**

> *"I think there is a feeling that women are quite grateful, rather than thinking they deserve to be paid more. We don't negotiate and we are quite reasonable, whereas men can be quite unreasonable in their expectations. I know I was quite reasonable and fair when I was negotiating. I was thinking about other things that were going on, the size of the company, the role, the fact that I wanted to do it and it was a bit of an opportunity. I was quite happy with the role so accepted the salary. Whereas men would think, 'I'm absolutely worth that, so they should pay me for it.' It is about self-belief and knowing you are worth it. I can't speak for all my colleagues, but I think the role is more important than the salary. It needs to be reasonable, but it is not a deal breaker.*

> *I'm wondering whether the new generation is going to be better at that. What happens between teenage years and moving into the job market? I see very confident teenagers that don't always translate into confident adults. Thinking about those that I've worked with, all of a sudden they've been happy to*

be subservient." – **Gill Adams**

I have heard so many 'reasons' why money is not important to women, but I firmly believe it's just a self-protection strategy. We must see beyond society's gendered beliefs and focus on the reality of our worth and potential as individuals. Of course, we can maintain our pride in doing our jobs well. But we can reject the proposition that rewarding this with the commensurate money, position, power and influence is unimportant. Why should someone with the same capability and potential as you earn more than the value of a house extra in his working lifetime? Why should you do a dull job that's beneath your capability because someone else asked for better before you believed you were ready to ask? Why should the word 'power' sit uncomfortably, if the truth is that you are in a big role, managing vast resources, huge budgets and / or complex, leading-edge and highly significant projects?

> *"I think that if you consider it a one-time conversation, you are going to have a tough conversation one time pretty easily. Picking the right time to talk about it does not brand you as a whiner. I think the reason we don't want to do it is because we're scared that people will think this is all we're about. And it goes against our grain. Women pride themselves on saying, 'It's not just about the money.' We are afraid of having a conversation that is just about the money. But we've got to push it. If we don't push it, it isn't going to happen. There's an assumption that your pay cheque is incremental.*
>
> *Because once again you are representing, not only yourself, but you are carrying a flag for the whole gender. So we have a tendency to question our abilities and our potential for being successful to a fault. Our greatest fear is to go into a job and not be successful, because that not only lets us down it lets all women down. Therefore, before I put my hand up for this job, I want to make sure I can really do*

it. Because I can't afford to fail. This whole notion of not being able to fail is what causes women to be more reluctant to self-promote or even believe that they have the potential, because they want to make sure they are not going to fail.

I think most of what happens here is subconscious. It is based on what we are taught and how we are raised from a very young age in terms of what we are supposed to do and what we are supposed to be good at doing. I think what happens is that it ends up projecting itself into how we behave as adults in the business world. I have spoken to many women about this and there is always a look of recognition in the audience. So, I think there is not a real strong level of awareness that these things happen."
- Anna Catalano

It'll never be exactly the right time.

A third critical dynamic is that many women tend to wait far longer than men to go for the next role. They believe – or want to believe – that promotion and special opportunities will be presented to them when they are ready for them. That would probably work if meritocracy existed or if men had the same attitude, but for the most part, they don't. And the scenario of men going for jobs when they have 20% of what it takes while women wait till they have 80% has a widely recognised basis in reality. So, while women wait to be sure that they will be able to do the role well, their male colleagues go for it. And with a confident pitch, strong negotiation and persistence, they secure these opportunities leaving women behind them with their jaws on the floor, saying to an empty room, 'what about me?'. This clearly means that men get on faster, learning and developing once they are in the new role. Repeating the cycle again and again, progressing faster and earning more than the women that were once their peers. Research by Catalyst.org shows that making senior people aware of their contribution and value, i.e., self-promotion, is the most significant lever women can pull to address differences in pay and the rate of promotion compared to male peers.

And while there is a complex set of reasons behind this deeply uncomfortable topic for many women, the good news is that it's actually relatively easy to confront and address. Many women I've worked with, even briefly, have gone away, and with genuine ease, secured a higher salary, from a single digit percent increase to 90% and even 100% in some memorable instances – as well as a range of other benefits such as promotions, new opportunities, training and sponsorship.

I wonder what difference earning even just a few percent more on your annual salary and a bigger bonus would make to your life.

> *"I think Imperial, at college promotion levels, is fair. I think if you get put into the college promotion process, there are quite a lot of women sitting on the big promotion board, so it is fair. Women aren't disadvantaged in any way. But there is a lot of evidence that women are less likely to push for promotion. I write around to the heads of department every year and remind them that women will have a different publication pattern and that women push themselves forward less and that they should take account of this in the departmental decisions. We've got lots of data on that because the Americans have just done this huge report called 'Beyond Bias and Barriers'. The National Academy in the US did it. What this does is look really carefully at all the reasons why women are underrepresented in science and takes them apart. It says that we have dealt with all the obvious things, so what are the rocks below the surface which keep women out? In the end what they conclude is that it's the cumulative effect of very slight differences. Women are less likely to push for promotion, so they will be a bit slower getting it.*

> *I think it is more about men and women having*

a different mindset about all of this stuff. Men are obsessed with earning money. The role I sit in now is deputy principal of the business school. They [men] are all trailing in here asking for pay rises and you don't often get it from women. That is part of what I talk to women about." - **Prof. Dot Griffiths**

Me: Positive self-promotion, includes such things as going into your annual appraisal and asking for more money.

"I have never done that in my life.

Me: My theory on this is that we could close or narrow the gender pay gap dramatically if we could enable women to do this.

Having promised us [me and Keith] a bonus last year, Keith negotiated. I would never even have thought of asking for a bonus last year when we merged the businesses; I would just get a bonus for my results, that is it. He managed to negotiate for both of us a guaranteed bonus. Then they backtracked on it and said we were only going to get part of it. He still managed to negotiate a bit more. I was amazed. I would never have thought about it. The only time I have ever used external factors was when I pushed them for that job, but that wasn't about money. I could have made it about money because of what this guy had done. The other guy had released a lot of salary information and I realised I was being paid less than the male director. I could have said 'Unless you give me... then I'm not staying.' I have been very poor at that and I think I could have earned a hell of a lot more money if I'd been better. Just merging with Keith made me realise. He is on 30% more than me just as a basic salary and then he got all the other benefits on top of that. If I'd been better at it, I should have been earning 30% more.

Me: How much more could you have earned?

Loads. Probably a quarter of a million or something.

I would have paid off the mortgage. That is frightening. I was just grateful. They would give me a pay rise and I would say thank you. 'Thank you, I didn't really expect it this year.' I just understand if I don't get one. The last two years we have had a pay freeze. Fine. Even though our business has made a quarter of a million pounds profit and we are one of the three companies in the UK that has done it.

[later, at the close of the interview...]

Me: Is there anything, in summary, that women should think about?

"For a woman to get on now and forge a career, the key thing that you have said that I think I could have done better is the positive self-promotion. I do think the women who work for me...actually I don't really like it when people come and demand money from me, I don't like it at all...I would much rather give it. I have one of the girls here who has been really forceful, and I have ended up giving her five grand because she pushed for it. She will go far. I do see that that is a really important thing and one of the things that I've struggled with." - **Sally Wells**

Sally's estimate of how much more she could have earned has been validated by research that has shown that the loss of earnings a female manager experiences across her career, relative to an equivalent male manager, is equivalent to the price of an average four bedroomed house (in the UK) today.

"Men are driven by ego, especially in the workplace where it all comes out. If you interview a man, his CV will say – and he will tell you – that he can do

everything that you are asking for. He can do a lot more. A woman will say, 'Well I haven't done that bit, but I can do that.' You will get honesty. Men will say they can do it all. They will go into meetings and pontificate. The peacocking goes on and they will use their physical presence to pose.

You clearly can't work on the basis that you need only do a good job. You clearly have to get out there and communicate and meet head on. You can do it in your own way, you don't have to match the behaviour, but you have to be fairly assertive. Women should know that." - **Charmaine Stewart**

There are two types of personal promotion that I recommend for your strategic focus:

A: ***Pitching for significant specific opportunities*** such as a pay rise, a promotion or a new job for which you can plan and prepare to get the outcome you want.

B: ***Ongoing personal PR.*** This is making sure that you are known for the value and benefits of what you do and deliver, by the people that influence your access to opportunities (see also, Chapter 21 on managing stakeholders).

A: Pay rises, bonuses, promotions, special projects, assignments

Re-learn how to ask, and make it a habit.

Child: *"Mummy, can I have an ice cream?"*
Mummy: *"No, not now sweetheart."*
[20 minutes later]

Child: *"Mummy, **please** can I have an ice cream?"*
Mummy: *"Not now darling"*
[10 minutes later]
Child: *"Mummy, [shirt sleeve tug] **please, please,** can I have an ice cream?"*
Mummy: *"We'll see."*
[5 minutes later]
Child: *"Mummy [continual shirt sleeve tugging] **please, please, pleeeease** can I have an ice cream?"*
Mummy [remembering the consequences of sticking with 'no' last time and reading the determined expression on the child's face]: *"Oh, alright."*
[Moments later] The child is enjoying an ice cream.

Had that child asked for a '99' [a whipped ice cream in a cone with a chocolate flake] the chances are that they might have got one, but even if she didn't get her number one choice, she would at least have got an ice cream. If that child had asked for a less exciting ice cream, then that type of ice cream would be the best they could have expected. However, if they were 'just' a very good little child all day, but didn't ask for an ice cream at all, then they might have got a 'you've been very good today' at the end of the day, but they wouldn't have got an ice cream!

As children, we're brilliant at asking, and we persist until we either get what we want, get something similar, get the option 'banked' for next time, or get told unequivocally that it's out of the question. Children will wear down their carer's resistance until they get what they want. They may resort to tantrums and tears, and carers know this! Every parent, guardian or carer knows well that sometimes you will give a child whatever it is just to stop them asking, to prevent a melt down and to get a bit of peace so you can get on with whatever you were trying to do.

In many workplaces getting what you want requires a very similar process – you have to let people know what you want and the consequences if you don't get it, and not be put off if at first you don't succeed.

The consequence of consistently and compellingly putting yourself forward is that you get considered when decisions are being made about tasks, about projects, about roles, about money, about training and development. And the better you package and present your *professional value proposition*, relative to what matters for these tasks, projects, roles, bonuses etc, the more likely it will be you that gets them, along with all the material and psychological benefits that come with them. You can make it a 'no-brainer' that you get chosen, so there is effectively no decision to be made. This can be a great relief to those responsible for organisational changes, project management, and appointments, as they have one less component to have to work out because you've given them the solution. In some cases, it's not only about existing opportunities, but it can also mean that opportunities are created for you because the key people know exactly what you bring, what you want, how much you want it and how well you will perform given that opportunity.

Have a read of Lin's story below. It's my absolute favourite for bringing this theory to life.

"I went on this management programme last year, at the end of the course, as part of the self-learning, you have to consider, 'How am I going to change myself?' I am sitting there thinking 'I don't know.' I'm only going to be with Shell eight years maximum. I want to retire when I'm 55. That is the plan. I can't actually tell my boss that I've been on this great expensive course and I'm going to retire in eight years.

So I thought, 'What can I say that will make them think I am really inspirational and ambitious?'

After some deliberation I thought I would tell them I wanted to be on the executive team because that wasn't going to happen. In my final wrap up session, I sat there feeling really uncomfortable and I said, 'My goal is to be on the executive team. I've got the brains, I've got the qualifications, I think you should put me on it.'

I didn't hear anything for three months and then the VP came in and said, 'I have decided I'm going to put you on the executive team.' I said, 'That's very nice of you. Thank you very much.' I thought, 'Gosh is it really that easy? Why have I been worried about doing it all of these years?' I did it tongue in cheek. I didn't do it expecting it to happen." – **Lin Phillips**

Lin would never have asked for that promotion under normal circumstances, but not only was she successful in achieving a level that she thought she would never achieve, but it was hers within three months. **The difference between never securing that incredible role, and securing it almost instantly, was simply asking, and doing so with clarity and conviction**.

If you think you'll get the remuneration package you merit without asking for it, you are wrong.

In the early stages of our careers and in a few very tightly defined and measured professions, employees are paid and promoted based on clear, measurable and unambiguous objectives. However, in most jobs from the entry interview right up to MD (or the equivalent), what you earn is down to what you negotiate. If you start lower you stay lower.

> *"If women are paid less than men in the same positions, those salary disparities can persist even if the employees perform at the same level."*
>
> **Director of Compensation, Google.
> June 2017 (statement made during a
> Federal Court case)**

Your starting salary is usually your most significant scale of opportunity. Yet the impact of being exposed to evidence of being valued less is also felt here. Research in Silicon Valley by recruitment firm hired.com, identified a gendered '*expectation gap*'. Comparing over a hundred thousand job offers they found that women expected less than men for identical roles by an average of $14,000, and this expectation gap increased in line with the perception of job roles having higher male to female ratios.

UK gender pay gap figures that show that the average hourly pay gap in the private sector is around 16% but that rises to 50% in a range of sectors when factoring in the discretionary components of pay (such as annual bonuses). Discretionary elements of a package are yours to lose if you wait to be rewarded without any direct and consistent effort.

When I was a line manager in the corporate world, I had an amount of money I could allocate to my teams every year as pay increases and bonuses. I was told what the average percentage increase would be across the business, and it was up to me to decide how to allocate that money. Like most line managers, I worked on the assumption that individuals ask for more as a matter of course, so I would anticipate a negotiation and present a lower offer than I expected to settle on in the discussions. If a strong case was put to me that I had made the wrong preparatory judgement and an individual should receive a higher increase, I needed to have the contingency to do so. However, if I didn't spend all my budget then I was doing my own job well – delivering tight financial management.

> "*The company's position is 'don't give' and the woman's position is 'don't ask'. We avoid confrontation and feel grateful for any reward, or indeed no reward, but to have that role. Many women feel very exposed and overanalyse*

the implications of possible outcomes – dwelling on the negative 'what happens if it all goes wrong?' - Anon Interviewee

Women have to work harder than men at self-promotion to compensate for biases.

I've shown that the psychology of decision-making means that judgements are flawed. A study featured in McKinsey Quarterly (D. Lovallo, 2010) based on a survey of 2,207 executives reported that 60% believed they made as many bad quality as good quality strategic decisions. The awarding of pay rises, bonuses, promotions, special assignments, new job appointments and so on, are subject to the same issue – systematic errors of judgement caused by cognitive biases.

The harsh reality is that for many roles women are less likely to be on the opportunities and rewards radar and if they are, they will be further away from the sweet spot. This makes the case much stronger for taking a strategic approach to self-promotion, and doing so with skill, tenacity and forethought, in order to open decision-makers' eyes to possibilities other than the usual suspects and to consistently provide the evidence that they deserve serious and objective consideration.

"The other angle I work on is that this all comes into play when you have formal groups who make the decision on who should be promoted. Every decision that's made in a company on who should get a promotion is made by a group of people sitting round a table usually. That could be three or eight people. The makeup of that group and the lack of diversity around that group is the real problem. Because when your decision-making group all thinks one way, your likelihood of picking someone

who looks very different is greatly reduced. So you've got formal structures that enable the same decisions to get made." - **Anna Catalano**

Figure 22: Self-promotion self-assessment.

You know how this works now. So, assess where you currently sit against the following question and identify if you would benefit from moving up the scale, and if so, how far.

Q. As a matter of routine, do you put yourself forward for pay increases*, promotions, special projects or other benefits and opportunities?

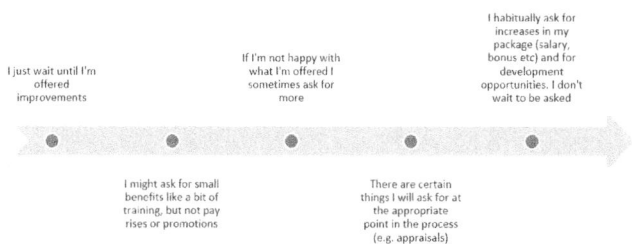

I just wait until I'm offered improvements

If I'm not happy with what I'm offered I sometimes ask for more

I habitually ask for increases in my package (salary, bonus etc) and for development opportunities. I don't wait to be asked

I might ask for small benefits like a bit of training, but not pay rises or promotions

There are certain things I will ask for at the appropriate point in the process (e.g. appraisals)

*If you really have no influence over levels of pay increase (cannot even challenge your performance rating) consider the question in relation to promotions, special projects or other benefits and opportunities.

"Men for some reason are able to de-personalise it. Women are not. It impacts who they are. For men it is work, but it is not them. That is interesting, because the flip side is that with men, when it comes to the positive things it is all about them. Whereas with women, when it comes to the positive things, they will say that they contributed. So, on the positive side men say it is all about me. On the negative side women say it is all about me. There is a huge difference in that dynamic." – Peggy Montana

Overcome any anxiety in asking for what you want, by replacing fear with facts.

We've seen that anxiety about asking for more, bigger, better or to simply be included comes from societal evidence and micro-messaging about gendered expectations, not from facts about the reality of an individual's performance, experience and attitude. These are the real determinants of what opportunities and rewards we merit. And the good news is that you have already done the work to identify and articulate all the facts to support your case powerfully, clearly and compellingly. You can use the professional values proposition template (in Chapter 14) to assemble and tailor your content for specific pitches.

Asking for a pay rise, bigger bonus or a promotion is a process you can learn, like any other.

Ruth Waring (below) illustrates the benefits of formally learn how to negotiate. And now, more than ever before, access to this type of information and independent training is incredibly easy.

"A lot of this is due to the male model that is used, which is assuming you will go in and argue your ground for more money. The onus is on you to say, 'I'm worth another five grand, give it to me.' Women do not work like that. I think it is a completely flawed expectation of businesses that they expect you to do that, or that they reward people for doing it. I am amazed that still goes on.

It is one of the areas I had to think about when I went self-employed, because you have to be able to go into an organisation and say, my rate is £XXX a day, or my rate is £YYY a day or whatever is appropriate to the work, and not expect to be lashed out of the room. You have to be able to hold your ground and negotiate. For a woman who hasn't done that before, that is quite tough. Certainly, when I was in paid employment I was guilty of just taking whatever was given to me and being quite grateful for it, not going back and saying, 'If you want me to do that job I want another £5,000.' I just didn't work like that.

I had to teach myself negotiation skills. I have always been very embarrassed about negotiating in the past, which I think is a traditional female trait. Trading with hauliers I found really embarrassing, but I had to completely get over that. I had to be prepared to overcharge people, so that if you do get battered down to a lower rate you still make enough money to survive. One of the things I challenge myself with at the moment is do I charge enough? Should I charge more than £XXX a day? It is difficult to know what you are actually worth. You need to know what you want to achieve. I want to be doing *work that I enjoy doing. I want to be getting out of bed in the morning and feeling happy.*

Me: When you say you find negotiating fees uncomfortable and you just had to get over it, what does it take to get over it?

When it is your business you know you have to do it. When it is somebody else's business, I just found that element more embarrassing. That maybe illogical. It may be about growing up and accepting that if I want to be an amazing businesswoman, I have to be able to negotiate. One of the things about business is you have to be very upfront about money and you have to mention it when it is a bit uncomfortable. You have got to say, 'By the way my day rate is X.' You have to mention it when nobody wants to mention it. I have had to really teach myself to be totally and utterly up front about how much money they are going to pay me, so I don't get in a mess with rejected invoices and things like that. I wouldn't say that there was a moment when I realised, but I think as I've got older, I've just found it easier.

Me: Would you give women a tip on that sort of area?

Go on a course. Then you are applying the techniques you have been taught, so it is not so embarrassing or difficult then. You do X, Y and Z and find that it works." – **Ruth Waring**

Starting with baby steps is better than trying giant leaps.

Starting small is the surest way to develop this into a consistently successful and comfortable practice. It's just less scary and so you're more likely to try it. Then you will experience the reality that it's easier and more effective than you thought it was going to be. You find that there are not going to be the career-stopping pushbacks you may have subconsciously anticipated. So, build up your confidence, practise your technique and create a body of evidence that proves it's OK to ask, by starting with small requests. For example, ask for half a day's external training – a small, off-budget investment in you; or ask for a piece of software to support your role; or ask to be a part of a specific team or project.

With each of your initial asks, notice what the result is, how the request was received and the truth about how difficult it actually wasn't in reality. Be very aware of what your objective was and how that compared to the outcome. Did you get what you wanted? More / less / different? Then consider what you can learn from these small, safe experiences and what they inspire you to do as the next step up.

Remember when you make these mini pitches not to start the conversation with 'I know it might be a bad time but...'. Leave the reasons 'why not' to the person making the decision. They won't be as creative as you, and they may have been waiting for you to speak up for so long that they'd almost given up hope!

Some key principles for success.

1. *Do **your** homework* so you can prove why you fit the bill for a specific role or why you merit the level of

remuneration you are asking for. Have knowledge of the external market dynamics in terms of supply and demand, rewards and related responsibilities and also understand the context and needs of the organisation and the implications for this role.

"It is absolutely preparing your case. It always is. Fail to prepare, prepare to fail basically. I would prepare my case, research the industry. I would even write to friendly headhunters and say, 'Off the record, in this industry what is the going rate?' The going rate is different from industry to industry so UK benchmarks aren't always helpful." – **Colette Dunkley**

"I think the other thing is understanding the position your boss is in. I think this is where women do go wrong sometimes on the pay thing. They go in having wound themselves up and having got stressed for weeks to ask almost apologetically if they might possibly ever conceivably have a promotion or a pay rise, but they don't quantify what they want. They don't give the boss a solution and bosses are busy. Understand the problems your boss has got and how you can make life quicker and easier for yourself and them. Go in with a piece of paper with a proposal, saying 'I have done these six things. I think I deserve a promotion. I think this promotion is worth this amount of money and I would suggest we split it this way between pay and bonus.' They will say 'Thank you very much' and you will get a much better decision. I think knowing how to promote yourself in a way that is supportive of the people above and around you is very important." – **Mandy Pooler**

2. ***Close your expectation gap and never be the first line of negotiation.*** By this I simply mean, don't be the one to decide what the organisation can or can't afford, and then adjust your pitch downwards based on the view you have formed before you've even opened your mouth. After all, if you position yourself as worth less than you are, people might assume you are worth less than they had believed. Pitch for what you wanted at the outset and prepare your case, using that imagined pushback as an objection to prepare how to overcome.

3. ***Have a clear case.*** Make sure this includes clarity on what makes you stand out (your point of difference). Remember, you don't have to do this in isolation – you can bounce your case off your sponsor, mentor, coach, respected colleagues or savvy friend.

> *"Some people might say it is arrogant to go for jobs that you don't have the skills for. One friend said to me, 'You have always had a belief in yourself and applied for jobs that most of us wouldn't have gone for. It's a step up and you know you are up against the best, and they are probably all blokes. And you haven't worked in the industry.' She is a leading divorce lawyer, but that is her view. I think she is probably right. I would go for it. I would research it first and I would really make sure I had something different to add.*
>
> *Why have I always done these things? I was brought up in Liverpool and Australia, by a Liverpudlian Dad who had to fight his way in the world. He was always a self-starter and made his way in the world by spotting job opportunities that he wasn't always 100% matched to. He'd read up about it before the*

interview, find his own angle and win the job, because he had to.

One of my three favourite quotes is Woody Allen's, '99% of all successes in life are due to just having turned up in the first place'. You have to go for things, then you can help shape things.

I read somewhere that women look for a 95% match against a job description while men look for a 65% match. So, my approach has always been, look, I'm not going to be a 100% match to this, so let's look at where I do match and then let's think about other things that I can bring to that company that may not be written in that JD. Job descriptions are general frameworks. People grow into and develop their roles bringing their own uniqueness to them. Most people bring to the party more than what's on that JD.

Explain how you match, but also highlight other things where you can add value that perhaps they haven't specified.

Of course, good negotiations need to present a win-win situation rather than Me v You." – **Colette Dunkley**

"I guess up to now I've been in a system that's reasonably formalised; once you've got your performance rating everyone within that performance rating would get a certain increase (with exceptions). I now know that there are people who have tried to negotiate a bit more. I fought for my ratings. I have said, 'I believe I'm this rating because...' I have been happy to do that." – **Maggie Stilwell**

4. ***When it's significant, be prepared to move on or turn down an offer if it's not good enough.*** There are times when it is right to have made the decision in advance that if you don't get what you are pitching for, you are prepared to move on or reject a lesser offer. This gives you greater strength and commitment in your discussions, increasing your likelihood of success. It also allows you to prepare in advance for the eventuality that you need to make another choice, enabling you to set the wheels in motion to make that happen. Clearly, if your analysis shows what the outcome should be (i.e., what you are pitching for), but it doesn't come about, and you are not provided with robust justification that you can accept, then pursuing a different course could well be the healthiest outcome for your career and you.

5. ***You are doing them a favour.*** You are giving your organisation the opportunity to keep you engaged and happy, while benefitting from your talents. Your position is, 'of course I'd rather stay, but clearly, I have to do the right thing by my career, as anyone would.' You are doing them a huge favour by letting them know, in advance, what they need to do to keep you. They don't need to try to guess, and they don't even need to do the leg work of finding out what the market rate is. What a brilliant outcome for them.

> *"I remember I was earning £18,000 a year and I was 28. I said, 'I knew my market worth was probably £8,000 to £10,000 more. I remember that after I pressed for a pay rise, they increased me to £22,000 or £23,000. I was then headhunted and left for £27,000. Then fifteen months later I returned to the previous company on £37,000. I doubled my salary in less than two years. You need to know your worth and take a level of risk.*

*Then there was becoming General Manager. I
was prepared for that, because I'd been Sales
Director and Marketing Director and had
many roles in between. But it was getting that
job that was tough. It's not that you aren't well
qualified for it, it's getting the actual offer. For
that John [the incumbent] pushed my case a lot
with Corporate.*

*He championed my cause but at one point I had
to resign. I said, 'I haven't had any reassurance,
so I'm going to go.' I was going to set up my own
business. I did a bit of a small revolt; who would
blink first. They came back and said, 'We will
guarantee you will get the job when John goes.'
They honoured that."* – **Karen Guerra**

*"I got a call from the UK CEO who said,
'Want to build another building?' I came over
for a formal interview and said that I'd be
willing to consider it, which was totally untrue
because I was desperate to do it. Then I was
sent down the way to see the HR director and
negotiate my salary and I basically held out for
an astronomical sum of money. I said, 'If you
don't want to pay me, that's fine, but if you
don't you can find somebody else.' They really
didn't have any choice, so they ended up paying
me an astronomical sum of money, which was
fabulous. Another five years of my life, another
building."* – **Sara Fox**

6.   ***Use Pareto's Principle the right way round. Don't wait
     till you can do 80% of the role before pitching for it.*** It
     is all too common that women wait till they feel they
     have 80% or more of what it takes to do the next job,

before they go for it. In comparison, men repeatedly and successfully go for it when they have more like 20% of what they perceived it takes. If you are one of these people, dare to try for the next opportunity earlier. Keep focused on the evidence of your track record, and what it says about your capability and potential, and what they mean in terms of outcome benefit to the organisation. Remember the example of Lin Philips at Shell! At worst you'll have demonstrated your interest, at best you'll get the role you deserve, and the pride and confidence to enjoy the new role and to go for it even sooner next time.

"Men go for it when they have 25% of what they need, and women wait till they're sure they have 85% – I would have done that in the past but now I believe that I've got nothing to lose.

I went for the Traffic Commissioner role too early as a way of registering my interest. I had the interview and I got it! Then I thought 'Oh my God, what do I do now?'" – **Beverley Bell**

It seems that men tend to go for things and believe in themselves more. They will go for promotion when they've got about 20% of what it takes, and women will wait until they've got about 80%. Or 110%. Then they wonder why they are passed over for being overqualified. I've seen the confident male and they don't even know how much they don't know. I've seen that many times." – **Marion Cowden**

B: Ongoing personal PR – the habit for staying on the radar

This section and the following two chapters (*Reputation* and *Stakeholder management*) are very closely related but have distinct differences that require separate consideration, assessment and the development specific plans to accrue all the possible benefits that they offer.

"Public relations (PR) is the way organisations, companies and individuals communicate with the public and media. A PR specialist communicates with the target audience directly or indirectly through media with an aim to create and maintain a positive image and create a strong relationship with the audience." (Institute of Public Relations, 2020)

Personal PR therefore aims to create and maintain a positive image and relationship with your workplace audience including gatekeepers of career opportunities. Ongoing personal PR uses salient opportunities to appropriately and positively profile the work that you do, its value and impact, with the people that matter.

You don't need to be 'in-yer-face' or aggressive about it. You can be reasonably subtle, but you must not be invisible, and you should establish these connections so key people associate you with the work you do and the outcomes it delivers. There are simple, painless ways to consistently do this, they aren't rocket science, but they make a significant difference. In many organisations things move so fast that today's news and today's stars are forgotten by tomorrow, so if you don't maintain this PR you will fall off the opportunity and decision-making radar.

By maintaining this awareness, you are doing your organisation and the stakeholders in their success, a real service. There are real and meaningful benefits to the right people in an organisation knowing who can do what; how well; what their potential is; the directions they are interested in taking in the future; and what support they might need to get there. It enables the planning and management of their human resources with greater success and less risk. Many larger organisations have dedicated departments to define their talent strategy and run their process, so they have the best chance of optimising the potential performance of the organisation. However, if the key decision-makers in this process are vague about your strengths, ambitions and potential, they will be far less able to put your name in the frame for the work that you want and merit.

To be successful at your personal PR you must be alert to awareness raising opportunities and plan how best to use them to get the right information across. Ideally, you develop ongoing habits that ensure your name is always on the radar to meet your short, medium and long-term career goals.

Figure 23: Ongoing personal PR self-assessment

This is your opportunity to identify your current situation and decide if it's where you want to be. If there is a gap, use the examples shared by my interviewees to stimulate your thinking about what you could routinely be doing to close this gap.

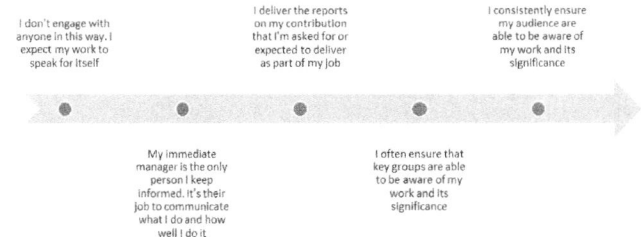

Being effective at personal PR means getting into a mindset to habitually spot and appropriately use opportunities, which will forge and maintain positive relevant associations. This keeps you on the radar for any opportunities that may emerge. Given that this is more of an indirect self-promotion approach, it can mean that they can be quite left-of-field, as they can include those that you could not have known about, targeted or predicted.

A simple but effective recommendation for subtly staying on the radar and forming positive associations with your work was made by communications expert Colette Dunkley, and this was simply to habitually put your name on documents as the author (project leader, etc). This ensures that presentation documents, case studies, proposals and any other significant communications which could be referred to independently in your absence are easily associated with and linked back to you.

> *"There is a little bit of a line to dance here. You need to make sure the right people know. The ones that ultimately can affect your career and can make the decisions to make your plans go ahead, get implemented and be successful. The right people need to know. I do not recommend blowing your own trumpet, because it is a dangerous game. We all know people who do it and they fall on their swords. But put your name on the bottom of the documents that you write and imprint it, so they know you are the authority on the subject.*

> *Importantly, you also need stakeholders to know you are part of or lead winning teams. You are a driving force for success and the teams you work in are energetic, inspiring and shine brightly.*

> *Ultimately, we all need to create a personal*

brand; even inside a company you personally have a brand. What is different about your brand? What teams and strategically significant wins are consistently associated with your brand?" – **Colette Dunkley**

We know that women tend to be more collaborative than men and will often showcase the work of their teams – which is to be applauded as a great Transformational Leadership approach – but you must also incorporate a reminder that you led that team. Valuing your role doesn't detract from the value others in the team receive for their specialist input, and the wider audience will be clear that the impact of this team was enabled by your leadership and development skills. So, with presentations of your team's work, you should introduce your role as a natural part of introducing the role of others and introduce it first, in whichever medium you are communicating about this work. I'm sure that's what you'd like your team members to do, if you were mentoring them! So, be their role model.

There are many types of work and functions or specialisms with less obvious performance measures and fewer opportunities for status updates. Lavinia Carey (below) demonstrates that if the right measures and reporting aren't in place to enable your work and its impact to be easily made visible, then you should be proactive and create what's needed for the purpose of personal PR (and stakeholder management). Don't sit there and wait for someone to come up with it – if it's your interest, you need to make it happen.

"When I was applying for the job at [name withheld] I said that I wasn't very good at blowing my own trumpet. Because the way I've been brought up is to be modest, not to be boastful or to be pushing myself forwards. It's not an attractive trait to be pushing yourself forward and trumpeting your successes. I'm a traditional

English person. I realised that if I didn't start doing a bit of trumpeting and jostling, that I was going to lose some opportunities. Sometimes when somebody is coming up behind you and overtaking you, you think, 'How has that happened?' Then you realise it's because you didn't claim the authorship or ownership of that success. Therefore, I have developed, over the time I've been here, a means of reporting that does say, 'I've done this and I've done this' because if you don't, people don't credit you with the success. Particularly because I haven't got a sales target, which speaks for itself.

When it comes to my annual review, I find myself in the uncomfortable position of having to put down on paper what I have achieved, otherwise they wouldn't know how to measure my year and my worthiness of an increase or a bonus. I have to tell them. So that is something I've had to develop." - **Lavinia Carey**

Your attitude and natural curiosity will speak volumes.

Charmaine Stewart's experience shows how important your mindset is to gain the opportunities which can make huge long-term career impact. An open, interested and can-do attitude clearly means that you will be known to be someone who can be approached with opportunities. So, your attitude is a message that constantly communicates and has a key role to play in your personal PR approach.

"I think one thing that probably got me noticed a bit more (and this is not just a UK cultural thing) was that I was very interested in doing different things. I was interested in the world

around me. Any special projects or opportunities, I was up for. I always expressed interest and tried to get involved in those things. I guess I wasn't explicitly trying to get taken notice of, but I guess you naturally do, because it is not in that traditional model. It is well received if you are interested, show some passion and some energy, delivering and proving your worth, your capability and execution side and binding those together, that does get you noticed.

Someone would come and talk to me about a special project and I would show interest. If I hadn't said yes to some of my special projects I would never be where I am today. I didn't measure myself and I didn't get rewarded through being in a box. I had an inherent desire and interest in doing interesting work. I pursued those opportunities and was able to get myself noticed through those opportunities, deliver through those opportunities. And one thing leads to another." **- Charmaine Stewart**

In addition to a generally positive, interested and open attitude, the example below provided by Sara Fox demonstrates that it can really pay off if you sow the seeds of interest by stating what you'd like to do if the opportunity ever comes up, so that if it does, your name will be first on the list of potential candidates.

"I'd been there about a year and there was a call to arms. Periodically there would be a firm wide notice and in this particular instance it was to say that our Australian practice had just picked up a load of new clients and they were looking for additional consultants. I went along to the practice manager and said I'd like to put my name down for Australia. He

said, 'Now Sara you don't understand. These transfers are for professional staff'. Technically researchers were not professional staff, using McKinsey's terminology. It wasn't meant to imply that I wasn't professional. I said, 'That may be, but if they need lots more consultants, then they probably need lots more research assistants as well. He said he didn't think so. I asked him to send a telex. Just to get me to shut up he agreed to send a telex. About three or four days later he called me into his office and said, 'it's as I thought, they have a researcher. They are very happy with him. They really just need professional staff.' Two months later he called me into his office and said, 'Are you still interested in going to Australia?' I said, 'Yeah, but what has changed?' [...the incumbent researcher had been sacked]. – **Sara Fox**

So, there are a wide range of ways to create and maintain a positive image and understanding of what you do for the organisation and its stakeholders. And it's clear that they can be both subtle and really effective in making the connection to significant new opportunities which could be pivotal to the rest of your career, as these examples have shown.

Making it happen:

Which of these approaches do you think would be valuable for you?

Is there anything else that you need or want to do to develop and maintain your professional profile?

Chapter 20

Define and consistently deliver against your ideal professional reputation

Your reputation is what people *believe* they know about you. It refers to how people describe you in your absence, and it can be important in opening doors that are beyond your reach. Equally it can inhibit your progress if your professional reputation hasn't reached the right ears, or it has but not about the right things or in the right light.

The bottom line is that with many opportunities, your reputation will reach decision-makers and influencers before you do. This applies to many internal roles, and clearly the whole field of true head-hunting is driven by reputation and recommendations. So, you will never know the impact of a reputation which isn't what it could be (in reach or content), because you'll never know which opportunities you could have been offered or connected with if you'd focused more on building your best possible reputation.

Your reputation can be thought of as a tweet-length summary description that is used by others to describe you as a professional individual. As such, it's subject to the distortions of a chain of third-party representations, biased assumptions, and skewed views of you due to limited direct experience of you. Ensuring that you manage your reputation successfully, so that people carry and communicate an image that reflects best on you, requires two key things:

- Being clear on the few critical professional characteristics that you want people to hold in mind when they think of you.
- Your consistent delivery of those characteristics in all aspects of your working life including publicly and professionally accessible social media.

Some people refer to your professional reputation as your 'brand' – a distillation of what you stand for and what values you represent. That may be a useful strategic approach to managing your reputation although some people find that too contrived and leaning too far towards creating something that could be inauthentic and rigid.

A professional reputation can cover a range of characteristics: capability, attitude, behaviour, values, commitment, results, qualifications, experience, network, ethics and so on. Different fields of work will value and prioritise different characteristics. So, it makes sense to understand what these are and to know how you stack up against them. You don't have to be a clone of what you see in people doing work that you aspire to do. You can – and should – be the person you respect and do it your way. Apart from anything else, it's hard to project and sustain an image that isn't authentic.

> *"Any system has a human element, so whoever is sitting on the interview panel exerts a lot of influence. The higher up you go; they have made their mind up long before. The higher up you are, without a doubt, it is not about how you perform on the day. It is about a whole range of soundings and assessments that have gone on in the run up to that. I do think at the more junior level it is about competency, because you haven't built up a reputation and people don't know you so well. It is those highly sought-after posts at the very top.*
>
> *I think you have to maintain your integrity as a female, and I have always done that. I have always tried to maintain my personal reputation. That has been one of my drivers throughout my whole career; my personal reputation, how do others really see me.*

It is very important in all its guises. It precedes you. Wherever you are going, they will have done their research and know about you. Before I came here, they had all Googled me and spoken to ex colleagues. They had all done their research. They even knew my children's names. They knew all about me before I even stepped in the door. They want a boss they can be proud of; someone who is going to represent them as a group and represent the organisation and fight for them. They want somebody with credibility. They don't want somebody whose reputation is tarnished in any way.

Dad said to me very early on, 'Keep yourself to yourself.' You should always be aware of how you are perceived by others. It is very true. That advice has stood me in good stead. You have to define how you want others to see you. It doesn't happen by accident. I always wanted people to see me as being a very honest individual, who worked incredibly hard and achieved results. Those three things have been my mantra. The other one is people having trust and confidence in me. If they like me it is even better; but they don't always have to like me. I have long got over that.

With the police, externally I would make sure I knew all the key community members, politicians and any of the key government individuals that I needed to know. I built myself an external reputation, which has held me in good stead." – **Sharon Kerr**

Figure 24: Professional reputation self-assessment

Given the question below, where do you currently see yourself, and how does that compare with where you want to be?

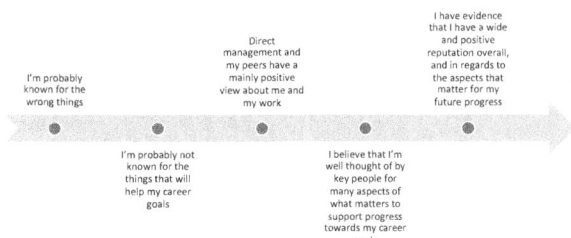

Be clear on what you want to be known for and why. Keep it simple.

Your reputation is, more often than not, a reflection of your core professional values and standards. These are things you believe are fundamentally important, so even when you are under significant pressure you will still act and behave according to these principles.

The women I interviewed consistently spoke of one to four characteristics that they felt strongly they wanted to be, and were, known for. These had helped them secure the positions and opportunities they aspired to.

> *"I worry about my reputation. I don't care if people don't like me, but I really care if people don't respect me. If people don't like me that's fine, but if they don't respect my work, I'd lose sleep over that."* –
> **Morag Blazey**

363

"I do what I say I am going to do. 'Please can I have this factory closed down by December 1st?' That is all you have to say to me, and I'll just get on and do it. I have always been hot on delivery. They know I mean what I say." - **Barbara Harris**

"I came with the real credibility of somebody who knows the business, who had been through mergers before, had done sales and understood marketing." - **Sara Lewis**

"I would always stand up to be counted, and I would always say if we had got it wrong or if I had got it wrong, and I'm doing X, Y and Z to resolve it – which is definitely how I built my relationships with the retailers. I'd built my credibility on being somebody who could be trusted." - **Gill Adams**

"I have never actually applied for a job. I got headhunted into publishing. Somebody knew of me and had recommended me for a role.

Yes, I think I am lucky to have built up a good reputation in this industry. Certainly in one sector of this industry. That has helped me in getting all the jobs. Knowing the connections between people has helped me, and my reputation has helped me progress my career.

There was quite a lot of PR about me. I had done PR before on the trade magazines, so people know who I am. But when I was made redundant from Crone Corkill they ran a piece on it in the paper. 'Big shot made redundant' type of thing.

Me: And then the phone rings?

Yes, it did actually." - **Sally Wells**

How are you actually known now?

Your reputation is based on the perception of others, which is something which is not easy to control, but you have significant influence over it. Once you've defined what you want to be known for, you need to understand what the difference is between where you want to be and where you are now. Then determine the scale of the task, and where to focus your efforts. It's easier to assess how you are perceived in organisations which include 180° or 360° feedback in their appraisals, but harder in other organisations, and harder still, yet possible, beyond the walls of your organisation.

Research has shown that women in the workplace receive less feedback than men, so this means that you may have to construct situations that enable people to feel comfortable talking about how you are perceived. In reality, this only requires a few select conversations with key people. Having this type of conversation can have wider long-term benefits, as it creates a stronger connection, develops the agenda about your aspirations, and shows that feedback you receive will be positively received and acted upon.

> *"There is a fine line for women between being a bitch and a bimbo. I discovered that, especially in the male dominated industry that I was in. You must really walk a wire. Because if you fight every single battle you get the reputation of being someone that nobody gets along with. You have to balance that out with being walked all over."* - **Anna Catalano**

External perspectives depend on your reach beyond your organisation. If your remit does extend externally, you may be known within professional bodies and networks or recruitment organisations. Informally picking up on topics of common interest with key individuals ('just wanted to give you a call to get your view on…') creates an opportunity to get a feel for how you may have been seen (if at all) and gives you an opportunity to start building the relationship and guiding it down the best path.

> *"People say I'm terrifying sometimes, and I hate that. I don't know if it's a new job title that suddenly*

makes you become this being that has to be obeyed, and no longer an interesting, engaging person. That is not who I want to be. Being respected is more important to me than being liked, but I would never want to have a negative impact on anyone or be unapproachable.

You have to be careful about perception becoming reality. People see me as a strong person with definite and strong opinions. Sometimes I'm refining my thinking as I'm talking, but because I tend to talk in definite language people think I've made my mind up. So I've learned over the years not to stifle input from my team by putting my views out there too early in a conversation. I found that hard at first, as I get passionate about things, but I learn so much from my team. I think sometimes it is just an aura you inadvertently give off, because I definitely don't know everything, and I do worry more internally than people realise." – Claire Walters

If you find out that your reputation is not what you want it to be, there are options to guide others' understanding of you, towards creating a more accurate and appropriate version. Before you develop a plan to address anything that you perceive to be problematic, just pause for a moment and check:

- Is this belief about you really a problem? It may just have been communicated in terms you wouldn't choose, but are still representative of something that is actually positive and valuable.
- Does it really matter? If you have the sort of reputation described by Claire about being tough, is it really an issue or something that could be a professional benefit, despite it sitting slightly uncomfortably at a personal level?
- Can you really do anything about it? There may be characteristics ('feisty', 'bossy', 'too serious') that are not what you want, but may be hard or impossible – or perhaps

wrong – to address. Don't waste your efforts and energy trying to correct a perception that's not in your control. It's worth working on making sure that other characteristics also come to mind when someone describes you, 'she's quite feisty, but she always delivers, and clients are loyal to her'.

"It is so easy to typify women into being mouthy or emotional or strong willed and feisty. Why is it wrong to be feisty and driven? 'She is a feisty, driven woman. There must be something wrong with her.'

I had a reputation for people fearing me. There is obviously the odd experience that has been shared as to why people might be scared of me. I do think that working on your reputation and thinking how you want to be portrayed is important. Those little moments of losing temper or losing calmness, you always look back on them and wish that you hadn't. It is good to learn from those. Even wanting to burst into tears, which is something that I had been tempted to do years ago. The only way I felt I could deal with the emotion was to burst into tears. That is another thing that is a reputational risk.

But you can't get to know 400 people personally. The people who I work with closely know that I am a very warm person, but I can definitely be seen as cold and hard, I'm sure." - **Dana Skelley**

Some dos and don'ts

1.   Do start as you mean to go on.

First impressions last. When you start in a new role or organisation, try to ensure you know what impact you want to make. Create your own guidelines to help you show that, so you establish the best first impression from which you will build an ongoing and consistent reputation.

2.   Maintain high professional standards – regardless of those around you.

Workplace standards are getting more and more relaxed (just think of how dress codes have changed), but this should never be confused with standards of professionalism. You should determine what you think is the right standard for you. If others are late for meetings, you don't have to be; if responses to communications vary in standards of presentation and timeliness, yours don't have to. However, if you find your standards are being dragged down, it might be an indication that the organisation you are with – or the part you are currently in – is not the right one for you, as their values don't match yours.

3.   Do correct misconceptions when you can and if you need to.

"In court people call me 'love' rather than Ma'am or Commissioner which can be down to nerves and I put them straight. But when someone called me 'love' to put me down on day

2 of being in the role, I came down on them like a ton of bricks. I showed them who was the boss. It flew round the industry.

Strong women have very negative stereotypes though strong men have very positive stereotypes – but it doesn't bother me." - **Beverley Bell**

4. Do avoid workplace relationships.

When I worked for the Mars organisation, they had a simple and clear rule that everyone was made aware of from the outset, and that was that if you had a relationship with a colleague, the more senior of the two had to leave the business – no ifs or buts – that person had to leave. That sort of clarity was helpful, fair and defended people from unwanted attention from more senior and more powerful colleagues. Obviously that sort of organisational stance is rare, and most leave it up to individuals to work it out.

There are a range of difficulties with having relationships, both during the relationship and afterwards (if it doesn't work out). However, the longer-term issues are harder to tackle because those are the issues related to your reputation. I suspect that the normal societal unfairness operates around men being seen as heroes for playing the field, with women being viewed in demeaning and derogatory terms.

"I absolutely don't recommend dating somebody in the office if you are on a career ladder. Firstly, it can hack off all the other people. Secondly, I think colleagues take you less seriously as a rational, objective person and see you through a more personal and emotional lens. Of course, we need a balance and to bring our whole self

> *to work but we are there to work and need to prioritise the success of our organisation. The perception you portray should be one that prioritises the business.*" – **Colette Dunkley**

> "*Don't poke the payroll – never use sexuality or have a relationship at work.*" – **Rebecca Salt**

5.   Don't 'let your hair down' too far, or too often.

Depending on the type of work you are in there may be fewer or more opportunities to have fun with colleagues. It is certainly fine – and often important – to socialise (see Chapter 22: *Build your social capital*) and have a bit of fun when you are on the way up, but you must make sure that this doesn't conflict with the profile of the role or roles you want to be considered for in future.

Take a leaf out of the most fundamental rule of interacting with the media – nothing is off the record. Nothing you get up to with colleagues is disconnected from work, despite any agreements along the lines of 'what goes on tour stays on tour'. You should exercise restraint and be careful when you let your hair down, as reputations – particularly women's – are lost more easily and quickly than they are won.

My best advice is just don't get drunk in a professional setting – co-workers may feel like friends when you are out, however, these are professional relationships first. And if you do get a bit tipsy or just relaxed and matey, don't over-share i.e., talk about things or opinions that are best to remain private.

> "*If you step out of line even a tiny bit as a woman, you will get talked about. I've always advised my teams to be very careful at the Christmas party i.e., have one drink and then we will all go somewhere else as a team. Stories*

abound about people who ruined their careers at corporate events by getting drunk in the wrong environment with the wrong people. I have seen people get sacked as a result of what has happened or been said at Christmas parties. They were not at work the next day or ever again." - **Colette Dunkley**

6.   Don't 'dis' people

A fact we learn as children, usually to our cost, is that the best way to spread information is to say 'don't tell anyone, but...' And it's not just children who love to share secrets or juicy gossip. So be very guarded if you are considering being less than objective about someone in your organisation or connected to your organisation. Be aware that many people are connected, so if you unfairly criticise or undermine someone, it may well get back to them and with consequences for you.

Making it happen:

What have you identified as your immediate priorities to develop or extend your professional reputation?

What else is important to you?

Chapter 21

Proactively manage the stakeholders in your success

Stakeholders in your career are the people who do or could benefit from the work you do now, and the work you could do in future. Stakeholders include people who actually benefit and those that perceive they do or could. While this group will include peers and more junior colleagues, the key ones in the context of having your best career are people in roles that connect to other areas or functions adjacent to, or beyond, your immediate area or even organisation.

There is compelling evidence that shows that careers progress more rapidly when people actively manage their stakeholders. These individuals or groups are vital as they can both open and close doors.

> *"I was aware of stakeholders, as in those who needed to be aware of the value I could add and who needed to have a good opinion of me in order for me to be considered worthy of sitting at a table or being part of a peer group. I think it's almost like getting something through the board. If you are going into that board meeting without having prepared your stakeholder support, then you are going to fail.*
>
> *I suppose I did work on my stakeholders to enable me to get signed up as head of supply chain, because*

if I had just worked in isolation it would never have happened." – **Gill Adams**

Through stakeholders understanding the value of the benefits you deliver, and what it is about you that is significant to them, you stand to gain recognition, support and access to new opportunities. You can think of stakeholders as gatekeepers to a range of opportunities, as they can link your talents and potential to other things they perceive could benefit from your involvement. Things such as in specific projects, leading initiatives, taking on a specific role, managing specific clients or sectors or geographies and so on.

However, like all of us, stakeholders will have plenty on their plate, and if you don't raise your profile and develop your professional relationship with them, you are missing the positive, but potentially fleeting, opportunities they have the access to and influence on.

"Everybody wants something. Find out what it is and connect your desire to theirs." – **Sharon Kerr**

Stakeholder management is closely connected to and intersects with *personal PR* (Chapter 19) and *professional reputation* (Chapter 20). However, stakeholder management is a more highly targeted and specific activity. Stakeholders and their success have a direct connection with the work you are doing (or should be doing). This allows you to develop, directly control and drive a targeted strategy to support your current career ambitions. These people may be unaware of the link you share or the value of your role, and how well you deliver it (relative to others), and until they do, neither of you will have the opportunity to really maximise how that connection benefits both of you. Beyond that, stakeholders can also have a significant role in enhancing and extending your professional reputation and represent an important source of formal or informal mentoring and / or championship (sponsor) support.

The rebranding of BP was one of the highest profile in corporate history, and it was led by one of my interviewees, Anna Catalano, who had established a strong, trusting relationship with a critical stakeholder, the CEO, John Browne. He was clearly aware of her strengths and awarded her with this enormous role.

"I got to know the CEO John Browne. We started talking about the rebranding of the company. He decided he needed a head of marketing. He had never had a head of marketing in BP before. So I was moved into the marketing job after a very short time in the other job. That's when we rebranded the company."
- Anna Catalano

The concept of working on relationships at a different level to delivering the day-job may feel all rather Machiavellian and uncomfortably deliberate. But given the vast array of articles, books and training courses on stakeholder management, you can be very comfortable with this as an everyday practice, and even core to a number of roles. Obviously, the choice is yours and it needs to be compatible with your values. There are clear benefits to opting in, and opportunity costs to opting out. Now you can be clear what they are, so your decision will be an informed one.

"You may need to do something extra and personal to build relationships with people. I've approached people in the lift (and been approached by others) to say, 'There's something I really want to talk about with you. I know you're really busy. Can I talk it through over lunch with you?' This would just be in the canteen with the people I needed to know.

I do think you have to build relationships. People like people. The emotional side of our brain says we need to spend time with people we know and like and the rational yet informal environment frames it in the right context.

You need to make sure the right people know about your skills, passions and drive. The people who can affect your career, involve you in key projects or help you succeed." **- Colette Dunkley**

"You've got to manage and network upwards.

I think it is a huge mistake that women make.

They think being good at your job is enough. It is a fraction of what you need to do.

I've seen a lot of very confident women, who have a lot of self-belief that they are very competent, but don't understand the 'political' side of it.

They just think they will get noticed because they do a 'good job'. They're totally results focused. They make fantastic employees, because they'll meet the objectives, achieve the numbers, but a lot of them don't understand that is actually not what it's all about." - **Karen Guerra**

"I had an experience with an Asian lady that I mentor a couple of months ago. They had set up a different framework in the business when they went to work globally and virtually. Even though she had responsibility and accountability for a certain piece, and it was global, they said, 'We want the Americas people to speak to the Americas people, we want the Europeans to talk to the Europeans.' She followed the rules; she followed exactly what they had told her. She was responsible for the work, but she let the interaction in the US be with the American representative. She got 'killed' for it, because they didn't see her, and they didn't know her impact and influence, all they saw was the spokesperson who was 'making all of this happen'. So, we started talking about what had happened. I said, 'Why did you do that?' She said: 'I was told that was how the organisation was supposed to work.'

Me: Is that a culturally Asian approach?

Yes. That is the rule. I told her to stop doing it because that was what got her into the mess. Her boss was seeing the delivery, so he was happy, but her stakeholders were only seeing the other person and not seeing that she was the actual person delivering. Therefore, when it came to rating time she got killed by the other stakeholders. It mattered because they owned the business. We sat down and I told her to stop following that rule and tell me what it was she was going to do to be able to be in front of the stakeholders on a regular basis, so they knew she was the one who was driving that delivery." – **Peggy Montana**

Figure 25: Stakeholder development self-assessment

This assessment has two parts to support you in narrowing down where you might need to focus your efforts. Carry out the usual process of identifying where you are now and where you need to be. However, it's important to note that you have to achieve your goal in question A (mapping your key stakeholders) before you can reap the benefits of doing well in question B (engaging with them for your mutual benefit).

Q. A. Do you have clarity on the key people (inside and outside your organisation) that can influence your career success?

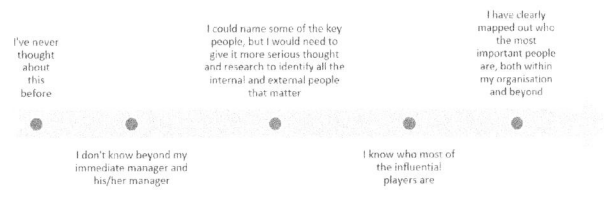

Q. B. To what extent are you engaging with these key people – the stakeholders and gatekeepers of your success?

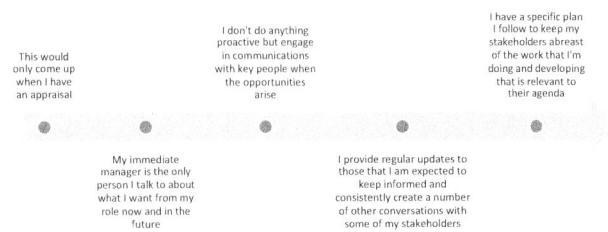

A 6-step approach to stakeholder strategy development.

Stakeholder Mapping is a strategic approach that enables you to articulate who your stakeholders are; it helps you identify the intersect of their interests and yours; and it provides the framework for you to plan how and when you will engage them, and with what goal.

The following simple 6-step process takes you through the steps of mapping stakeholders by type of goal, prioritising them within an action planning matrix, and stimulating thinking about your approach to communicating with priority stakeholders.

Table 4: Stakeholder relationships, goals and benefits

Goal Type	Stakeholders (individual/ group)	The intersect between what you do and what they need	The specific benefits they could bring to you
Job Role Stakeholders			
Career Stakeholders			
Other Key Area Stakeholders			

1.   **Identify and differentiate your job role, career and other stakeholders.**

Stakeholders can be within your organisation or beyond it. The first step in identifying and organising them for your planning purposes is to focus on your main goals – whether you are looking at short-term successes in your day-to-day role or looking beyond for access to career opportunities. Hence, I make the distinction between Job Role Stakeholders and Career Stakeholders and, depending on your specific field, there may be other goals that are also important, so I have given you a third category, 'Other Key Area'. Clearly these will include some of the same people, however, you will have different agendas with them depending on which of these goals you are considering, thus they have separate strategic areas for your planning purposes.

2.   **Identify what your stake is in their success – the intersect (connection) you share.**

Initially it can seem quite obscure when you try to work out what your real or perceived stake is, or could be, in their success. So here are a couple of questions to prompt your thinking and help you to identify where this or these intersects might be:

- What would happen if you didn't do what you do [that connects with them]?
- What impact would it have on them if you did it better / more, or if you did it worse / less?

3. Articulate the ways in which your stakeholders could benefit you.

Try to articulate what this individual or group could do to your benefit. This might be anything from sharing information and providing advice, to more active endorsement and championship of your ambitions. This is where you will need to consider their role, its connections and level of influence and sphere of decision-making. It's important because stakeholder support is more successful and more easily given when they are clear on what support is required of them, on what basis and to what benefit(s).

4. Plot your stakeholders on the action planning matrix.

Use the matrix below to prioritise your stakeholders using the dimensions on the axes, namely their level of influence, and their level (or potential level) of vested interest in the benefits you bring through the success (or otherwise) of your role. Once you have done this you will see that there are indicated actions against each quadrant of the matrix, and you should consider this as the basis of your strategic stakeholder plan.

Figure 26. Stakeholder Mapping and Strategic
Planning Matrix

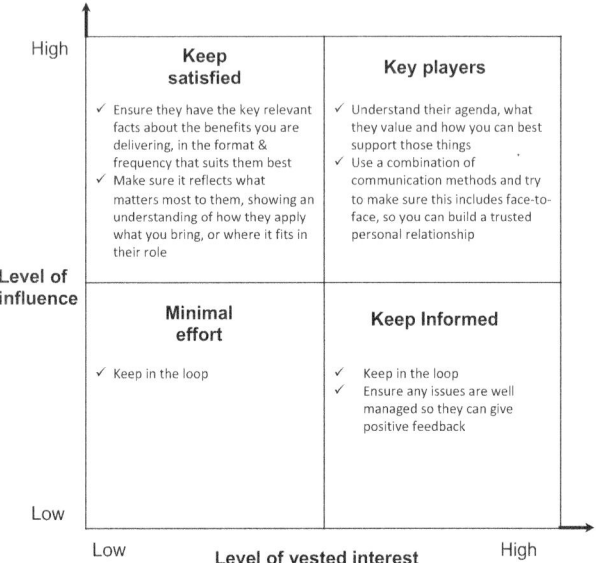

> *"There are certain people you need to get and keep on your side. Then there are other people you know you are never going to win over but you try not to upset them too much."* – Sara Fox

5.   Communicate.

Today it's very easy to be distant and impersonal when we communicate, but taking the time and trouble to have closer conversations will result in a stronger, more personal, more positive and trusting connection. Talking in person is better than a video call, which is better than a phone call, which is better than a WhatsApp or text message, which is better than an email, which is better than a LinkedIn comment, which is better than a LinkedIn 'like', which is better than a tweet!

Don't take the easy route. Take the personal one.

It may seem scary or inappropriate to approach people you aren't used to working with, but people very quickly open up when given the opportunity to talk about what matters to them and interests them, and how you can support them in their success. Starting from this point feels a lot more comfortable for many women and brings better results according to some of the most successful business networkers.

> "How do I engage with this odd person who isn't like me, who I have some kind of business connection with? Did you watch the match last night doesn't come naturally as an icebreaker. Actually, we probably have to take a bit more risk in trying to create some of those and get over our imaginary barrier of thinking, 'Why would they want to have a business relationship with me? Am I necessary to their success?' I do think we probably put this barrier up where we think, 'They have this relationship with all the other men, so what would my role be?'
>
> What do great relationships look like? They look like trust and candour. They look like shared interests. All very professional, but great relationships are important for good and fast decision-making, great alignment and resolution of differences.
>
> The other top tip is probably your point about relationships. It is about really identifying the

people who are in a position to respect, admire and support you and so work really hard on those relationships. We [women] are never going to have the team factor; I can't have a great relationship with everybody in my football team. We have to pick the striker, pick the central defender and have a great relationship with them. They are the pivotal players on the team. That is a really hard thing to do because it requires women to be quite calculating and generally we are not." – **Sarah Lewis**

When positive relationships have been developed, your objective is to gently, subtly or directly ask for the support or advice to make progress in their realm of influence. Benefits are likely to have accrued along the way just by virtue of actively cultivating the relationship, however, with certain goals, you need to open up the topic and ask. You have created the best possible conditions, so you are likely to be pushing on an open door.

6. Review.

Create the opportunity to stand back and evaluate what you have been doing, who with and how it has been going. Ask yourself if you are achieving what you had hoped for. What benefits have you accrued since you started implementing your plan? Then assess which people and approaches have been the most effective and update your plan in the light of these insights.

Making it happen:

What has been your biggest learning in this section on stakeholders in your career?

What's the significance of these insights to your future (short, medium and long term)?

Chapter 22
Build your social capital

'Capital', in the world of finance and business, refers to assets of significant value. Personal capital includes things like significant savings in stocks and shares and the portion of the value of your house or flat which you actually own (i.e., that has no mortgage against it) i.e., the money you can convert from bricks and mortar to cash should you need it. You build capital through wise investment. That means careful research perhaps to find the right property; or to find the right funds to invest in. It works on the principle that you invest now for a bigger payback later.

Social capital refers to relationships of significant value that you have invested in and built up over time. These are relationships that you can call on if you need to, as social capital is characterised by a tendency for people to support each other. The 'social' shows that this relationship is not primarily built in a work environment. It develops by spending time with people informally building a relationship, finding common ground (with work as the first common denominator) and gradually building bonds of trust and friendship. The term 'social capital' emphasises not just informality, but a wide variety of quite specific benefits that flow from the trust, reciprocity, information sharing and cooperation associated with social networks, but most importantly, a sense of mutual obligation and support.

> *"It's where the King-making gets done. Where trust, confidence and relationships develop."* –
> **Sharon Kerr**

At home you may build social capital with neighbours through taking time for conversations and taking interest in what they are doing and what's happening in their lives. Then when you go away on holiday, they'll say 'yes' to a request to put out your bin, water your plants or feed the cat, just as you'll say 'yes' when they ask for your help, and you'll be prepared to make a concerted effort to make sure you do what you said you would do for them.

At work you build social capital through investment of time with colleagues from any levels or functions, with clients, suppliers and so on. Social capital is typically built at the pub, wine bar, coffee shop, at the game (football, rugby, golf, etc and watching or playing), industry events, customer entertaining, around off-site training, conferences and so forth.

> "Social capital is vital. It is not after hours; it is part of the job. I'm afraid you have to think about it as part of the job and organise your home life around it. I think it is the only way around the boys' club. I actually think on a personal level you miss out if you don't go to the pub for a drink. You don't have to do it every night, but you do have to do it sufficiently to be in the gossip, in the know and are seen to be friendly. With clients, particularly, the only way to really build a relationship with a client is out of hours. You have to do it. Some of the great highlights of my life have been at sporting events. Women have this bizarre thing about, why would I want to go to football? Just try it would be my advice. It is something that you can learn to love and enjoy. Some of the highlights of my career have been at those events.
>
> I have always thought, maybe because advertising is such a socially driven business, it is the best way to build relationships with clients. The sad thing is because of the economy, at the moment people can't afford to do it anymore. You find you have much more remote relationships with people because of

it. Even if the clients weren't there, I have enjoyed the sporting events so much. Don't knock it, suck it and see. Don't whine about the golf, go and organise something yourself that you want to do. Don't just knock the social thing and say you can't do it because you are a working mum. You won't get on if you don't do it.

Me: What difference do you think it made in terms of getting on?

I think people get to know you better. I think people get to trust you more and vice versa. All business is about relationships. It is very difficult to really get to know somebody if you only ever see them in an office. It is as simple as that." **- Mandy Pooler**

"It thus appears [from research] that social capital can be even more essential to managers' advancement than skilful performance of traditional managerial tasks." **(A. H. Eagly, L. Carli, 2007)**

Leadership psychologists Alice Eagly and Linda Carli (cited above), are referring to research showing evidence that people can get more tangible benefits from building these sorts of relationships in this way than doing a great job, and certainly, it's easy to bump into anecdotal evidence supporting it. In this high-speed world where decisions about who to involve in tasks, teams, projects, promotions and new roles are made with little time for reflection, there is no sign of this becoming less significant.

"I've had people say, 'Have you considered Joe Bloggs for that job? He's quite good.' The two of them had met somewhere and got on well. You can see those kinds of things happening. Often it is based on quite short exposure to these people they are recommending, not that they have seen two years' solid good work. You often find out they haven't got much real experience of this person at all." **- Anon Interviewee**

So, social capital is the wealth of relationships you can call on, or that simply pays back, that's created through social interactions. The more social capital you build the greater the opportunities you are connected with, and the more support that you will be given both directly and in your absence, i.e., being spoken about or recommended when relevant situations occur. The return on the social capital you build can be experienced even decades later.

An informal environment is critical for creating social capital outside of the office, as the organisational hierarchy breaks down. The CEO happily talks football with Jacinda, the junior in accounts. They can have a laugh, taking the mickey out of each other's football teams, thus forming an enduring bond. When the CEO is then in a situation when he (based on the majority of situations) needs a certain financial report, for example, he will pick up the phone and call Jacinda. The CEO could have called any number of people, but he knows Jacinda. He feels he trusts her and sees her as the equivalent of a 'good bloke'. Jacinda now has a direct line to the board and visibility she would never have had if she hadn't been able to chat with the CEO informally, over a drink after work.

In the social environment, information flows informally. Football blends into talking about the latest political shenanigans, families, pastimes, politics, projects, clients, people and so on. You'll find out about stuff you would never have known except by stumbling across it in casual conversation.

> "I think it is something you should try and do. I think to isolate yourself is missing out on that knowledge. You don't have to behave in an inappropriate way. All throughout my career I have belonged to all sorts of groups and I have never been highbrowed about joining my male colleagues. I think it is overegged a bit about this football. Yes they touch upon that, but when they get females within the group (certainly with the groups I have mixed with) the conversations are inclusive. Tonight, I am supposed to be meeting a whole range of ex colleagues and they have taken the trouble to ring me up. You become part of the

group instead of an observer. Sometimes I call them up to have a meet. You don't have to be subservient; you can actually call on the social. You don't have to be the one who gets the invite. I think it is useful." – Sharon Kerr

Figure 27: Social capital self-assessment

Identify where you are now and where you feel you would like to be ideally, given your aspirations.

Q: Are you actively building social capital in your work-life sphere, including with the stakeholders and gatekeepers of your success?

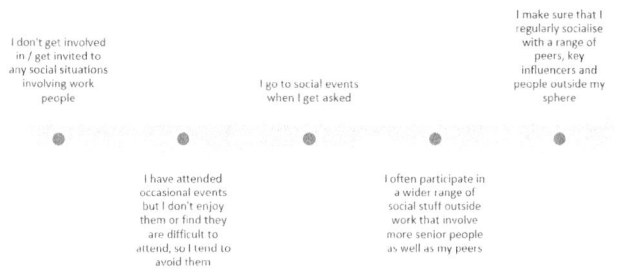

I don't get involved in / get invited to any social situations involving work people

I go to social events when I get asked

I make sure that I regularly socialise with a range of peers, key influencers and people outside my sphere

I have attended occasional events but I don't enjoy them or find they are difficult to attend, so I tend to avoid them

I often participate in a wider range of social stuff outside work that involve more senior people as well as my peers

Be strategic & creative, because it's harder for women to access traditional opportunities to build social capital.

Building social capital is another key differentiator in the success men currently enjoy compared to equally well-qualified women. Conscious planning is needed to get involved in social situations that seems effortless for guys, or to create even better alternatives.

> *"I have found in many countries throughout the world, eating together, or drinking coffee is extremely important. This where all the bonding and socialising happens.*
>
> *Taking time out to chat about politics, about the world, about the rugby match, about fashion and what was going on. It is really important to take time out of work life and learn about other people's lives. The French and the Turks are particularly good at getting this balance just right."* - **Lin Phillips**

There are four things which make building social capital difficult for women that can be successfully navigated, if you find they are relevant to you.

1. Women often don't get asked to regular social events or ad hoc occasions. There are assumptions about women not being interested in certain types of activities (football, rugby, beer, certain types of night club) but often, it's just that women aren't front of mind when opportunities for such things pop up.
2. Women are often put off by the social situations in prospect, just as the guys assumed. The prospect of standing up for hours in a beery-bar or freezing in the football stands just doesn't appeal to many women.
3. For the women that are mothers, who are yet to establish the necessary shared-parenting strategy with their partner, it is often simply not possible to nip to the wine bar after work or to go to a football match at the weekend.
4. Many men struggle to open up a conversation with

women, due to either lacking the social skills or making assumptions about what women talk about. It's easier and more comfortable to avoid the risk of such a challenge. They forget that, as work colleagues, there are loads of work-related conversation openers that can get the ball rolling. However, as Gary Ford, leader of many male allies programmes and one of the authors of *The Accidental Sexist* (G. Ford, 2020), pointed out to me, many men struggle for conversation beyond football with anyone.

> *"Be strategic about it, that was what I was taught. Who do I actually need to build that relationship with? That may be why women have to prove that they are better, because how else do you get noticed? They work very hard at the job and at being very good at what they do, so that they can get recognition in that respect. Because you don't get the chance to go off and play rugby. You don't have people saying 'of course you can do that because you're a good chap.'"* – Gill Adams

Getting in on the work social scene.

There are a range of ways to address the issue of not being included in the socialising that happens in and around your organisation, but be reassured that once you get involved, you'll just become part of the fabric of these often ad hoc social groups and occasions.

The two main strategies appear to be **to just sharpen your elbows and push your way in**, as Fiona Hagdrup describes below. Much like kids in the playground, you just have to make the assumption that you're part of the group, and they will assume the same thing once they look round and spot you. Alternatively, or additionally, you can **create your own social capital building opportunities** as Sara Fox and Collette Dunkley describe. The latter has the advantage of being closer to the type of social situation you'd prefer.

"You've got to do it. I hate it, but you've got to do it.

Me: Do you have any particular approach to it?

I was in a very lucky position when I was at Swiss Re, which was that as the project director I could define the social circumstances within which most of it happened." **- Sara Fox**

Clearly the first step is to find out what currently goes on, and when. Then you can work out how you can get involved – do you really have to be invited or can you invite yourself – 'are you guys going over the road after work today' – or just pitch up (do they really go around inviting each other, or do they just have a habit or routine which they follow?).

"Men would rather be in a bar just chatting. They like that, so it's not a stretch for them like it is for us. It is kind of dull. I'll do it because it's important and it's easy enough to muscle in. It might mean that you need to use a bit of a back door route to get in. These things are quite cyclical, once you are on a list you tend to get invited again." **- Fiona Hagdrup**

Get creative if you really don't like the sort of places that social capital is built.

Most of us have experienced the fact that at certain stages of your career it pays to participate in things that aren't fun but are a means to an end. At least with building social capital you have choices about what you do or don't participate in, and now you can make those choices with greater knowledge of the costs and benefits to your career.

"I've often been the only woman but I'm pretty confident so I can handle it. Women can give as good as they get these days.

The worst thing you can do is back out. You choose to exclude yourself and that will have an impact." - **Jane Walton**

It is worth challenging your assumptions of what you do or don't like doing, as you may just find you're wrong. Often, it's really not so bad once you get involved – it seems worse from the outside. As Sharon Kerr recommended – give it a go, to find out what it's really like, before you make up your mind. Also, as Claire Walters shows, it's absolutely fine and appropriate to have boundaries that you won't cross.

"I do enjoy things like dinners, awards, football matches and rugby matches, so I have never felt like I've endured social events. People do sometimes get a bit out of hand, but you learn to deal with that by talking robustly, pushing back and setting boundaries. Looking back, I wonder if I should have done more on some occasions to set people straight, as the only woman at an event – to make it easier for those who came next. You try to find the right balance, but don't always feel like you get it right." - **Claire Walters**

"I have a problem with all of that because I'm not interested in soccer. I do know a lot more about rugby because my family know about it. I go racing, which I've found is something you can talk about, but I've only come to that later on. I don't play golf. I prefer things like the opera and ballet, which not everybody likes doing. So that is difficult.

Me: Is that important?

I think it is sadly. But I can talk a bit of the talk. Only because I've learnt to. But I'm not comfortable with it. I would never dream of inviting somebody to a rugby match. I might accept an invitation.

The partner at A and O, who had two children, is a sailor, which is sort of genderless, and she did a lot of

*her socialising, as far as I could see, in that way. That
was a good point of contact. It helps to have something
other than children to talk about."* – **Claire Maurice**

You have to plan ahead, to be able to develop social capital when you've got childcare commitments.

In *To have your best career you have to address your home front strategically* (Chapter 15) we looked at how important it is to negotiate terms at home to ensure that you have the flexibility to respond to last minute(ish) work requirements as well as opportunities to socialise or network with colleagues and other key people in your work-life. You and your partner (or childcare provider) need to be clear on the way it will work for you, either on a regular or ad hoc basis, whereby you can change domestic arrangements late in the day to respond to needs or opportunities, but without stitching-up your other half. This could be to enable evening socialising immediately after work or longer commitments at weekends for such things as football, rugby, sailing, the theatre or golf.

And if you are a single parent you have to move up to another level of advanced childcare planning to participate in work-related social activities. Or do something like I did as a management consultant, and create a brief, after-work, single-drink routine that takes place on the same day of the week or month. It meant I could plan the cover I needed, and so could other people. And the single drink on Friday at the close of business concept meant that most people could justify, and look forward to, that brief time to unwind before heading home and starting the weekend.

In both sets of circumstances, it helps to have thought through and identified who it's important to build social capital with, so that you are able to make decisions based on what represent higher priority opportunities, i.e., to be able to say, 'if Fred, Ginger and Rogers and Hammerstein are going to be there, then I want to be able to go'. You can use the information you built up in your Stakeholder Development Plan to help identify which groups of people or individuals it would be advantageous (and perhaps interesting and fun) to build social capital with.

> *"I have been quite lucky in that I have been quite social with my work colleagues all the way through my career, and I have been able to go for a drink after work, given the setup I have got. I have been able to say, 'I won't be home until 8.30 tonight.' I would usually work until that time, so I might go to the pub instead of working and I would be home at the same time as usual. I do think that helps in terms of people realising I am a person the same as them, not this strange woman. I can talk about the same things as them. The football thing is great because I am a season ticket holder to Fulham football club with my son.*
>
> *I do think it can be very difficult. A lot of women don't want to go to the pub with the blokes and they do have to rush off home. I do think that is a disadvantage.*
>
> *Now I don't socialise. I have been here for nine years. A lot of my peers are still here and they already know me from socialising in the past. I think they feel it is perfectly understandable and reasonable that I'm not down at the pub with them all of the time. I think it is important, and I have been lucky in that regard."* – **Dana Skelley**

Diversity delivers a big payback in social capital too.

Although your stakeholder group is a good core group to prioritise, it's better to try to extend your thinking more widely to create a more diverse spread. Research on this topic from University of Chicago Booth School of Business confirms the importance of a diverse network: "*Indeed, it might not be who or what you know that creates advantage, but rather more simply, who you become by dint of how you hang out. **The disadvantaged hang out with folks just like themselves, while the advantaged engage folks of diverse opinion and practice.***"

Building social capital is different to stakeholder development and personal promotion in that you are not marketing yourself – here you are simply building relationships, and the topic of work need not crop up at all. These relationships have a very different basis with no direct or immediate goal. In fact, if you go in with a blatant agenda, you will defeat the object of building mutual trust and support.

Building social capital is not like a networking event either. Just pitch up and try to enjoy yourself and exercise an interest in people. People love to talk about themselves when they get the chance and, as trust develops, within an informal environment they'll talk more about topics you may never normally get to hear about.

Try to remember key information people share – family names, interests, adventures, clients, projects, so that next time you can ask again, and this reinforces that you're interested in them and what they do and so the bond will deepen. If you are genuinely interested, you'll find this a lot easier!

Managing socially inept men.

I have witnessed first-hand, many times, the agonies of otherwise eloquent men who seem to have no idea how to talk to a female colleague in the absence of a focus on a specific work task. Like some cartoon character with a string of thought bubbles, I've seen a rapid set of options of opening statements whizzing through their minds, questioning whether they're appropriate and dismissing them, leaving them blank, and at a complete loss. They seem to think they have to speak to you about an entirely different set of topics to those they'd use with male colleagues.

In fairness, the same challenge can come up for many people if you ask them to initiate a conversation with a person that they perceive to be from a completely different sphere of life or work. A person in middle management may be at a complete loss to start a conversation with a board director; an accountant might worry about how on earth to talk to an engineer (and vice versa!).

"I still think this is the most difficult area for women to crack. The main reasons: one is the time issue we have just talked about [finding time given family commitments], secondly it is actually quite difficult to know how to behave in that environment, and thirdly – and I feel a bit bad about saying this because it kind of puts the blame onto blokes, there are very few men in senior positions who have friendships with women other than their wives. They have lots of mates who they have known for years. They play squash with them and they have known them from college or university. Therefore, when they are out on business they know how to behave because they are with their mates.

If you put a woman in the mix they don't know how to treat you, because they have no experience of that. Usually, if they are out socially, they are mixing with other men's wives, their wives' friends and they have a place for them. I just see an enormous amount of social ineptitude when you put a woman in the mix, which means it is incredibly hard. If you get to the point where they find it comfortable to have you there, you have fallen into that very interesting box that is called 'one of the boys'. Being 'one of the boys' is either an unsustainable position to be in or actually it is a bit derogatory. I still haven't, and I don't know of any senior female leader who has, cracked that little conundrum. I do think that that semi social environment is still an important place where very important decisions about people and their future get formed. I don't know what the answer is. I think if you were to say, 'What is the one thing that is going to stop women being successful?' I would probably have that pretty much at the heart of the issue." – **Sara Lewis**

Many of the women I interviewed talked about the barriers that exist when sport isn't considered to be a common denominator, which creates a sort of social exclusion as guys talk over you or round you. Unfortunately, it's down to you to find a way to break in and help these guys to include you and to discover other topics that are also good to talk about. However, sometimes it is a case of if you can't beat them, you have to join them.

"I have no problems talking about sport. My knowledge is superficial, but I know all the right words to use in the right order." – **Lin Phillips**

"I've had a Queens Park Rangers season ticket since 1986. My football capital is right up there. I think this was really helpful for me. It is tragic. People pretend they are an Aston Villa fan because they think they have to. Men pretend it too because they think it gives them some social currency.

I'll be invited to football jollies. I've been invited to the World Cup, and it will be me amongst the blokes. It was something to talk to me about. They could put me on their jolly list. The other men there would have something to talk to me about. They would be worried that if they couldn't talk to me about football I would resort to periods and makeup. So that was always a source of great relief to people." – **Morag Blazey**

Some social capital building watch-outs.

Being of the 'opposite' sex and generally in the minority on these occasions, it means that there are a number of things that need to be factored into your decision-making and behaviour for the best (and safest) outcome:

- Try to avoid one-on-one socialising in the evening – it's too easy for people to get the wrong impression (the other person, other colleagues, other person's partner). So, keep one-to-one situations during the day and try to avoid significant activities – 'grab a coffee' rather than go for a fancy lunch.
- Don't get drunk and make an arse of yourself – the guys may do it, but it'll be your reputation that gets, and stays, tarnished.
- Be careful not to see these social situations as another environment for finding a partner. Yes, many relationships do start at work but don't treat this as an opportunity to find Mr or Ms Right.
- Avoid flirtatious behaviour and avoid dressing in a way that makes people see you in a different light (a sexual one). That'll be the way they see you when you get back to work and that would be intensely counter-productive.
- If someone makes a pass or starts to chat you up, take immediate action to stop it. Walk away, change the subject or help them out of the hole they've fallen in by making out that you thought they were trying to be funny. Then try to avoid a situation where that might occur again – don't be left drinking or talking one-on-one, stick with a group. It's incredibly hard to deal with in the moment, but it's critical to nip it in the bud and act decisively so it's clear that their behaviour is not welcome and will be fruitless.

Chapter 23
Network with integrity

Networking works. Networkers' careers benefit compared to those who don't. If you chose not to engage in networking, it probably will cost you opportunities – both in terms of access to new and different roles as well as new and interesting insights and perspectives. This chapter may alter your perceptions about networking and give you the incentive and courage to dare to try it if it's something you've avoided in the past.

This chapter is called *Network with integrity*, because it's a different take on networking. A way that works better for everyone and which is far more acceptable and even appealing to many women. And if you are already a networker, this chapter will present you with ideas on how to expand the ways you do it to increase the range of benefits you'll get from it.

> *"I have a very good friend who is 45, she has just had twins, and she has seven non exec directorships. Two or three of which are governmental, and the rest are PLC. She has got those all through her network. Headhunters do the interviewing but it is all academic. It is because she has been recommended for the job. I thought it was enough to have the headhunting network, but I was wrong. You need the business network."* **- Karen Guerra**

Your career's roots and wings: support networks and professional development networks.

In this chapter I will show you the importance of two different types of network. Firstly, a *support network* – a small number of people, which is likely to predominantly be other women, who can understand the challenges you face and offer both practical and emotional support to get you through some of the lows and the frustrations you encounter. These are the roots that will keep you strong, fed and grounded when storms may be raging around you. And secondly, *professional development networks* – contacts and connections inside and outside your organisation which could support your development, by opening up your mind to new perspectives, and your career to new and different professional opportunities. This is the networking that gives you wings to take you to places that you couldn't otherwise access.

Bear these realities in mind, when you wonder what the point of summoning up the effort is:

- 70% of roles never get advertised. This percentage gets higher the more senior the role.
- It's your way to access roles, organisations and job locations you'll never encounter otherwise.
- You limit opportunities if you limit who knows you, the stuff you work on, and what interests and drives you.

You can't buy a product if it's not on the shelf.

Any product has to be within customers' sight and reach, if it's to have a chance of being sold. The same goes for accessing career opportunities – they are out there, but if you are not in sight or within reach of those who can connect you to them then they'll get connected to someone else. So, networking is an essential strategy for putting yourself 'out there'. 'Out there' can mean a variety of different environments which vary along the 'scary-scale'. You can review your options and choose where to get involved, depending on how you feel, how practised and or comfortable you are, and how much freedom you have to participate.

"I spent a year after this merger, eventually becoming very unhappy in the environment. The firm tried to accommodate me by having me report to an accounting consultancy partner who was working from one of the other offices, but it wasn't going to work. I was sufficiently well connected in Auckland, where I was then living, through my involvement with the professional association, so I knew other partners around town. I started talking to the other firms about changing jobs. I was in dialogue with two other firms about possibly going to work for them. Then I had my doubts, thinking, 'Why are these going to be any different?' At that point I was in conversation in Wellington with a colleague from my audit days. I said I was looking for a job and even considering moving to Wellington. He said that the Department of Labour was looking for an Internal Auditor. He'd been on the panel and they hadn't found anyone. He said I'd be perfect. That is how I came to make the next move. So again, timing, opportunity, networking.

[at another stage in her career] I wasn't actively on the market. I had coffee with a friend. While we were in the café, she ran into a friend of hers who is a recruiter for Korn Ferry, the international recruiting firm. I was introduced and gave her my card. She said, 'I'm looking for a Chief Financial Officer.' And so that is how that one came about.

I tend to see networking as much more about putting together two people that should be talking to each other. It is not about me. It is about if I am talking to you and you mention that you are looking for something and I can say, 'You should talk to...' That is what networking is. If I am going to invest time with someone, I actually want to do it because I enjoy their company, not because of what I can get out of it. There have obviously been, in my own case, useful by-products, because I have been in the right place where someone has spoken to me and introduced me to someone and that has led to something happening.

When I do stop and think about networking, it is networks that have made the difference in a number of places." **– Marion Cowden**

Networking covers the vast range of activities (no longer just the old-established 'working' of crowded rooms), which enable you to build a range of contacts that you would not normally encounter during your working day. Men have known the importance of networking and used it successfully for centuries or even millennia, hence we have the cliché, 'it's not what you know, it's who you know', and the power of the Old Boys' Club.

A considered or just open approach to networking can enable you to discover and access new career areas (sectors, levels, geographies, organisations) and new job opportunities (with competitors, with customers, with partners, with suppliers, with new organisations). It can also provide a fast track back into work should redundancy strike, and help you explore and secure the best options when returning to work after a period of extended childcare.

"I've become a bit tired with it and it feels a bit manipulative. I'm no stranger to that of course. It might be an age thing. I've lost interest in it, yet I know I need to do it. It will go in bursts. I'll go for ages not going anywhere or doing anything, and then a wave of desperate, ingratiating behaviour in order to restore relationships that I've let wither a little bit. I was much better at it before and cared a lot more about it before. Now I'm in a lot of danger of letting it wither for too long. It's crucial, it's important. These are the people you will draw upon to help you professionally when you least expect it."
– Fiona Hagdrup

However, just the word 'networking' can send cold chills down the back of many women. Many dread the prospect as they envisage walking into a room full of strangers and trying to force their way into a conversation in order to try and get something out of it. Despite the perception that women would be natural networkers, it appears to go against their logic and integrity around what it *should* take to get on. Many women see networking as artificial and contrived (which it clearly often is) but also somehow dishonest, using relationships for personal and / or business gain. So, recognising and respecting that viewpoint, this chapter presents approaches that work with women's integrity and still deliver the benefits.

> *"Women are good at networking in depth with a few people. They are not good at wide and shallow. They are good at narrow and deep.*
>
> *I see some old school friends from 40 years ago. We walk in and start up a conversation and away we go.*
>
> *Women are not like that. They want a much closer relationship. That is what I think. It is better networking. It is higher quality networking."* - Simon Hughes

Sort out your roots – invest time in nurturing a support network.

Having a great idea turned down...An incomprehensible decision that goes against your work, your team or just you...Management seeming to be behaving like Muppets...Every door you push at appearing to be stuck shut...Something that's important to you has gone wrong because you couldn't get the resources you needed...

There are times when you just want to talk with someone who understands what you are experiencing, or who can see things from your point of view, given that they are likely to have faced similar situations. These are times when it's great to have access to someone who can shore you up when you are feeling under pressure or even undermined. They can help to reset your self-belief, boost your resilience, and keep you sane by helping you work through, or providing a different perspective on challenges and frustrations. It's important to have sources of support who can understand your work challenges in a way that family and friends just can't.

These people are your support network, and they can make all the difference to your ability or will to keep going when you feel your back is against the wall, or when you want to celebrate or acknowledge 'wins' the significance of which others would struggle to understand, or when you just need a confidante.

> *"I have a significant number of strong female friends. I can go to these women with problems and share them and they can give balanced, unbiased advice in complete confidence. They are people whose judgement I respect."* – **Beverley Bell**

It's the same for men and women, but if you are one of only a few women, or the only woman in your area of work, it's likely that you will face challenges and issues that male colleagues won't experience. Hence, they will find it harder to see or understand, and may find it harder to provide appropriate support or advice. This means that you'll benefit from nurturing a few professional relationships with people who can 'get' what you face and what you do. They needn't be in the same organisation, sector or even country, but they do need to be people who you respect.

These days it's hard not to fall over women's professional networks – networks for specific companies, professions, levels, locations and interests. The majority are well facilitated and thoughtfully managed, cognisant of new attendees' feelings when joining. Many are easily accessible in terms of physical and online location and in terms of their timings (family friendly). The wholesale move to online events during the pandemic has shifted the game for women, as the networking culture of this environment is far better in many ways, making it much more comfortable and easier to take the first steps to meet people and then get to know them. So, you have choices, and the prospect of better network cultures.

Nevertheless, don't discount your male colleagues as sources of support. You probably have many more of them to choose from. Seeking advice or a different perspective on a problem is a great way to create new bonds and enter their inner circle.

Figure 28: Informal professional support network self-assessment

Use the question and scale below to identify where you are now and where you would ideally like to be, to inform your priorities and planning.

Q. To what extent have you developed informal supportive relationships within the workplace that you can call on with work-related challenges?

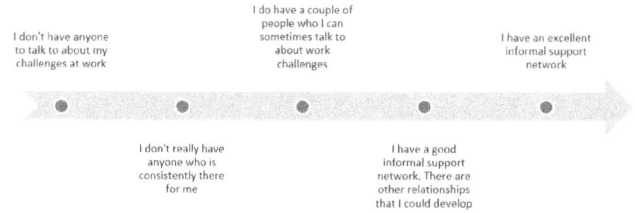

I don't have anyone to talk to about my challenges at work

I do have a couple of people who I can sometimes talk to about work challenges

I have an excellent informal support network

I don't really have anyone who is consistently there for me

I have a good informal support network. There are other relationships that I could develop

It's prudent to think about your support network consciously and strategically and to nurture these valuable relationships. 'Nurture' is the key word. These are important relationships, and they must be mutual relationships of support and respect, where you are there to reciprocate with time and attention for the other person when they need it.

You should dedicate time to such people. This doesn't need to be often, or even face-to-face, but it does need to be thoughtful and centred on them, as this is a real 'do unto others' situation – you can't expect support back that you wouldn't genuinely and readily wish to give.

Perhaps you know who these significant people are in your working life, but maybe you need to stop and think about who is or has been there, and who you are there for. When you know who these people are, you can take greater care of the relationship. If you find you are without this supportive network, then it may be time to think about gently developing one.

These relationships require the greatest integrity. They need to be trusting, confidential and without agendas, unlike other networking or stakeholder relationships.

The higher you climb or the more specialised you become, you'll find fewer and less frequent opportunities to build these relationships, and yet, they are probably more important in these circumstances than ever. So, it makes sense to nurture and maintain the special connections you make as your career progresses, so that if you need to pick up the phone or share a glass of wine to explore a challenge or just feel better by talking about it, you have the option to do so.

> *"We have a group of women partners who meet. I did find it important to have a group of women who I liked and respected in my network at work. I do find that that has been a big thing for me in helping me feel at home and comfortable with getting to this level. I can look at them and see they are doing things in a way that I really respect.*
>
> *One thing we haven't talked about here is loneliness. I wonder if this is more of a female sensation than a*

male one. It can be very lonely leading. Work hours can make for a lot of loneliness. It is something I have maybe only become aware of more recently. If you are leading all day at work and you are coming back late on the train, it is dark, then you come back to the house and your children are in bed, your husband is still working, that can be a very lonely day.

Me: As a leader you can't be mates any more with other people.

No. That is a challenge for me sometimes.

Me: What does it mean? And what do you need?

You need good friends and habits which re-energise you, which you actively seek out and commit to as if they were as important as eating and sleeping.

Me: At work?

At work is better in the sense of being able to understand the particular work issues that you might be dealing with. But you need good friends out of work too." - **Maggie Stilwell**

Making it happen:

What steps could you or should you take to enhance your informal professional support network?

Professional development networking.

I call this type of network and networking 'professional development networking' because it's not just about the career opportunities that you can stumble across in conversation with new people or old contacts. It's also about the opportunity to develop your knowledge, your insights and the range of perspectives you have, along with the arguments and counterarguments, around different professional topics, political topics and many others. Hearing new viewpoints, new anecdotes and news about what is happening in, around and beyond your profession is really powerful; interesting information that you simply won't encounter if you restrict yourself to your internal work environment.

> *"People have made a huge amount of money writing about the fact that if you talk to people you find things out, I think they call it networking!"* – Lin Phillips

These opportunities can be hugely valuable at many levels, not least because you get to meet different and genuinely interesting people who can give you a new angle and insights, and these could even introduce you to fields of work that you never knew existed before.

> *"Networking actually helps you build who you are. I'm a huge networker. I love connecting people and I believe it grows me and it grows other people. I see no downside to it at all, introducing people to one another. I think one of the most important things about networking is building confidence.*
>
> *And if you don't start, it gets harder and harder to do it. Because everybody around you is doing it.*
>
> *Some people view networking as manipulative and political.*
>
> *As soon as the merger happened, I became a mentor to as many British women as I was to US women. A lot of British women asked me about networking and said, 'Doesn't it seem a little manipulative?' I*

don't see it that way. I see it as an opportunity to strengthen your content of what you know, because you network with people who know things better than you do, as well as meeting people who might collaborate and do things with you. Men kind of do it naturally.

I don't see much of a difference between networking and friendships. Women always have more friends because we make friends. We keep in touch with people, and we make friends. I see it as an extension of my friendships.

Me: So you go in with a philosophical point of view.

Yes. I do. I don't see it as any more than that. I am very willing to help a friend do anything. I view networking as another facet of friendships that I have. I don't see it as being political or manipulating at all. I don't know if that's a model that all women have. It is certainly one that is very important in business.

I have met some of the most brilliant people. I think the main benefit is not necessarily the contacts and the phone numbers that you get, but it actually changes your perspective on the world, in terms of opportunities that you have to work with people and to learn from people. I view it as a learning experience." – **Anna Catalano**

Figure 29: Professional development networking self-assessment

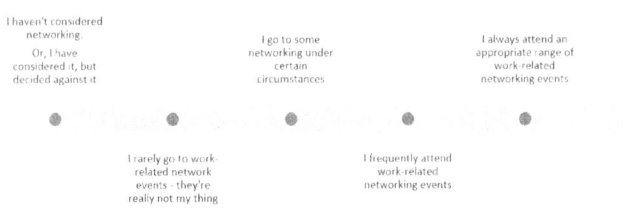

Develop a personal code of conduct: network with integrity.

What was enormously clear from my interviews was that most of these women decided that they had to do networking their way, and that meant with great integrity and sincerity. They focus on people with authentic interest, from a point of view that it's about finding out how they could be of help to them, rather than what they could get from them, which results in genuine relationships. These were the 'terms of engagement' with networking which made it valid and acceptable, and grounds on which this networking could be positively embraced.

So, this is networking from a different premise to the traditional one.

Research published in an article called *Capabilities of the Consummate Networker* (N. Anand, 2007) showed that the second most effective networking strategy is what they called '*match-making the right capability to get things done*' which is about making connections between other people for their mutual benefit. It results in great outcomes which, in turn, raise the profile of the 'match-maker', as a pivotal creator and enabler, a strategic thinker who can identify opportunities and make them happen. This is the sort of model preferred by my interviewees.

In case you were wondering, the most successful strategy, according to Anand and Conger, is what they called '*developing the king-pin capability*' which is about targeting the most influential (but not necessarily the most obvious or senior) person in relation to one's areas of interest.

> "*I have made a personal decision about networks. They are very important in my business as your network of potential work referrers (who you know in the lawyer market and corporate market who can refer work to Ernst and Young).*
>
> *I made an early decision that there was no point in my trying to keep up networks with people that I didn't enjoy being with. I figured out that if I don't enjoy being with them, they sure as hell don't enjoy being with me either. So are they likely to give me any work or be in a relationship that is positive in my life for any other reason? Probably not. I am afraid I try and cultivate true friendships and relationships, because I have got on well with someone rather than working-the-room for its own sake.*
>
> *Me: Do you think you bring in less business as a result?*
>
> *I'm not sure whether I would bring in more business if I had a different approach. Possibly, but at what cost? The risk is it wouldn't give me what I need in terms of thinking about my own life and the quality of what I am doing daily.*
>
> *It became very clear to me that I did have to demonstrate that I had a network and that I had people that would give work to me. Therefore I had to find a way that I was comfortable with.*

Otherwise, it is too draining and tiring to keep doing things that don't gel with you in some way." - **Maggie Stilwell**

"I am crap at networking. At the end of the day in the UK a lot of opportunities come down to who you know rather than what you know. I do have a network, but it is a network of friends and valued, trusted work colleagues who I admire for whatever reason. I admire their business acumen, I admire their achievements, and I like them as friends. I cannot bear to network with people that I don't like." - Sara Fox

"I've never been particularly good at networking, unless I can see how it could grow the business. I think I have relied a lot on reputation.

I got invited recently to sit on a round table. It was inconvenient from a diary perspective, but I thought I needed to broaden my thinking and who I interact with. It was really good. It's great to meet people with similar challenges who talk about the hard stuff in a safe environment.

I did a Senior Executive course at a business school, and we have an annual reunion with people from all round the world. I find that so valuable as we all know and trust each other from spending four intense weeks together. We talk about our challenges and new roles, and we give each other lots of advice. It's fantastic to know that whatever we expand into I know someone I can call who works in that market or industry.

From a business perspective networking through dinners, drinks, breakfasts etc is how a lot of business gets done at a senior level. From a personal perspective, when I want to make the next move in my career it's easier if you know a lot of people." –
Claire Walters

You can choose the type of networking that you are most comfortable with.

There is a massive range of ways to engage in professional networking, so the following list is just a sample and a few minutes of online research will reveal a range of opportunities that will fit with your career needs and interests, geographical location and availability.

- Industry or professional events
- Women's professional networks (by sector, specialism, location, organisation)
- Interest group networking events (either within your organisation or profession or beyond)
- Conferences
- Training courses (within or beyond your organisation)
- Keeping up with people you meet through your working life (college alumni, former colleagues, customers, clients, suppliers)
- Social media. There are many social media networks and groups within them that provide quite astonishing access to people, information and opportunities. However, be thoughtful about communications where there are blurred lines between your professional and your personal networking. And be thoughtful about what you express, and how you express it, given this footprint lasts a long time, as many politicians have found to their cost. Once you've

established a good virtual connection, move it towards something real by picking up with them directly – not just via DM (Direct Message) but by having a Zoom, phone or in person meeting.

> *"I can remember the first time walking into a conference. There were hundreds of people in there (or it seemed like that) who all knew each other, and I was the only female, apart from the women pouring out the coffee. The only reason I have got over that is because I now know so many people. I remember thinking, 'Who shall I go up to and talk because no one is going to come up and talk to me. Shall I pick a nice friendly looking old bloke or a really good looking one?'*
>
> *I have overcome that because I have built up those networks now. It didn't take too long to build them, but it does take a bit of hard graft initially."* **– Dana Skelley**

Domestic responsibility restrictions on your extracurricular activities mean you have to be highly selective.

If you are going to have to be selective, then you need to be strategic in developing and nurturing your network. You should start by specifying what outcome(s) you really want from networking. This will enable you to identify the sort of networks that could deliver against that objective, and then you can narrow it down to the absolute priorities.

> *"I was very, very selective. I should have done more, but family becomes a priority.*
>
> *I think this is very important and a lot of women are not very good at it. Because it comes to a point*

when you've got a family, that is all private time that you've got to use. Men are very good at it; they just don't come home. My husband was rubbish at it too because he always used to come home to be with the family.

The ones that are good at it, go to that drinks function, they go to that dinner; they do all of that in private time." - **Karen Guerra**

Some tactical tips.

- Take the plunge – it can even be fun after the initial acclimatisation, and many networking events are now so well structured to make it easy, enjoyable, informative and productive.
- Have an objective before you go to an event. You have chosen to go there for a reason.
- Be curious. Try to find something interesting in everyone you talk to (this will encourage you to listen well, and to ask good open questions to find out more about them).
- Always find something to ask of a person, based on what they have said – it shows genuine interest and creates rapport.
- Always keep your mind and your ears open.
- At face-to-face events it's normal, and expected, to move on from one conversation or group to other people, so don't stick to one person or group for the whole event. If you are unsure how to engineer a departure, listen to what others say to enable them to politely move on.
- Try and maintain relationships even when life seems quite overwhelming – even if it's just an occasional phone or Zoom call.
- Collect and organise the contact information you gain, so that you retain information that matters about those individuals. Include thoughts on where you could be of

reciprocal value. Identify when you should connect with them again and put it in your calendar.

If you still just can't face networking.

That's fine. You've read through the options and the opportunities, and if it's still not for you then you are now fully aware of the implications. The good news is that you are making a positive and informed choice and in doing so you are actively in control of your career and the balance with your non-work life. You know what you are doing and why you are doing it.

Choosing not to do something is often as powerful and important as choosing to do something. It means that the pressure that has been lurking there in the back of your mind to do something that didn't sit comfortably for some reason, is now off. You've made the decision so you can now relax and enjoy your time the way it works best for you.

Chapter 24

Get a mentor to navigate your role. Get a senior sponsor to get on

Catalysts' analysis of their longitudinal research project involving over 4,000 male and female MBA graduates (from top providers worldwide) over more than ten years, factoring in industry type, career experience, education, aspirations and whether they were a parent, showed the following:

- Women were paid an average $4,600 per annum less for their first role after MBA graduation.
- Women had lower-level management roles than their male counterparts.
- Women had lower levels of career satisfaction.
- Yet more women than men had mentors.

Subsequent in-depth interviews of a subset of this sample (who were engaged in mentoring programmes) and a further stage of the broader study (Catalyst, 2010) were used to drill down further to identify what was happening. There were three critical findings:

1. Women were receiving a more passive feedback and advice style of mentoring while men were receiving a more active, championing style in which the mentor used their influence to advocate (i.e., publicly support, recommend and promote) for their mentee. In other words, they act as their sponsor.

2. Women's mentors were more junior than men's and therefore had less power and less influence.
3. Men received 15% more promotions (but the same number of lateral moves) confirming that their supporters had more traction in the organisation.

The message of this large-scale research is clear – mentors are helpful, but sponsors are better for accelerating career progression and accruing the financial benefits that go with it.

Likewise, my interviewees were in no doubt about the value and impact on their careers of having a sponsor or mentor (or, in a couple of cases, an executive coach instead). They spoke of a range of tangible and material benefits which accelerated their progression in just the way that the Catalyst research analysis demonstrates.

However, my research has made it clear that there are several other benefits which arguably have more fundamental and more far-reaching impact across women's careers, as they have a profound and lasting impact on their inner momentum – their self-belief, self-esteem and self-confidence.

Firstly, a sponsor or mentor can be a vital and rare source of objective and respected insight into your true levels of capability and potential. In Parts 3 and 4 I've demonstrated why it so difficult for women to recognise and value their strengths and the extent of the impact this can have on limiting career fulfilment. To have a source of accurate feedback which you believe is a phenomenal asset, as you will read in the following interview excerpts.

Secondly, a sponsor will push you into situations in which you have to use this capability and stretch up into your potential zone. This means that you do the things that you doubt you can do and that, left to your own devices, you might pursue much later, if at all. The evidence shows that when women stretch up to these opportunities they succeed. They deliver. They thrive. Just as their sponsor knew they would. But the step-changing benefit is the evidence that individual women get from doing what they thought they couldn't. They get a massive boost to their confidence – their real, inner confidence. And this creates a virtuous cycle, as once they've experienced successfully stretching up to something scary and making it work, the next step up looks far less scary and often positively exciting and worth embracing.

So, the impact of a mentor's insights and a sponsor's demonstrable belief, as well as clear and constructive feedback, and putting you in a position to do and deliver more than you thought you could, can be truly pivotal, with an impact that can last a lifetime.

> *"At Saatchi the person who hired me was a guy called Ray Burden. When I was leaving I remember doing a leaving speech and saying at the end (it is theatre, and it was like my Oscar speech), 'This is for Ray who hired me and believed in me and every day told me I was bigger and better than I thought I could be.' And because he did, I was. I always carried that with me when I had people who were looking up to me as their leader. Most people, and I do believe this, are capable of being as big as you tell them they can be. If you tell them they can be giants, I genuinely believe that most people can come up to that. I carry that always with me. That was how he made me feel, that I could do anything, even though I didn't feel it inside. I guess you don't want to let someone down who believes in you, but there is also that sense that maybe you can do it."* - **Miriam Jordan-Keane**

> *"I worked with Mike for 10-15 years. He was extraordinarily supportive and empathetic and caring. A very remarkable leader. The clichéd way of describing Mike would be that he was in touch with his feminine side. I don't like that phrase, because I think that implies a certain amount of cliché about what constitutes feminine. I just think Mike was a remarkably good leader.*
>
> *I have never met a man with a higher emotional intelligence than Mike.*

The really extraordinary thing Mike did for me was when I went to tell him I was pregnant. At that point I was the number two in the media operation. He said to me, 'You will come back won't you, because we want you to run it when you come back.' It was the biggest vote of confidence – though slightly scary – you could have as a woman going off on maternity leave.

He convinced me that I had all the skills to have a big career. He encouraged me. This sounds terribly Freudian, but in the same way that my father had said I could do anything, Mike would say I could do anything.

I think he did it in two ways. He was a very honest critic. When you didn't do something well, he would be the first to tell you. That gave him enormous credibility because it meant you could believe him when he told you that something was good. He didn't unilaterally praise. I've sat in some very tough meetings with him where he tore to shreds what I was doing. But what he did do, when he said you'd done something well, he would tell you why. He had very good analytical skills. He was very good at deconstructing something and saying, 'This was good because…This could have been better if…' He made it very real in terms of promotion, reward, opportunity, tangible evidence of giving you the next step. In that sense you had the evidence." – **Mandy Pooler**

The irony is that, as ever, there are challenges for women in securing either formal or informal sponsors or mentors, as men tend to be drawn to supporting men and women often struggle to ask for help. Additionally, the three key characteristics of a potent mentor or sponsor are that they are mature, secure and senior, which is a rare combination in many working environments where egos and personal power and profile so often get in the way. This just means that finding one and securing one takes focused effort, but the paybacks are worth every ounce of effort.

> *"I kept getting more money. He kept promoting me. He would be supportive verbally. He made sure my profile was raised. He made sure I was involved in his management meetings. Even though I started off as a fairly lowly positioned individual, he included me in all the business discussions. It worked fine and they started to trust me and believe in me."* -
> **Barbara Harris**

> *"A sponsor needs to be senior. A sponsor is your champion. Someone who gets how good you are, and at what, and is clear on where that talent should go and what it should do. They will put you forward for stuff and fight to ensure you get it rather than someone else. They'll push you to do things that may be scary because they know you can do it.*

> *So, a senior sponsor will secure you critical opportunities you wouldn't otherwise get, and will build your confidence faster than you could, by putting you in situations you might shy away from. You'll find you can do it and will grow.*

> *They do help with your confidence. Quite often you don't realise how good you are until you change job. You forget how good you are. Having a mentor, whether it is overt or just somebody you talk to or who you respect professionally, just helps you order your thoughts. Quite often you muddle through things, without taking the time to talk problems through. A mentor is there, listening, and they might have some good ideas. There are people who I will have lunch with every six months who are the equivalent of mentors. You learn a lot of interesting things. I enjoy their time. There is this guy at the top of a radio network, who now has a portfolio*

and works in a private equity firm. He works in the radio industry and I've done a lot of consulting in the radio industry, that's how I know him. He gives you confidence somehow. The way he talks about stuff. He makes you think you can do it. Men love talking about themselves and how they do things, so you learn a bit from them. I've certainly learnt from having meetings with people like him. If you can do this in an unstructured way, just tapping into people is really helpful, rather than tying yourself into one person as your mentor. You can learn from lots of different people who do things in different ways. People love giving advice. I do. I love it if somebody comes to me and asks me what I think." **- Morag Blazey**

Figure 30: Sponsorship and mentoring self-assessment

Read the following question and consider which status on the scale below most accurately describes your current situation. Given the benefits described in this chapter, do you want to change that status to a different level on the scale, and if so, to which level?

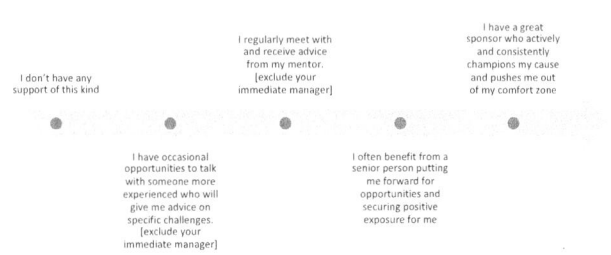

Decide whether a mentor or a sponsor is better for your current aspirations.

And while the actual title is unimportant, you do need to understand what is meant by mentor and sponsor, in order to know what to look for or specify, to secure the right support given your current needs and ambitions.

The term 'mentor' comes from Greek mythology. The story is that Odysseus (King of Ithaca) entrusted his house and the education of his son and heir, Telemachus, to his friend, Mentor. *"Tell him all you know,"* Odysseus said. A little-known fact in this story is that Mentor was not a man at all, she was actually Athena (goddess of wisdom, courage, inspiration, civilisation, law and justice, strategic war, mathematics, strength, strategy, the arts, crafts, and skill) who disguised herself as Mentor to provide this guidance and advice to Telemachus.

In modern parlance, 'mentor' means someone who imparts wisdom to, and shares knowledge with, a less experienced person. A mentor is someone who can show you how the things you need to do are done, because they've done them before (or seen them done successfully before), so they are sharing this knowledge to enable you to understand how things work and therefore what you could or should do. A mentor is a guide who gives feedback in the context of what works and how to do better. They can assess your capability and advise you on your personal potential in an objective way, in relation to the organisation and your technical or professional specialism. A mentor is a translator of the organisation's culture: *'when this is said or done, it actually means that, and so this is what approach or response is really required.'* So, a mentor has a valuable role in enabling you to read the signs around you to equip you to successfully navigate the organisation's culture. It's important to understand that in its pure sense, a mentor is not someone who is there to open doors for you, fight your corner or represent you. So, a mentor can only get you so far. Hence, in formal mentoring situations it's really important to be clear on the mentor's expectations of their role to work out if they will be able to deliver what you really need.

And there is an additional watch-out that has emerged from my latest research (Parkes, *The Credibility Crunch. Sat Nav to Success Research Report*, 2020). Organisations are increasingly seeing the importance of mentoring and individuals are also pushing for them as a core component of their professional development. Hence mentoring programmes are now available in many organisations. The problem is that managers and leaders who are expected to put themselves forward as mentors are often ill-equipped to do so. They lack training in what mentoring is and how to deliver the role successfully. The result is that a significant proportion of male and female mentees are reporting no benefit. A mentor who doesn't understand their role can be more of a liability than an asset, so seek to establish whether a mentor put forward to support you has the will and the skill to make a positive difference.

From my research I concluded that if women are seeking a mentor, it's better to have a male mentor. However, this was both hotly contested and vehemently supported by my interviewees. The Catalyst research I referred to at the beginning of the chapter showed that the most critical component was the seniority of the champion, but they also found that the gender of the mentor didn't make a statistically significant difference.

> *"It is critical that you have a male mentor. Not necessarily someone within the organisation. Although I would say you should have somebody internally and externally. Don't have a female mentor because then you think 'She's got where she has got, therefore I can follow in her steps.' You can go and see a female member of staff and get an overview of how they got there and pick up some tips. But you have already got the traits of a woman, what you want to understand is how the male mind works, because they are fundamentally different. That is what makes you a more rounded leader, you are able to see things from different perspectives, therefore you can anticipate where you will get support and where you will get blocks and why."* – **Sharon Kerr**

There are two reasons why I say your best option is male. Firstly, the knowledge that they can share not just the formal stuff, but also the informal culture which will usually have evolved according to male workplace norms and to which men have greatest access. They are therefore best placed to help you interpret attitudes and behaviours to enable you to engage successfully with the organisation. Secondly, and very simply, there are more men than women at senior levels, so you have a better chance of finding one who has the time for a mentee / protégée. You'll have a wide choice in terms of the areas they cover, so you are likely to get a better fit with your needs. As you will recall, one reason female leaders are perceived to pull the ladder up behind them is that they have to decline requests for support from other women, but this is simply because they're inundated by requests and can only help so many people before it affects their own ability to perform. So, while it might feel more comfortable to ask a more senior woman for support you would have more choice and a better potential result (in terms of a 'yes') if you seek out senior men for support.

However, this is all about giving you comprehensive insights and options for you to make the best choices in your circumstances. And, as with an appointment to any role, you have to look at the outcomes you want and look for evidence that the person has the potential to deliver them.

> *"I think one of the reasons you have a mentor is because you want someone to advocate for you. You want someone to show you the ropes, but you want someone to advocate for you. Based on the profile of people who are advocating, you've got to have male mentors. Because otherwise you're not going to have anyone bringing your name up in a meeting. I think that the thing you've got to be really careful about when it comes to mentors is, you actually don't want anyone to tell you how to act. You need to make that decision yourself. You want someone to tell you how things work. There is a real difference between, 'This is what you need to do' and 'This is how things get done.'"* - **Anna Catalano**

"It is someone who understands what you bring to the table and the worth of what you do and will support both you and your work within that organisation and then perhaps match opportunities for work to you. I don't think it is about exploring personal attributes in the workplace. I think this is why I don't agree with the term 'male mentors'. Maybe some people have had them, but I never have. I have never been able to sit down and have a conversation with a male that I couldn't have better with a female at work. I would sit down with a woman and say, 'I've got this problem at work. How do I solve that?'" - **Charmaine Stewart**

"The way you were treated was a function of your sponsor.

I had a male, much older boss. He supported me, promoted me and facilitated changes. He believed in me. He made sure I presented my work. I got the exposure, and he gave me a sense of self-belief. He had nothing left to prove. Unlike other men where so much comes down to what they need to get for themselves. He was genuinely altruistic. He gave me opportunities to do things (he could have done himself). He told me I could do things that terrified me, but he said I could, so I did." - **Jane Walton**

Table 5: Mentors vs sponsors (Ibarra C. A., 2010)

Mentors	Sponsors
Can sit at any level of the hierarchy.	Must be senior managers with influence.
Provide support and feedback on how to improve and other advice.	Give protégés exposure to other executives who may help their careers.
Help mentees learn to navigate corporate politics.	Make sure their people are considered for promising opportunities and challenging assignments.
Strive to increase mentees' sense of competence and self-worth.	Protect their protégés from negative publicity or damaging contact with senior executives.
Focus on mentees' personal and professional development.	Fight to get their people promoted.

Sponsors and mentors appear to do subtly different things, but this can make all the difference if you want to secure the work and environment that is most exciting and engaging for you. One tells you how things work and therefore what to do to navigate your role successfully, the other actively pushes you forward by using their platforms and influence to secure opportunities you could not otherwise access. However, both roles could be delivered by the same person. The most critical differentiator of the impact this person can make on your career is their seniority – the higher up they are and the greater reach and influence they have the further you will get, and the higher will be the rewards you reap, materially and psychologically.

> "Then once you get noticed, the important thing is to get sponsorship from as high a position as you

can get. Executive sponsorship is really important. Ultimately that is usually a male. I have been very lucky through my whole career. I have found that sponsorship. I didn't go looking; people have come to me and have realised my worth, and valued that, and therefore sponsored me through that organisation.

Me: What does that mean in real terms?

That means everything. That is the difference between success and failure. It is like any standard project or programme of work; if you don't have the right sponsorship within the organisation, you are not going to achieve what you need to achieve. You can do all the hard labour down here, but unless you've got the communication, engagement and the distribution and knowledge channels, you are not going to achieve anything.

Me: What do you mean by distribution and knowledge?

In organisations you've got lots of people working down at a certain level and you can transfer knowledge across, but unless it actually comes across the higher level and then disseminates down, you are not going to be successful. From a personal point of view, you have to find that executive sponsor. Ensure you have one. And from a project and programme point of view you must have that. Once you have got your executive sponsors, they earmark and recommend you for other things. Again, one thing leads to another. People at senior level have a very good vision of what is going on and they know the opportunities. If they can match the people with the opportunities, that is a sign of a good leader. If you are in that sphere that is great. That to me was the way I could get there. That has been of enormous benefit to me. I am working in BP now and have

been with them for three years. I work for myself still. I got into BP through someone I worked with, one of the executive sponsors I worked with 10 years ago in this country, who has since moved on." –
Charmaine Stewart

What to look for and what to avoid.

We've seen that the consensus of opinion is that a mentor or sponsor should be senior, mature and secure, so that they are beyond the need to grab the glory for themselves and are at a stage where they will enjoy supporting rising potential and sharing the benefits of their experiences.

"I would change the word 'male' for 'powerful and influential'. I personally don't think the sex of the mentor affects it. I think it is about having someone who is much more senior and experienced than you, who believes in you and says, 'Yes you can do it, try it!' Male or female, I think that has a huge effect on your self-belief and confidence. If somebody is actively doing that you are getting experiences you wouldn't otherwise get, you are crashing through some of those limiting fears and self-beliefs that mean you come out a better leader." –
Maggie Stilwell

If you are looking for a mentor, they can be internal or external, and you don't need to stick to just one source of wisdom on how to navigate your role and challenges. And while there are many employers with formal mentoring programmes, there is no need to wait to be part of one. Mentoring is a very natural extension to a conversation with a more experienced colleague or contact and it is something you can embark on without wider permission and without fanfare. You just look around at who might provide those insights and create the opportunity to open up a conversation around this subject. The key is to keep in mind what sort of support and outcomes you are looking for, so that you can be clear on who might be a great fit. When you reflect on this, you may well find you already have someone who mentors you, but you haven't considered the conversations and relationship in that way before, and if that is the case, you have the opportunity now to constructively build on what you already have.

Your line manager can give you advice on how to do your job well, but bear in mind that they have a specific agenda. So, it is best to look beyond those people that need your focus on particular things rather than purely having your progress in mind.

> *"You don't actually walk into a room thinking 'I need a mentor.' If you find one grab him or her. Be on the alert for a mentor for sure, but you can't write a job description for a mentor, it doesn't work that way. It is all about chemistry, it is about being in the right place at the right time, it is about finding somebody who is nurturing and supportive and recognising that is what you have found, and taking advantage of it, and using it for what it is worth, which is a huge amount."* - **Sara Fox**

> *"It is funny because when they were trying to find me an external mentor, they really struggled to find somebody, because everybody was too staid, everybody was too thoughtful, everybody was too much into predictable corporate activities and my world was chaotic. I would be spinning ten plates at once; there would be high levels of risk that I was managing. I was always on the edge of a crisis; not personal, but there was always a crisis running. I think it took them two years. I ended up with Keith Edelman, who was then the managing director for Arsenal. He did all of that innovation for Arsenal; sold off the old ground and built the flats, created the new stadium, brought in Emirates, the sponsors. He is a really creative man. He held the purse strings and was the businessman behind the whole operation.*

Big football, big money, and big stakes, he was great. He didn't believe in policy or HR. He was a hire and fire man. He was absolutely dynamite. I used to go to him and say 'This is my strategic thinking for this year. This is where I think I want to focus out. These are going to be our primary objectives.' He would quality assure my thinking from an external point of view. That was great. A mentor has to be right for you, not just male, because you have to be able to strike up a comfortable and confident relationship. I see that a lot in reverse, with males seeking out females. They seem to be sought out a lot to be mentors by ambitious males who want to become more rounded and want a different perspective. There is a merging of need really." - **Sharon Kerr**

Women are less visible to potential senior sponsors, so put your head proudly above the parapet.

The role of a sponsor is to take 'high potentials' in the organisation and ensure that their full potential is realised to the maximum benefit of the organisation and its stakeholders. Sponsors are the champion of talent optimisation and critical to an organisation's ability to deliver shareholder and / or stakeholder value. However, as we have seen, unconscious gender bias means that men are assumed to have the potential to be leaders while proof is needed (by way of evidence of performance) from individual women to show they will be able to succeed in those roles and levels. Organisations and their stakeholders need women to have their voices amplified by those whose voices already carry significant credibility, in order to help ensure that female talent is considered equally and advanced accordingly. A key responsibility of a sponsor is to bring this awareness and objectivity to the decision-making table.

This is a classic Catch-22 situation for organisations and for individual women. Sponsors are needed to champion female talent but will struggle to recognise their potential due to their own unconscious bias and the natural familiarity that leads to men gravitating towards championing other men.

So, given the scarcity of organisations which really recognise these issues, let alone successfully address them, it rests with individual women to overcome any lack of self-belief to break through this clear and critical barrier. Ironically, to gain access to this pivotal source of inner confidence, women have to suspend any disbelief in their capability to clearly demonstrate their high-performance potential, and / or an existing track record as a high performer and make their aspirations patently clear.

Catalysts' rigorous and extensive research (N.M. Carter, 2011) has shown that **making your achievements known and making it clear that you have ambitions to get on is the most pivotal strategy in accessing the support and resources that accelerate career progression and secure the remuneration that goes with it**.

However, there is a common concern among women around asking for help. Namely that if you ask for help it's an admission that you haven't got what it takes. This is an understandable concern, but it is counter-productive and ill-founded and just puts up another barrier. Asking for advice or another perspective has a range of direct benefits above and beyond the solution or insight you may have been looking for.

- You learn what you need to know without the iterations of trial and error in trying to get there independently, which can burn time and credibility.
- You can access resources beyond your reach (authority and / or budget).
- You may get more than just the support and advice on the immediate matter in question, as people typically talk around and beyond the topic.
- You will have created another valuable connection and sometimes these people are the experts who will want to take this part of your challenge off your plate, and then bring the solution back to you.
- You will also gain further support, because the sponsor, or

specialist whose advice you've sought, has invested their views and recommendations in the matter, and will want to ensure it succeeds.

"Women's view is that asking for help will be seen as a weakness. But it's about the way you ask. Do you use apologetic language – 'sorry, but I need help' – or do you re-frame it in men's language?" – **Anon Interviewee**

I don't believe that you have to change your style into something more masculine in order to ask for help, but I do believe you have to frame the request in the positive. That will often mean putting it in the context of the need of the wider task or function or organisation, and putting it across with confidence that the person you are asking can help. Bear in mind that, while you benefit from the support, the key winner here is the organisation / function / project, and that is the proposition to take to a potential supporter, advisor or sponsor.

If you are offered this type of support, you should take it.

Women who have initially worried about what it says about them, have found the benefit outweighed any initial concerns about the perception of others. Additionally, as Prof. Dot Griffiths points out, when male leaders get the opportunity to listen to women and understand first-hand the challenges that they face, the whole organisation gets to benefit. This is consistent with the findings of the FTSE 100 Cross-Company Mentoring Programme reported on in *A Woman's Place is in the Boardroom*. (Graham, 2005)

"We did a thing on mentoring. It was just for women. We got a lot of stick from our women. They said, 'Why have you set up something that is just for women. I can manage perfectly well in my career. I don't need this kind of help.' Young women didn't want to know. 'I don't want anything special. I'll get there on my own. You lot belong to a different generation.' There were some who found it helpful, but on the whole we got more hostility than positive reactions.

The one really powerful thing that came out of it was the male mentors who suddenly saw the world through a different lens." – **Prof. Dot Griffiths**

Making it happen:

If you have identified that gaining the support of a mentor or sponsor will deliver significant benefits, what are going to be the main planks of your plan to achieve your new objective?

What specific benefits do you want to gain from the relationship?

Chapter 25

The biggest challenge is being heard – the quest for credibility

'credibility': from the Latin 'credibilis'
meaning worthy to be believed.

Have you ever been in the situation where you're in a meeting, and you put forward a solution to something that's being discussed or a really important point, and it's as if you were in a parallel universe and not actually in that meeting? No one responds to what you've said. It's as if you hadn't said anything. And then, a few minutes later one of the guys says exactly what you'd said. And this time it's different. 'Great idea Mike', 'we need to build that in', 'fantastic solution', 'you'd better get started on that straight away'. Your jaw and your motivation are on the floor. Your idea and your opportunity gone.

In my view, the most fundamental obstacle for women is the issue of not being heard. It is the most pivotal issue because if women cannot be heard, how can their value, capability and potential be recognised, understood and applied? How can women be fairly compared with their colleagues if it is only the voices and words of male contributors that are heard? How can women be considered for project leadership, high profile assignments or promotion?

> *"I do remember being in the situation where you are in a meeting and you make a point, and about two minutes later somebody says, 'As John's just said.' I've noticed that quite a few times. You think you've made a telling point and five minutes later a man is credited with that point. I don't think it is deliberate. I think they genuinely haven't heard that you made it."* – **Anon Interviewee**

This isn't just important for individual women. It's also a critical issue for organisations and their stakeholders (including the shareholders of businesses), since if they are unable to make resourcing decisions drawing from all their available talent, then they simply cannot be performing at the level that they could and should be. As you've read in earlier chapters, analysis by many highly respected consultancies shows that the bottom-line performance of companies with a critical mass of women at the top is very significantly healthier than those without.

> *"It happens to us all. We sit there and say it, and nobody takes any notice, then two minutes later a man says it and they say 'Oh yes that's a good idea.'"*
> – **Prof. Dot Griffiths**

Not being heard is the consequence of all the dynamics that we have been exploring, and it's the biggest barrier to women's career fulfilment as it represents more than not being heard in a meeting; it is any form of voice, from your CV and job application onwards. However, it comes as the last strategic challenge to address because, in addressing all the previous ones, you have been making the strategic and nuanced changes which increase your visibility and your credibility, which result in putting yourself right in the sweet spot on the radar. Once there, your way ahead is far smoother and easier, and your choices and options are wider.

Figure 31: Being heard self-assessment

Below are two sequential questions about this topic. The first asks whether you are speaking up (contributing whenever you could or should) and the second asks if you are being heard i.e., if your contributions are being valued by recipients.

Q. a) To what degree are you confident that you 'speak' up (i.e, contribute via any means: presentation, conversation, email, proposal speech) when there is a contribution you could / should make?

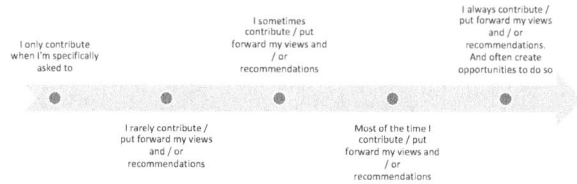

Q. b) Thinking of when you make contributions, to what degree are your contributions heard, recognised and valued? Evidence of this will include: being asked for more information; clearly listening while you speak; referring to your contribution with your name as author; asking you to lead an initiative in connection with this topic; referring others to you as the specialist; consulting you on related matters; rewarding you, specifically citing these areas, and so on.

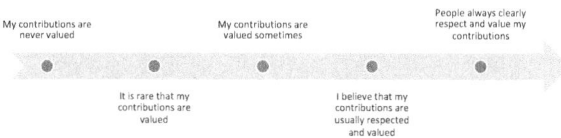

Understand why and when you may not be heard, to anticipate and head off the issue.

So, what's going on if you were not heard but your male colleague was when the content of the suggestions was the same and only the gender was different?

It comes back to human psychology again, rather than anything personal, as this is about what our senses are trained to tune in to, or out of, based on our expectations. It's an unfortunate by-product of how human brains have evolved to try to make sure they don't get clogged up in details that they don't need in order to save processing power for what they are needed for most. Our huge subconscious brain (relative to our conscious brain) focuses our attention on what it has learned to expect to be important, and tunes out extraneous sensory information. This can be quite literal if you think of a crowded room where we manage to focus on one conversation, despite many other conversations in close proximity. Until someone uses our name, which we instantly home in on. We have been subconsciously scanning other vocal data, enabling a vital bit to be fed through to our conscious brain to act on.

I didn't expect my 13-year-old daughter to know how to mend my computer, so when it crashed and I was busy swearing at it and fighting the urge to throw it out of the window, I was also dismissing a background noise going, "Mummy, have you tried clicking this?" She patiently and quietly waited while Mummy went berserk. When I finally calmed down, having failed with every option I pursued, I tried what she'd suggested: and bingo, problem solved. So much time and temper wasted – if only I'd considered her worthy of listening to. If only I'd considered and valued her intelligence, her experience with technology virtually from birth, formal education in IT, and her less limited thinking. If I had, I'd have heard her at the start of the process. In fact, there would have been no process.

The reason this all happened was that I didn't expect to hear my daughter because of my assumptions about a 13-year-old's capabilities and expertise. I made an assumption that a child couldn't solve what I packaged as an adult problem. My daughter's input was therefore not credible to me, so I didn't pay attention to her, and that was my loss. Fortunately, I was able to learn from that situation and fortunately she didn't withdraw future help on the basis of the horrible experience of being so stubbornly and rudely ignored.

The workplace assumption in the majority of cases is that men have the answers because they've been the only source of answers in the past. They've been the managers, the leaders, the scientists, the engineers, the academics, the doctors, the politicians, the businesspeople. Even the 'pink' functions (HR, Marketing) and organisations (schools, publishers) are populated by women, but often led by men. This means that we all expect them to have, or come up with, the answers, and we expect them to be the right ones, hence we listen to them before we listen to women. They have credibility by virtue of the expectations of their gender, which rides ahead of the reality of the individual's capability. The implication is that individual women may have to demonstrate why they should be listened to – why they are credible – before they can be heard. As we've seen in Myth 5 (Women aren't as good at Maths, IT or Science) this challenge is more acute in roles and at levels regarded as having to deal with significant complexity.

Social status acts as a proxy for knowledge status.

Psychological research into effective team working in primary schools showed the power of this stereotypically superior male knowledge status from a very early age, demonstrating the issue we observe in the workplace. Even in primary school today, boys are confident of their superior social status compared to girls; this superior social status was shown to act as a proxy for their knowledge status. In other words, boys are believed to know more than their female peers simply because they have superior social status. Boys were unwilling to accept the girls' approaches or solutions to the problems they were given to tackle under any experimental conditions. When the girl's knowledge status was equal to the boy's true knowledge status, the outcome was that the boy's solution took precedence. When the girl had a higher 'knowledge status' than the boy, a successful outcome (both at individual and team level) depended on girls using a variety of ways to explain why they selected their approach to the solution and how it worked. Clearly the situation is absurd and resulted in the process taking considerably longer than if the girl's knowledge status had been accepted.

Shocking but true, and it's the reality you have to navigate

This is the same dynamic in the workplace: social status can trump expertise. And the prospect of having to climb through these additional hoops to demonstrate your credibility, the quality of your thinking, the relevance of your experience and the value and worth of your contribution is quite depressing. However, it is better to understand the reality of what you may face and prepare accordingly, than to face the alternative of going unheard with the negative consequences for your psychological well-being and engagement, both in the moment and long term.

When I was a management consultant, I had a colleague who had the most incredible intellect and strategic ability. He was an Oxford graduate and had been Global Marketing Director of one of Britain's most famous and globally renowned confectionary companies. When he spoke in company and client meetings in his gentle, calm voice everyone seemed to hold their breath, to listen to every word he had to say. We met again earlier this year, some years after she had transitioned. She had a unique viewpoint, so I asked her, '*do you experience any difference at work now, as a woman?*' She said, '*Yes. Absolutely. It's much harder to get people to listen to what I'm saying.*' She still had the Oxbridge degree and the same stellar CV.

You can see now that the strategies of stakeholder management, networking, mentor / sponsorship and personal promotion all come together to support you in being valued, visible, credible and heard. Pursuing these strategies puts you in a better situation when you're sitting round that table putting forward your perspective or your proposal, because some of the key players will already be supporters and will already know why they should listen and what's in it for them. They'll also support and promote your credentials in forums that you can't be part of, but in which decisions affecting you will be made.

The other important aspect to remember is that it is not about you as an individual. In other words, it's not personal. The fact that your work contributions may be recognised less than your peers is no reflection on your capability or potential – it's simply a reflection of people's conditioning which results in this unconscious bias towards men in the workplace.

Belinda Gooding has the track record of an exceptional marketer. She developed and honed her skills with the best in the global consumer goods industry and these were enhanced by her instinct and passion for great food. She made her mark through results, and hence, she reached the top. Board director of Dairy Crest and then appointed to Managing Director of Duchy Originals, which was owned by HRH Prince Charles via The Prince's Foundation. Belinda is now a non-exec director of several companies as well as CEO and owner of her own organic products company. Under her leadership at Duchy Originals the profitability of the business soared, money which was fed into HRH's charities.

Belinda was the first person I interviewed for this book, and I may face beheading for treason for telling this story, but I hope HRH and his team will not take exception, and instead, support me in trying to demonstrate and address an issue driving inequality.

When Belinda decided to move on from Duchy Originals after seven years at the helm, she agreed to work with Prince Charles' team at Clarence House to select the new MD. This was a process that she had been through herself and an interview process on behalf of the future King of Great Britain and Head of the Commonwealth is bound to be memorable. So, she had a clear recollection of how she was tested and challenged, how she was required then, and at so many subsequent points, to provide bullet-proof supporting evidence to support her proposals, needing to drill down to a fine level of detail. So, it came as a great shock when the guy that succeeded in getting the job, talked in broad brushstrokes about controversial ideas. These seemed to gain instant support and were progressed without being probed for detail. But worse still was the apparent acceptance of his conceptual recommendations to take the brand into territories and product segments which were diametrically opposed to the existing, highly successful, uniquely appropriate and desirable royal brand positioning. From Belinda's view point these changes spelt disaster and her loyalty was torn at the prospect of seeing all that she had built with her team over the years being lost along with the core proposition. Belinda was right to be worried. The business failed, the charities were left unsupported, and the intellectual property and master brand licence had to be given to Waitrose (the premium UK grocery retailer), as the only way to keep the brand alive and as many of the suppliers as possible in business.

The reason Belinda told me this story was that she felt it was a stunning example that no matter how senior you are as a woman, your work and recommendations still lack the credibility of a man. As a woman, even as a Managing Director, you still have to prove that your words carry weight, that they are justified, using evidence and explanation. As a man, it's assumed that you are right. That is the default position.

While this story took place a number of years ago, you may recall the 2020 Sat Nav to Success Research data shared on page 98, in *Myths and Mantras* showing that the credibility gap (measured via the *Contribution to Value Gap*) persists for women all the way up the ladder but closes for men when they step from entry levels into middle management.

> *"It is interesting that in terms of the senior management, I get treated very differently now to how I was treated before I became a Professor - before I would always be asked how my children were. Even when you are asked the question you know they are not listening to the answer, they have just asked just for the sake of asking a question. Male colleagues would be asked about a piece of research. It is very interesting. It is as though they know how to relate to women in terms of social things outside of work, but not as colleagues.*
>
> *The title of Professor is something that people defer to and it is actually quite useful. What you find is that people will listen to you because you are down*

as Professor Kirkby. Whereas when I was Doctor I was almost dismissed because I was a woman. It is useful because people start to listen to you.

We are opening a building that I got all the funding for on Monday, and I am sure that to start with, I will be taken for the secretary. You do find all the time that nobody can believe that you are in the role you are in." – **Prof. Karen Kirkby**

If you do experience these situations, it knocks the wind out of your sails, and makes it tougher to stay energised, focused and driven. This is one of the reasons why it's important to focus on the work you are most passionate about. You need that connection to something that really matters to you to help pull you up out of the troughs and enable you to keep going (see Chapter 10: *Harness and hold on to what drives you*). This is also why it's good to have a professional network (Chapter 23) of confidantes to whom you can speak to gain reassurance that it's not you, that you are doing the right things.

You can make yourself seen and heard. Start by identifying the pinch points.

In the previous section I explained more about the psychology behind this frustrating phenomenon. It's really important to understand the reasons why it happens so you can anticipate when being heard and valued may be a challenge – which situations and circumstances are most likely to be problematic – so that you can develop a plan to head the issue off at the pass and do all you can to eliminate or minimise it. It's also important for your sanity!

Making it happen:

So, the next task is to home in on the situations and mediums in which you need to be heard and valued, but are not, or not enough.

· Is it in meetings, if so which ones? What is their make-up – who is there and what is the meeting role, goal, focus and subject matter?

· Is it in written communications? If so, to, between or with whom? What type of content and purpose?

· Who is getting listened to if not you, and by whom?

· Who needs to value your contribution and hear you?

Now, if you've narrowed this down, the next critical question to pose of each of the pinch points you've identified (asked of you broadly in the first Being Heard self-assessment), is:

· When it matters, are you actually speaking up (or putting forward your point in writing) when there is a contribution that you could or should make? Or are you being tentative or even remaining silent?

Clearly, you have no chance of being heard if you are not actually contributing when the key opportunities arise. When y<u>ou</u> perceive or believe that your contribution isn't as good or as credible as others then you are much less likely to take what feels like a risk by opening your mouth or putting your thoughts in writing. If this is the situation then read or re-read Chapter 9: *Challenge any limiting beliefs* and Chapter 19 on self-promotion to help you get to the point where you can 'dare' enough to put your contribution forward. Make a start by using communication vehicles that are less scary, or test less intimidating environments until your confidence builds (on the basis of the positive responses and positive outcomes from making that effort) to the point where you can contribute in all the forums and use all the media that matter to your role and your future.

Demand respect – look and sound authoritative & never undermine yourself.

If you have reflected on the pinch points when your contributions appear to go unheard and you are confident that you are speaking up whenever you can or you should, then the next stage is to consider the range of strategies that should change the response you experience.

The first consideration is whether you are undermining yourself and inadvertently recommending that your audience doesn't listen. As described in *Challenge any limiting beliefs*, women frequently apologise for what they are about to say, are saying, or have said, and the same for what they have done, and plan to do.

'*You probably know more about this than I do, but...*'

'*I'm probably wrong about this, but...*'

'*I may not have thought this through fully, but I think...*'

I hear this every day in women's talk and written communications, in every area and environment of their lives.

Work hard to avoid saying anything to undermine your work and your worth. Try to spot and stop any inclination to do that. It can be hard, and it can feel unnatural, but with awareness and practice and the appreciation that there was never any need to apologise in the first place, the reality is that when you communicate with confidence, people react to that confidence, which will, in turn, make you more confident.

> *"Women know plenty about many subjects, but they whisper comments to themselves or their neighbours in meetings or at conferences, instead of speaking out clearly and loudly – as men tend to do. This is a function of their lack of confidence in a male dominated and defined culture.*
>
> *To be heard women must give their voices weight. Though not an admirer of Margaret Thatcher, I was impressed by her awareness of this fact, and that the work she did on her voice demonstrated. She went a bit too far, dropping it half an octave would have been better than dropping it a whole one. But she did get heard. She also worked on her body language. Women often look down and don't project in meetings or interviews. Watch how Mrs T stopped Robin Day in his tracks by looking him in the eye and laying a warning hand on his arm*!"*
> **– Barbara Follett**

*A reference to Prime Minister Margaret Thatcher silencing a dogged television journalist to ensure she could finish every point she wanted to make.

> *"You have to speak up. Your voice needs to be heard. Early on in my career I had to learn the art of polite interrupting. I don't know if you found the same thing as I did. I'd be sitting in a meeting and I'd say something, and nobody would pay attention to it. You've got a man next to you who says the same thing and everybody says, 'Oh great idea.'*
>
> *I think part of it is having the courage to say, 'I would like to make a point.' You actually have to draw attention to it. The problem with the dynamic is that the conversation is going on at the table and you are being ignored. You*

actually have to stop the dynamic and say, 'I would like to make a point.' Sometimes saying something like, 'I really agree with you Robert and I would like to add onto that.' That can buy you some points too. If you can show that you are building onto something that they are saying and give them a little credit, that can help too. Part of it is physical. You've got to be able to speak up. I get frustrated when women have little voices, and they physically can't be heard. You've got to be able to project your voice. You can't be too delicate about it." - **Anna Catalano**

Know your stuff and anticipate pushback before it happens.

Confidence and self-belief can be reinforced by having a thorough knowledge of your stuff. However, many women go way overboard about the amount they feel they need to know before they feel that they have the authority to make a point. There is a balance to be struck here, in terms of what you need to know and what you need to be able to demonstrate. A few choice offerings can deliver all the impact you need.

This is where you need to consider your audience – *what do they know and what do they want and how does that compare to what you know and what you can give?* Try to recognise when you are the expert or authority in the room i.e., the person with the greatest, more contemporary or most relevant insight, knowledge or experience, and be ready to gently, but clearly, reference this position, before you proceed with your contribution.

It may feel like a silly game sometimes, but to gain credibility you need to enable your contribution to be respected (and thus heard); to achieve that, there are extra loops you will have to jump through. One of those is presenting or dropping in a few key facts which help establish you as the authority. And, as Lin Phillips points out, don't assume that the questions you are asked are because people think you are wrong, they may simply represent opportunities to show that you are right! So, what can seem like challenging questioning may be better framed as an opportunity to calmly re-confirm your credentials.

> *"I think part of it is not to be afraid to have an opinion and to believe what you say. If you believe what you are saying, people will listen to you. It is no good being a shrinking violet.*
>
> *It is useful to develop the art of the killer questions, look to the place you know you would have missed or would have made a mistake, chances are no one will have even thought of it. My first boss was great at this; he would always look at my presentations and he would always find a bit that I had missed. It didn't matter what I put in front of him, he would go straight to the point that I didn't know the answer to. I asked him once, 'How do you always know that I've missed that point?' and he said, 'Because I would have done.' So, you've got to work out what you would have missed and put that question to them.*
>
> *My observations from working with the senior leadership team is that some of the guys always wanted to disagree as part of the ritual of the whole thing. It didn't matter what it was about.*
>
> *I found it part of the challenge, trying to work out why someone was disagreeing with my approach. If you are in the wrong frame of mind, the chances are you will react badly, but if you are in the right frame of mind you will think, 'Why did he just ask me that?' Then you can just say, 'Why did you just say that?' That puts him back having to explain why he said that. It is all about playing chess at the end of the day."* – **Lin Phillips**

Personal presentation makes a difference – so make the right difference.

Personal presentation is a significant opportunity to communicate a loud message about your professionalism, your credentials and your intent without even opening your mouth. This is about the way you dress and your body language i.e., your non-verbal communications. Together, these speak volumes both to others and to yourself. And it's important when you are physically present as well as virtually.

I recommend watching the Ted Talk by Harvard social psychologist, Prof. Amy Cuddy, *Your body language may shape who you are* (Cuddy, 2012) as she shares some compelling evidence that two minutes' preparation in a 'power pose' ahead of presentations, key meetings and interviews makes all the difference to imbuing your audience with confidence in your capability. It may sound deeply uncomfortable, so listen to what she has to say and see if it's worth considering for yourself. These simple steps certainly made all the difference to me when I appeared live on national TV on the early evening news for the first time, to talk about how to close the gender pay gap.

> *"I have natural authority.*
>
> *It's a way you speak, dress, hold yourself, your mannerisms. People listen to you and then you can bring in the touchy-feely stuff."* - **Beverley Bell**
>
> *"I think my physical dress sense probably hasn't changed much. I don't ever recall dressing to conform. But in my own mind I have always probably had the view that you dress in a certain way if you want to be held with respect in the business. I wear what I wear because it is my uniform for work, and I think people take me seriously when I dress this way."* - **Sarah Lewis**
>
> *"I think we all make judgements when people walk in the room, so I always try to look the part. At school I enjoyed acting. I tell everybody here, 'You've got*

to play the role.' I don't mean being a dipsy female, but you've got to stand confident, look smart. But I would say that to the men. I don't think it's different. I say that sort of thing to the men here as well. 'Have you cleaned your shoes?' I think it is something that people look at. I was the recruitment partner at Allen & Overy, and we used to have lots of training to make people aware that a judgement would be formed as soon as they walked in the room. It's the horns and halo effect within two minutes. You try to put that away and listen to what they are saying rather than being distracted by what they look like. But at least you can look smart and confident, and then you could be halfway there. You may, of course, talk rubbish, in which case they'll ditch you.

Me: People don't look to overcome stereotypes; they look to ensure that their stereotype is correct.

That is exactly what we had in the interviewing. You make up your mind and then spend the rest of the interview looking for evidence to back you up. I'm married to a head hunter. For me it was hardly an epiphany. But it does happen now when people walk into the room. I make a judgement and I've tried not to. But I do think it's a game. You are ahead of the game if you turn up looking presentable, and as if you care." – **Claire Maurice**

Make your communications concise, clear and unapologetic.

It may seem that it's hard to strike the balance between overselling your argument or point, and not giving enough evidence to make it. The right approach will vary by situation – by audience, by the type of meeting or conversation and its context and purpose, as well as the stage that this item has reached in familiarity, relevance, urgency and discussion. It's a judgement you have to make and adjust based on the situation and the response.

> *"Women over-explain. I'm a classic. I will over-explain because I will want to be seen as clear and transparent. On the whole, that's not what men do. I'm generalising, but it is not what they do.*
>
> *Nobody writes reports anymore. Nobody writes a recommendation on a page. What's the background? What's the current situation? The proposed solution, rationale and forward action. You used to write all that on a page. Now people expect things in three lines, particularly if being acknowledged is based on the corridor speech. Within that sentence, with two or three bullet points you need to communicate your worth.*
>
> *I was told in emails never to use the words could, would and should, but will, can and must. So, the British way of speaking is no longer acceptable. It has to be about action, statement; it must not be about hypothesis."* - **Karen Guerra**
>
> *"I have sat in lots of board meetings in different environments, here and at the Met. Men seem to make their point usually succinctly and clearly; women tend to waffle on and start hypothesising and going all over the place. There is something about presentation which holds us back. We talk too much and too extensively about an issue instead of just getting to the point.*

Me: What do you think is behind that?

I think we think differently, and we tend to want to explore an issue. Instead of presenting an issue and a solution, we like to explore our thinking aloud in a group. That is the way we normally operate – consultative. When you are in a board environment there isn't always the time for that sort of pontification. I have been irritated on occasion. I think I have learnt over the years to adopt a very clear boardroom style." - **Sharon Kerr**

To comment - for the sake of being visible – or not to comment, that is the question.

An intriguing debate that ran through my interviews was whether to copy the thing men are notorious for doing in conversations and meetings, which is to make an unnecessary point, or repeat one already made, simply for the purpose of making it known that they are there and have a significant role, lest anyone forget! There was a division between those who believe you must play the same game as the guys, and those who say to just do it your way and speak when you have value to add.

My own view comes from a slightly different angle. I believe we don't do what we see the guys doing because we don't feel qualified to make the point, as the area under discussion isn't our core domain. This comes back to women seeing their technical capabilities or areas of specialism as the limit of what they can speak about. They exclude, or fail to connect, the range of general competencies that enable them to perform well in their role i.e., such aspects as their communication, decision-making, influencing, strategic skills and so forth. Additionally, in our culture men are expected to know more and be capable of solving a wider range of challenges than women in most spheres of life. The fact is that men aren't born able to put up shelves, navigate airports or to confront bad service, but because it is expected they have to rise to the occasion; '*I don't know what to do*' isn't considered an option for men in our society. Men are supposed to be capable and decisive, and broadly speaking women aren't. Hence, they get less practice at it, and have less evidence on which to base a positive belief in their ability to take on and address things outside their direct experience. As a single Mum I've had to do everything from house decorating to cake decorating; every decision; all the planning for work, for play, for financial security. It's been a challenge, but it's also been a hell of an insight into the range of stuff we can all do, if we put our mind to it. As Ester Boserup, the Danish economist said, "*necessity is the mother of invention*".

Back to the question of whether to pitch in with a comment or not. I believe women should widen their view of what they feel qualified to comment on with credibility and authority, based on using their balanced judgement, direct or indirect insights or experience, or simply by applying their common sense. In doing so women broaden their credentials and the range of possibilities, as the people around them start to appreciate both the depth and breadth of the impact they can and should make.

> "*Men tend to take on a more dominant role and they can talk about anything and everything and have a position on it. I am not sure women are comfortable doing that. I have developed a style where I can talk about anything to anyone because I have learnt at the hands of masters. I think for new people coming through that is something they need to get to grips with. They shouldn't just sit there and be a dormouse until somebody talks about HR or finance or whatever their area is. Be a leader and contribute to the discussion. If there is something relevant to say and you have a view, then say it.*
>
> *I just steam in and say which things are troubling me without thinking about it. I don't dwell on it. You are up against a very tight deadline and I have trained myself to think like that because of my old job [Met Police Commander and head of the Flying Squad]. There is no point sitting on issues, you get*

them into the open and deal with them and then put them to one side.

Rise above it [the internal concern about not knowing everything / being the expert on a certain topic] and think about whether there are any unanswered questions or any areas that aren't particularly clear or explicit. We are not good at seeking out new or additional information. We tend to accept what is presented without probing. That can be quite dangerous, particularly if you are in a board environment, because you are then making decisions when you are not sure that you have all the information you need. My training in the police has been to get all the information you possibly can before you decide. So, I do think I am slightly different to some of your other subjects because I have been taught in a different way." – **Sharon Kerr**

Consider your audience and where you can be creative, in order to be heard.

"There are other ways to be heard rather than standing up and talking. We have five senses and men are probably pretty good at using one, and women are pretty good at using the others. I guess it is using our strengths as individuals and our strengths as women. There are differentiators and we've got to use them to our advantage. How are we heard? Maybe we don't have to actually go into a meeting or a boardroom and speak a lot of words in the next hour, but we can be heard by what we actually make happen during the next week. We can then bring that to the table for the next meeting. We are the people who are actually driving things forward and making things happen in a certain way.

It is understanding the differences in people and playing to that. That is the way to be heard. It is another way of defining that. Men don't even think about that. Men just come in and can be who they are, or what they think they should be.

This happened to me just a couple of months ago. I was invited to present to a leadership team meeting. I was invited to join lunch and then I was put on the last slot. So I had to sit there until five o'clock. They had been going for two days. I sat there and listened to all of this stuff. I thought, 'What am I going to do?' They were obviously thinking, 'Charmaine's session. Last session of two days.' I thought about what made me different, what I could bring to the room that made me different. Energy, because I knew that energy was really low by that stage. Things like physical position. Everybody had been sitting around the table, so I stood up and started walking around. One of the key leaders around the table was a South African, and they had just had an Australian dialled in on a call and I was a New Zealander. And I was the only woman. I stood up and I walked around and already I had done something different. I really liked my topic, so I told them it was going to be the highlight of the day. People don't say that. I then turned to the South African and said, 'And I would just like to thank the South African for allowing a New Zealand woman to have the final say.' At first there was silence and almost a sense of horror, and then they just burst out laughing. It was something I could say to break the ice, bring some energy into the room and crack a joke at my expense. And bing, I had all of their attention. I turned off the PowerPoint and spoke to them about what we were doing. My session over-ran by half an hour.

It is demanding that attention, but doing it in a more charming way rather than an aggressive way. You are different; you are going to bring some different qualities to the table, so you need to think how you can highlight that in a subtle way. I was able to use that opportunity. Ever since then I have had one on one conversations with those directors and they will come and have a chat, but I feel that I have got the power and that is why they are coming to talk to me about certain things. You have to use your difference to achieve your means, which sounds completely mercenary, and I don't mean it like that, but you find ways of working within your environment." – **Charmaine Stewart**

If you are not heard in key meetings, network your content or contribution beforehand.

I've discussed how women tend to adhere to the formal routes of communication – if the process or the protocol describes a certain way, that tends to be what gets followed (see Chapter 17 on understanding organisational culture). Whereas the cannier, or those more open to the informal ways the organisation works, will identify and create other opportunities to gain understanding, buy-in or approval from key individuals. Networking ideas and proposals before their formal presentation is productive. You can gain people's feedback, listen to their perspectives, answer queries and even amend or tweak your proposal and secure support. Instead of limiting yourself to springing it on them from cold in a more formal forum, and in the moment, where they may need to behave slightly differently based on their position and as a representative of certain 'territory'.

Your talent and potential are wasted if you are not heard.

It is possible, unfortunately, that despite your most tenacious efforts, your inputs and achievements go unheard and unrecognised. So, there comes a point when you need to make a choice purely for your own benefit. Ultimately if it doesn't work – don't waste your time and talents in a blinkered organisation or function or team – get out! Their loss will be your gain, when you use the opportunity to apply everything you've learnt here, to find the perfect fit organisation and role, and secured an enviable package in the process. And it'll also be that new team, function or employer's gain through embracing your talent and reaping the reward it will deliver. Or you may be able to set up your own venture where you can reap the rewards of your talent and latent potential yourself and do things on your own terms.

Making it happen:

Where has this final strategic area taken your thinking? What is your view on your priorities to ensure that you can effectively and rapidly close any gap between where you are and where you want to be?

How will you know when you've got to a better place? What will the evidence be?

What resources can help you make swift and efficient progress?

Chapter 26

In conclusion

The purpose of this book has been to enable you to gain clarity on what you really want from this stage in your working life, and then to help you understand the range of choices you have for securing the things that are most important to you – the roles, the respect, the support, the rewards, the future potential, the balance at home for the freedom you want, the environment, the fulfilment, the buzz.

What I have come to understand most clearly through the years of developing this book – the interviews and conversations and my own personal challenges – is that the most important thing is to do what is right for you. No one else but you can determine what that is. There is so much noise out there, pulling and pushing you this way and that way, trying to tell you what you should do and be, and what you shouldn't, making it very hard to find the best and most fulfilling path for you. Part 3: Your DNA for success was designed to help you gain clarity on what that might be.

I've also spent time talking to you about the psychology behind the challenges that women face in achieving fulfilment in their working lives. I've done that so that you can separate the truth about who you are and what you are capable of, from the influence of the gendered expectations and limitations that exist in our society. I've shared this with you so that you can 'read' what goes on around you and could impact upon you as well as 'read' your own thoughts and decisions in a new and more liberating light.

You'll clearly understand the reality out there, so you'll be able to anticipate, prepare for, and overcome these challenges, smoothing the path ahead. I've also done some myth busting to show you the truth behind the mantras repeated and accepted in our society which also limit women's opportunities and potential to get the most out of their working life.

In Parts 4 and 5 I shared the most potent and pragmatic strategies to increase your inner momentum and to drive your best career agenda, which I distilled from the almost 300 hours of interviews with the many generous women who freely gave their time and openly shared their stories and insights so that this book could make a positive difference to your working life.

Whenever people start using new methods and approaches, there will be some crunching of gears as they find what works best and feels most comfortable. The daring aspect of *Understand: Dare: Thrive* can be difficult, feel scary and unnatural, but it is how you access the change that you want. Being conscious, deliberate and reflective of your actions and their effects will enable you to continue to grow your portfolio of successes, whether they be micro, feel-good changes, or macro and career changing. The more you test and learn about what works best for you in the environments you work in, the more you can fine-tune your approach and the more continuously you'll achieve positive outcomes, and the positive energy and momentum that will flow from them.

I hope this book has empowered you to make positive differences already, and that you've been able to create a plan that will move you swiftly and smoothly towards the goals you've identified. Through your career and the different life stages that impact it, you can come back and dip into it to find insights and options that help, or the tools to review and refresh your plan.

Go for it!!

Bibliography

A. H. Eagly, C. N. (2019). Gender stereotypes have changed: A cross-temporal meta-analysis of US public opinion polls from 1946 to 2018. American Psychologist(3), pp. 301-315.

A. H. Eagly, L. C. (2007). *Through The Labyrinth – the truth about how women become leaders.* Boston: Harvard Business School Press.

A.J. Koch, S. D. (2015). A meta-analysis of gender stereotypes and bias in experimental simulations of employment decision making. *Journal of Applied Psychology, 100*(1), 128-61. doi: doi:10.1037/a0036734

Adenzato, M. B. (2017). Gender differences in cognitive Theory of Mind revealed by transcranial direct current stimulation on medial prefrontal cortex. *Scientific Reports*(7, 41219.). Retrieved from https://doi.org/10.1038/srep41219

Apicella, C. C. (2015). Testosterone and Economic Risk Taking: A Review. *Adaptive Human Behaviour and Physiology, 1*, 35-385. doi:https://doi.org/10.1007/s40750-014-0020-2

Ayton, P. (2010). Judgement and decision making. In T. O. University, & H. Kaye (Ed.), *Cognitive Psychology* (pp. 443 -445). Milton Keynes: The Open University.

Banerjee, R. (2009). Gender identity and the development of gender roles. In S. D. Littleton, *Children's Personal and Social Development* (p. 153). The Open University.

Bass, B. &. (2006). *Transformational leadership: Second Edition.* Mahwah: Lawrence Erlbaum Associates.

Bleeker, J. J. (2004). Girls' and Boys' developing interest in Maths and Science: Do Parents Matter? *New Directions for Child and Adolescent Development*, pp. 5-21. doi:doi:10.1037/0022-0663.96.1.97

Bostock, N. (2018, March 8). The rise of women in general practice. *GP Online.* Retrieved July 31, 2020, from https://www. gponline.com/rise-women-general-practice/article/1458988

Buttle, H. (2019, August 15). Analysis: A Level Results Day 2019. *Education Policy Institute*. Retrieved from https://epi.org.uk/publications-and-research/a-level-results-2019/

C. Seierstad, M. H. (2015, March 6). Lessons from Norway in getting women onto corporate boards. *The Conversation*. Retrieved from http://theconversation.com/lessons-from-norway-in-getting-women-onto-corporate-boards

Cambridge Dictionary. (2020). *Sponsor Meaning*. Retrieved from Cambridge Dictionary: https://dictionary.cambridge.org/dictionary/english/sponsor

Castilla, E. J. (2016, June 13). Achieving Meritocracy in the Workplace. *MIT Sloan Management Review*. Retrieved from https://sloanreview.mit.edu/article/achieving-meritocracy-in-the-workplace/

Catalyst. (2004). Women and Men in U.S. Corporate Leadership: Same Workplace, Different Realities? New York. Retrieved from https://www.catalyst.org/wp-content/uploads/2019/02/Women-and_Men_in_U.S._Corporate_Leadership_Same_Workplace_Different_Realities.pdf

Catalyst. (2008). *Advancing Women Leaders. The Connection Between women board directors and women corporate officers'*

Catalyst. (2010, December 1). Mentoring: necessary but insufficient for advancement. New York. Retrieved from https://www.catalyst.org/research/mentoring-necessary-but-insufficient-for-advancement/

Catalyst. (2014, June 10). High Potential Women in Europe. New York:, USA. Retrieved from https://www.catalyst.org/wp-content/uploads/2019/01/high_potential_women_in_europe_print.pdf

Catalyst. (n.d.). The Promise of Future Leadership: A Research Program on Highly Talented Employees in the Pipeline. New York. Retrieved from https://www.catalyst.org/research-series/the-promise-of-future-leadership-a-research-program-on-highly-talented-employees-in-the-pipeline/

Covey, S. R. (2004). *The 7 Habits Of Highly Effective People.* London: Simon & Schuster.

Credit Suisse Research Institute. (2012). *Gender diversity and corporate performance.* Zurich.

Credit Suisse Research Institute. (2016). *The CS Gender 3000: The Reward for Change.* Zurich: Credit Suisse AG. Retrieved from https://www.credit-suisse.com/about-us/en/reports-research/studies-publications.html

Credit Suisse Research Institute. (2019). *CS Gender 3000 report 2019.* Zurich. Retrieved from https://www.credit-suisse.com/about-us-news/en/articles/news-and-expertise/cs-gender-3000-report-2019-201910.html

Cristina Díaz-García, A. G.-M.-M. (2013, Dec 17). Gender diversity within R&D teams: Its impact on radicalness of innovation,. *Innovation, 15,* pp. 149-160. doi:10.5172/impp.2013.15.2.149

Cuddy, A. (2012). *Your body language may shape who you are.* Retrieved from TED Global: https://www.ted.com/talks/amy_cuddy_your_body_language_may_shape_who_you_are?language=en

D. Lovallo, O. S. (2010, March). The Case for Behavioural Strategy. *McKinsey Quarterly.* Retrieved from https://www.mckinsey.com/business-functions/strategy-and-corporate-finance/our-insights/the-case-for-behavioral-strategy

D. Storage, T. E. (2020). Adults and children implicitly associate brilliance with men more than women. *Journal of Experimental Social Psychology.* doi:doi.org/10.1016/j.jesp.2020.104020

D. Storage, Z. H. (2016). The frequency of 'brilliant' and 'genius' in teaching evaluations predicts the representation of women and African Americans across fields. *PLOS ONE, 11*(3).

Dalli, H. (2020, March 5). EU revives plans for mandatory quotas of women on company boards. (J. Rankin, Interviewer) The Guardian.

Davies, L. (2011). *Lord Davies Women On Boards Review*. London. Retrieved from https://www.gov.uk/government/news/women-on-boards

Deloitte. (2020). *Women In The Boardroom. A Global Perspective. Sixth Edition.* Retrieved from https://www2.deloitte.com/global/en/pages/risk/articles/women-in-the-boardroom-global-perspective.html

Eagly, J.-S. a. (2003). Transactional, transactional, and laissez-faire leadership styles: A meta-analysis comparing women and men. *Psychological Bulletin, 129*, 569-591.

Education Policy Institute. (2019, August). The A Level Gender Gap: Attainment and Entries 2019. United Kingdom. Retrieved from https://epi.org.uk/publications-and-research/a-level-results-2019/

Engel D, W. A., & doi:, 9. (2014, Dec 16). Reading the Mind in the Eyes or reading between the lines? Theory of Mind predicts collective intelligence equally well online and face-to-face. *PLOS ONE, 9*(12), e115212. doi:https://doi.org/10.1371/journal.pone.0115212

Equal Opportunities Commission. (2015, June). *Greater Expectations, Final report of the EOC's investigation into discrimination against new and expectant mothers in the workplace.* London: EOC.

Eurobarometer 465. (2017). *Gender Equality 2017, Gender Equality, Stereotypes,and Women in Politics.*

G. Ford, S. K. (2020). *The Accidental Sexist.* Rethink Press.

Graham, P. T. (2005). *A Woman's Place is in the Boardroom.* Basingstoke: Palgrave McMillan.

Hewlett, S. (2007). *Off-Ramps and On-Ramps: Keeping Talented Women on the Road to Success.* Harvard Business School Press.

Hyde, J. S. (1990). Gender Comparisons of Mathematics Attitudes and Affect: A Meta-Analysis. *Psychology of Women Quarterly, 14*(3), pp. 299–324. doi:10.1111/j.1471-6402.1990.tb00022.x

Ibarra, C. A. (2010, September). Why men still get more promotions than women. *The Harvard Business Review*.

Institute for Health Metrics and Evaluation. (2020, July 14). *Fertility, mortality, migration, and population scenarios for 195 countries and territories from 2017 to 2100: a forecasting analysis for the Global Burden of Disease Study.* doi:https://doi.org/10.1016/S0140-6736(20)30677-2

Institute of Public Relations. (2020, August). *www.ipr.org.uk*. Retrieved from https://www.ipr.org.uk/

J. S. Hyde, E. F. (1990). Gender differences in mathematics performance: A meta-analysis. *Psychological Bulletin, 107* (2), 139-155. Retrieved from http://dx.doi.org/10.1037/0033-2909.107.2.139

J. Woetzel, A. M. (2015). *How advancing women's equality can add $12 trillion to global growth.* McKinsey Global Institute. Retrieved from https://www.mckinsey.com/featured-insights/employment-and-growth/how-advancing-womens-equality-can-add-12-trillion-to-global-growth

Javanoic, R. B. (2005). Do parents' academic stereotypes influence whether they intrude on their children's homework. *Sex Roles* (52), pp. 597-607. doi:doi:10.1007/s11199-005-32728-4

Koch, A. D. (2015). A Meta-Analysis of Gender Stereotypes and Bias in Experimental Simulations of Employment Decision-Making. *The Journal of Applied Psychology, 100*, 128-161. doi:10.1037/a0036734

Lee, T. H. (2012, September 3). Gender Differences in Voluntary Turnover: Still a Paradox? *International Business Research, 5*(10). doi:10.5539/ibr.v5n10p19

M. Costa Dias, R. J. (2018). *The gender pay gap in the UK: children and experience in work.* Institute for Fiscal Studies. Retrieved from https://www.ifs.org.uk/uploads/publications/wps/MCD_RJ_FP_GenderPayGap.pdf

M. Curtis, C. S. (2012). *Gender Diversity and Corporate Performance.* Credit Suisse Research Institute. Zurich: Credit Suisse AG. Retrieved from https://www.credit-suisse.com/about-us/

en/reports-research/studies-publications.html

McKinsey & Company. (2014). *McKinsey Global Survey results Moving mind-sets on gender diversity.* Paris: McKinsey. Retrieved from https://www.mckinsey.com/~/media/McKinsey/Business%20 Functions/Organization/Our%20Insights/Moving%20 mind%20sets%20on%20gender%20diversity%20 McKinsey%20Global%20Survey%20results/Moving%20 mind%20sets%20on%20gender%20diversity.pdf

McKinsey. (2007, October 1). *Gender Diversity, a corporate performance driver.* Retrieved from www.mckinsey. com: https://www.mckinsey.com/business-functions/ organization/our-insights/gender-diversity-a-corporate-performance-driver

McKinsey. (2017). *Women Matter. Ten years of insights on gender diversity.* Retrieved from https://www.mckinsey.com/ featured-insights/gender-equality/women-matter-ten-years-of-insights-on-gender-diversity#

Meyerson, D. (2001). *Tempered Radicals.* Boston: Harvard Business School Press.

N. Anand, &. J. (2007). Capabilities of the Consummate Networker . *Organizational Dynamics* (36), 13-27. doi:3610.1016/j.orgdyn.2006.12.001.

N. Chambers, D. E. (2017). *Drawing the Future.* educationandemployers.org. Retrieved from https://www. educationandemployers.org/wp-content/uploads/2018/01/ DrawingTheFuture.pdf

N.M Carter, C. S. (2011). *The Myth of the Ideal Worker: Does Doing All the Right Things Really Get Women Ahead?* Catalyst. Catalyst.org. Retrieved from https://www.catalyst.org/ research/the-myth-of-the-ideal-worker-does-doing-all-the-right-things-really-get-women-ahead/

NHS Digital. (2012). *Infant Feeding Survey – UK, 2010.* NHS Digital. Retrieved from https://digital.nhs.uk/data-and-information/publications/statistical/infant-feeding-survey/ infant-feeding-survey-uk-2010

Nicola J. Pitchford, A. C. (2019, September). Interactive apps prevent gender discrepancies in early grade mathematics in a low income country in sub Sahara Africa. *Developmental Science, 22*(5). doi:10.1111/desc.12864

Nofsinger JR, P. F. (2018). Decision-making, financial risk aversion, and behavioral biases: The role of testosterone and stress. *Economics and human biology, 29*, 1-16. doi:doi:10.1016/j.ehb.2018.01.003

Nowrouzi, M. (2020, July). WhereIsMyName: Afghan women campaign for the right to reveal their name. *BBC News Afghan Service*. BBC.

Office for National Statistics. (2019). *Gender Pay Gap in the UK: 2019*. London. Retrieved from https://www.ons.gov.uk/employmentandlabourmarket/peopleinwork/earningsandworkinghours/bulletins/genderpaygapintheuk/2019

ONS. (2018, December 5). Labour market participation rates by age and sex, UK: 1995, 2005, 2015 and 2017. *ONS*. London, London, United Kingdom. Retrieved from https://www.ons.gov.uk/employmentandlabourmarket/peopleinwork/employmentandemployeetypes/adhocs/0093851labourmarketparticipattionrates byageandsexUK199520052015and2017

Parkes, D. (2020). *The Credibility Crunch, Sat Nav to Success Research Report*. The Women's Sat Nav to Success Ltd.

Parkes, D. (2020). *The Credibility Crunch. Sat Nav to Success Research Report*. The Women's Sat Nav to Success. Retrieved from https://womenssatnav.co.uk/survey-2020.php

Parnell, D. (2013). *In-House: A Lawyer's Guide to Getting a Corporate Legal Position*. American Bar Association.

Reilly, D. N. (2019). Investigating Gender Differences in Mathematics and Science: Results from the 2011 Trends in Mathematics and Science Survey. *Res Sci Educ*, pp. 25–50 . Retrieved from https://doi.org/10.1007/s11165-017-9630-6

S. Galdi, M. C. (2013, May). The Roots of Stereotype Threat: When Automatic Associations Disrupt Girls' Math

Performance. *Child Development*. doi:doi:10.1111/cdev12128

S. Nevadomski Berdan, C. Y. (2007). *Get Ahead by Going Abroad*. New York: HarperCollins.

S. Thorne and D, K. (2020, February 12). Gender Parity in the Boardroom Won't Happen on Its Own. *Harvard Business Review*. Retrieved from https://hbr.org/2020/02/gender-parity-in-the-boardroom-wont-happen-on-its-own

S. Vinnicombe, D. A. (2019). *The Female FTSE Board Report 2019*. International Centre for Women Leaders, Cranfield School of Management. Retrieved from https://www.cranfield.ac.uk/som/expertise/changing-world-of-work/gender-and-leadership/female-ftse-index

S. Vinnicombe, E. D. (2015). *Female FTSE Board Report 2015*. International Centre for Women Leaders, Cranfield School of Management. Cranfield School of Management. Retrieved from https://www.cranfield.ac.uk/som/expertise/changing-world-of-work/gender-and-leadership/female-ftse-index

Sibley, S. S. (2016, August 23). Why Do So Many Women Who Study Engineering Leave the Field? *Harvard Business Review*. Retrieved from https://hbr.org/2016/08/why-do-so-many-women-who-study-engineering-leave-the-field?registration=success

Sibony, D. L. (2010, March 1). The Case for Behavioural Strategy. *The McKinsey Quarterly*. Retrieved from https://www.mckinsey.com/business-functions/strategy-and-corporate-finance/our-insights/the-case-for-behavioral-strategy

Steele, C. M. (2010). *Whistling Vivaldi: How stereotypes affect us and what we can do*. New York: W. W. Norton & Company Inc.

Stipek, D. J. (1991). Gender differences in children's achievement-related beliefs and emotional responses to success and failure in mathematics. *Journal of Educational Psychology* (3), pp. 361–371. Retrieved from https://doi.org/10.1037/0022-0663.83.3

Stone, P. (2013). Opting Out: Challenging Stereotypes and Creating Real Options for Women in the Professions. *Gender and*

Work: Challenging Conventional Wisdom. Harvard Business School. Retrieved from https://www.hbs.edu/faculty/conferences/2013-w50-research-symposium/Documents/stone.pdf

Tenenbaum, H. R. (2008, July 1). You'd Be Good at That: Gender Patterns in Parent-fChild Talk about Courses. *Social Development, 18*(2), pages 447-463. doi: 10.1111/j.1467-9507.2008.00487.x

The Bechdel Test Movie List. (2020, July). Retrieved from The Bechdel Test: https://bechdeltest.com/

The Daily Telegraph. (2014, August). Retrieved from https://www.telegraph.co.uk/women/womens-business/11033725/Women-and-girls-are-vital-to-engineering-says-Sir-James-Dyson.html

The Economist. (2013, September 7). The Origins of the Financial Crisis – a crash course. *The Economist.* Retrieved from https://www.economist.com/schools-brief/2013/09/07/crash-course

The Hampton-Alexander Review. (2019). *Hampton-Alexander Review FTSE Women Leaders: Improving gender balance in FTSE Leadership.* The Hampton-Alexander Review. Retrieved from https://ftsewomenleaders.com/latest-reports/

The Smith Institute. (2011). *Unlocking Potential – perspectives on women in science, engineering and technology.* (M. Munn, Ed.) The Smith Institute.

Treanor, J. (2011, June 21). EU call for women to make up one-third of bank directors. *The Guardian Newspaper.* London: The Guardian. Retrieved from https://www.theguardian.com/business/2011/jun/21/eu-women-bank-directors

Tucker, J. (2004, Feb). The DNA of Culture Change. *Profiles in Diversity,* pp. 40-43. Retrieved from https://issuu.com/diversityjournal/docs/pdj_jan_feb_2004

Vanderkam, L. (2015). *I know how she does it.* Bolinda Publishing Pty Ltd.

Woolley, A. W. (2010). Evidence for a collective intelligence factor in the performance of human groups. *Science,* pp. 686-688.

World Bank. (2019). *Fertility rate, total (births per woman)*. Retrieved July 18, 2020, from World Bank Open Data: https://data.worldbank.org/indicator/SP.DYN.TFRT.IN

World Economic Forum. (2020). *Diversity, Equity and Inclusion 4.0 A toolkit for leaders to accelerate social progress in the future of work.* Retrieved from http://www3.weforum.org/docs/ WEF_NES_DEI4.0_Toolkit_2020.pdf

World Economic Forum. (2020). *Global Gender Gap 2020.* Geneva. Retrieved from http://www3.weforum.org/docs/WEF_ GGGR_2020.pdf

Yeatman, S. N. (2007). *Get Ahead by Going Abroad.* New York: Collins.

Yekaterina Chzhen, A. G. (2019). *Are the world's richest countries family friendly? Policy in the OECD and EU.* Florence: UNICEF Office of Research.

Young, S. (2017). *Micromessaging: why great leadership is beyond words.* New York: McGraw-Hill Education.

About the author

Diana Parkes is a social entrepreneur on a mission to provide women with the wherewithal to successfully navigate workplace inequalities and secure the roles, recognition, support and rewards they merit.

Her catalyst was a second experience of a board role for which she had a unique and exemplary track record within that company, going to a white male peer with no experience. Her determination to find answers led to a pioneering research programme, a psychology degree and establishing The Women's Sat Nav to Success Ltd, a business dedicated to changing career outcomes for women.

While dyslexia means that writing would normally be last on Diana's choice of communications options, Understand: Dare: Thrive. How to have your best career from today has always been central to her mission, because it ensures that as many women as possible can benefit from her empowering findings, as the most affordable and accessible route to this often life-changing support.

Diana is a single mum who now lives by the sea, having moved from London to Bournemouth to bring up her daughter.

Printed in Great Britain
by Amazon